HUMAN EXPERIENCE

A PSYCHOLOGY OF GROWTH

HUMAN EXPERIENCE

A PSYCHOLOGY OF GROWTH

RONAL G. POLAND, Ph.D.

*Psychologist, Denver, Colorado; staff consultant to
Bethesda Community Mental Health Center, Denver;
formerly lecturer at University of Colorado,
Boulder, Colorado*

31 illustrations, with graphic abstractions by
Karen Sweikhardt

THE C. V. MOSBY COMPANY

Saint Louis / 1974

Library of Congress Cataloging in Publication Data

Poland, Ronal G   1928-
  Human experience: a psychology of growth.

  Bibliography: p.
  1. Developmental psychology. 2. Adjustment
(Psychology). I. Title. [DNLM: 1. Adaptation,
Psychological. 2. Social adjustment. BF335 P762h
1974]
BF713.P64   155   73-12566
ISBN 0-8016-3955-7

TS/CB/B   9 8 7 6 5 4 3 2 1

TO **Els**

PREFACE

This book is designed for the beginning student and the human service worker. Some of the information contained here is substantiated by research. Some is speculative but based upon the conceptual foundations of the psychoanalytic-humanistic tradition. While a combination of research-based and speculative writing may challenge the serenity of some epistemologists, the people for whom the book was written may be provoked to discussions. Readers may find the book useful not only in the development of increased self-knowledge but also in the development of a better understanding of their relationships with other people, including patients and clients in a mental health setting.

This book is a survey but not a compendium. Its content is spread thinly over some areas and made specific and detailed in others. The choices of what to state generally and what to be specific about have been mine. They are based upon my experiences as a teacher in an office (a psychotherapist), as a teacher in classrooms (a lecturer and discussion leader), and as an individual human experiencing the turbulence of our times.

It is clear that there is a high degree of turbulence in our society, turbulence caused by a variety of factors that may become more clear to the historians of the future than they are to us now. Yet it is we who must contend with the storms of our long season of societal change. It is we who must adjust and cope and learn from the turbulence around us—and within many of us.

Because we live in an environment that moves in the direction of greater complexity, it becomes increasingly more difficult to understand. Our technological and interpersonal environment offers few anchoring points for the individual, and what anchorings there are may shift from time to time. Many relationships and bonds can be viewed as fragile and, at best, intermittent or transitory. Conceivably, it may be that the only permanent relationship one has is the relationship with oneself. But who is that?

"Who is man?" wonders Abraham Heschel and "What are we?" asks G. B. Leonard. "What are we to do with our lives?" We can, if we choose, contend with the storms or attach ourselves to our vast technology, concentrating only on what to do rather than on how to be. We can hide from living or we can choose to participate in life and, optimally, foster the development of a few reasonably durable and intimate relationships with a limited number of other people. But there are times when the turbulence seems to prevent the growth of anything beyond the most superficial forms of relationships between humans. These are the times, perhaps, when we feel the most lonely or the most alone. These are the times, too, when we may view more closely the quality of the relationship we have with ourselves.

Case studies included throughout the text cover a variety of people from a variety of circumstances. In all instances, the people and the circumstances are real. Names have been changed and so have a few of the details of each case in order to preserve the privacy of those involved. If the cases have anything at all in common, it is in these areas: (1) an overuse of defensive behaviors, (2) a disorganization of behavior to varying degrees, (3) an inability to effectively cope with change.

Change signifies some need for adjustment and adaptation. Thomas Holmes and Minoru Masuda* have developed some useful ideas about the impact of change on the physical and psychological health of humans. A partial listing of changes they identified as having impact is shown in the list below. Their original list is much longer. At the top of the list are changes that call for the greatest degree of adjustment effort. The bottom of the list contains a few items that require less adjusting, on the average, but they are changes in routine.

Death of spouse
Divorce
Marital separation
Marriage
Retirement
Death of close friend
Son or daughter leaving home
Begin or end school
Vacation
Christmas
Minor violations of the law

---

*Holmes, T. H., and Masuda, M: Psychosomatic syndrome, Psychology Today, vol. 5, no. 11, pp. 71-72 and 106, April, 1972.

Holmes and Masuda found that individuals who experienced the greatest changes in their lives usually became physically ill *after* the changes. The degree of illness seems related to the degree of change. Those who experienced great change had the most severe physical illnesses, which included heart attack, tonsillitis, ulcers, leukemia, and cancer. Changes provoke a need for adjustment; when living is loaded with too much change and when adjustment attempts do not work well, physical illness can and often does result.

The impact of change on physical health is portrayed in some of the case studies in the book. For the most part, however, the case studies stay within the realm of psychological difficulties. In almost all instances the matter of a clean and precise diagnosis is not spelled out nor is a specific course of treatment outlined. Also, some of the cases are fragmented, discontinuous, and incomplete because that is how matters really are. Neat packages of the classic diagnosis-treatment-outcome sequence happen from time to time in the mental health sector, but much of what is done seems sometimes to be untidy and unfinished.

I would like to express my thanks to R. Dean Lund of the University of Colorado and to Bob R. Baker of MCA Inc. for reading the preliminary manuscript and offering invaluable criticisms about it. In addition, I would like to thank Carl Hollander, Sharon Leman, Richard Cattell, and Mary Lou Malmquist for their consistent interest and continued support. My thanks also go to Karen Sweikhardt for her imaginative drawings that appear throughout the text. Most of all, though, I am grateful to the woman to whom this book is dedicated.

Ronal G. Poland

CONTENTS

HUMAN EXPERIENCE

A PSYCHOLOGY OF GROWTH

PROLOGUE

Several years ago these words were put down on paper by Norman Cousins (1971):

> The newspapers recently carried prominent accounts of a meeting of American and Soviet scientists for the purpose of "tuning in" on the universe. The meeting considered ways in which scientists could monitor the universe for signals from planets possibly inhabited by creatures possessing intelligence and advanced communications skills. If contact with other planets should in fact be made, and if the earth-dwellers are able to send and receive information, what shall we say of life on earth? [p. 30]

In Chapter 4 of this book, brief mention is made of the one-way message attached to *Pioneer 10*, the first spacecraft to travel beyond our solar system. The message contained in *Pioneer 10* was a note in a bottle set adrift on the seas of space. Cousins, in contrast, wrote about two-way radio communications with beings, creatures, perhaps living things as Monod (1971) has described living things. And if, or perhaps when, we make contact and establish communications with those outside the human family, what shall we say of life on earth?

We could say many of us live dismally poor lives in Asia, South America, and Africa—and in the United States. The far-away creatures might ask why that is so. We could mention our enormous network of schools, and we might admit the schools produce not only dropouts but also millions of bored, listless, or angry students. The distant beings may wonder how.

We could describe the development of the automobile and the engorgement of our cities and what seems now to be the coming decline of automobiles and the decay of our cities, a cycle that took less than one hundred years to complete. The creatures of the distant planet might begin to question man's sanity. We could, of course, try to reassure them with the idea that most of the time most people are normal on the planet. We could explain the meaning of normality, but after that message was sent, the creatures at the other end of the two-way interstellar radio communications net might simply turn off their sets and leave us alone. They might, however, be more charitable and continue to listen and to ask more about life on our planet.

If the dialogue continued, we could try to describe the mind of man, so imperfectly understood yet so capable of so much in the way of creative expression. We could describe ourselves with our own poetry. If that did not convey the essence of the treasures we have, perhaps we could transmit pictures of the works of Michelangelo or Picasso or Steichen and the

1

others among us who portray life visually.

We could communicate our own history, and we might try to send information about humans and the human condition as it exists at this present moment. But the present moment becomes the past in a rapid way, and we might have to tell our distant friends about the matter of change.

Wherever they are, the beings on another planet would be living at an incredible distance from us, and although our messages would travel at the speed of light,* they would take years to get from us to them. In that time, much of what we could say about our present lives would be obsolete, for our environment changes at a rapid pace. As Toffler (1970) has pointed out:

In the three short decades between now and the twenty-first century, millions of ordinary, psychologically normal people will face an abrupt collision with the future. Citizens of the world's richest and most technologically advanced nations, many of them will find it increasingly painful to keep up with the incessant demand for change that characterizes our time. For them, the future will have arrived too soon. [p. 11]

Our messages should point out this idea from Hippocrates, who wrote it twenty-three centuries ago: "It is changes that are chiefly responsible for diseases, especially the greatest changes, the violent alterations in the seasons and other things" (Ford, 1970, p. 256). Coupled with that is Ford's comment: "Violent alterations in the human environment have occurred at an increasing rate since the beginning of the Industrial Revolution" (p. 256).

Perhaps the most violent alteration in the human environment has been the rush of people from villages and farms to the city. This rush, this mass movement of humans, is connected to, based upon, and a result of the increase in the level of our technology. Not only are fewer people needed to produce food on farms, but more people are needed in the cities to produce the machines and chemicals that help people on farms to produce more. It is a circle or, more correctly, it is one of the circles of our changing society. Another circle has been described by Athelstan Spilhaus (1972).

When people live scattered and far apart, what they choose to do does not infringe on others, but what they have to choose from is limited. Cities increase the number of choices, but when people overcrowd into too few cities and these grow too big (as they are doing all over the world today), we reach a point of diminishing returns, and choices become more and more restricted once again. [p. 711]

Los Angeles has been famous for its rapid population growth, but Nairobi, Kenya, has grown at twice the Los Angeles rate. And Lagos, the capital of Nigeria, has grown at twice Nairobi's rate (Ehrlich and Ehrlich, 1970). The average population density of London is forty three people per acre, while in Paris there are 114 individuals per acre. In a ten-minute walk in midtown Manhattan it's possible to contact (however briefly) 220,000 other humans (Milgram, 1970).

In the far past humans connected with each other in face-to-face relationships. Now there are not only the face-to-face but also phone-to-phone, and as Doxiadis (1968) has described it, the head-to-feet contacts of apartment and dormitory dwellers living on different floors. He also maintains we have within our grasp a high number of potential human contacts, and because of that, we have a greater range of choice than ever before. We have, he says, more humans to pick from in selecting friends and acquaintances.

The multitude of potential human contacts is easily seen not only in the crowded cities but also in the crowded vacation resorts, crowded campgrounds, the crowded highways and commercial air routes that lead to and from the resorts and the campgrounds. There are crowds everywhere, it seems. Even the line of people waiting

_____
*Approximately 186,000 miles per second.

their turn for a drink at the water fountain in the park seems crowded, a longer line than last year's. There are longer lines, it seems, at ticket windows, hamburger stands, and supermarket check-out stations. And with enough crowding, an individual experiences *overload*. As Milgram (1970) states it:

> City life, as we experience it, constitutes a continuous set of encounters with overload, and of resulting adaptations. Overload characteristically deforms daily life on several levels, impinging on role performance, the evolution of social norms, cognitive functioning, and the use of facilities. [p. 1462]

Overload leads to a withdrawal, a pulling back, a turning inward. It leads to the development of superficial, transitory relations with other humans and a need for meaningful relationships with a few other people if the existence of self is to be maintained. Selectivity and exclusiveness in choosing friends become a way of life.

Yet, there seems to be no way out, no way of shutting off the crowding, for there is the intruding and impersonal computer. Miller (1971) has written about the use of computerized information gathered from course and grade transcripts from elementary school on through the end of the graduate school years. Tax returns and insurance company records are computerized, as well as military service records, Social Security information, psychological test results, hospital files, credit references, and voter registration data. The list of data sources is lengthy, but a central issue remains: privacy seems to be a thing of the past. The combination of crowded cities and the convenience of computers may seem to leave us standing naked in the sunlight. At first glance, it appears as though we have gone beyond merely participating in our own technology. At first glance it seems we have been captured and made a prisoner of that technology and everyone can see and know everything about us. Or can they? Weizenbaum (1972) doubts it. He writes about the impact of computer technology on society and of the "capture," saying:

> But the very asking of the question "Has the computer captured the essence of man?" is a diversion and, in a sense, a trap. For the real question "Does man understand the essence of man?" cannot be answered by technology and hence certainly not by any technological instrument. [p. 611]

In contrast, L. Stephen Coles (1972) states:

> Computer technology is a welcome and powerful addition to our box of tools for exploring our universe and ourselves. We have already formulated our human questions: Who are we? How are we unique? and so forth. If computer technology can help to shed some light on these questions, why should the answers be inhumane? [p. 561]

It is possible the answers can be no more inhumane or damaging to people than the questions. The core issue, it seems, is not so much the matter of questions and answers but the matter of their use. Who makes use of computerized information about people? Who watches over the users and who watches the watchers? And who is affected? All of us, in one manner or another. And all of us is an unwieldy crowd.

The crowded cities are crowded because of the influence of our own technology upon the lives of all of us. Our privacy is, perhaps, compromised by that technology, and often science and technology become targets. As Thackery (1971) has written:

> Many attacks have lately been made on the conduct of various scientific bodies, and of their officers, and severe criticism has been lavished on some of their productions. Newspapers, magazines, reviews and pamphlets have all been put in requistion for the purpose. [p. 27]

If the words seen stilted and old fashioned, it is because Thackery is, in fact, quoting Charles Babbage who wrote them in 1830. They fit today (Lang, 1972).

Science is an easy target, even though it never stands still. Science can be an easy target because it constantly challenges and unsettles those among us who prefer a stable and predictable world. It is an always unfinished effort. As Eisely (1970) has pointed out:

> Science, in spite of its awe-inspiring magnitude, contains one flaw that partakes of the nature of the universe itself. It can solve problems, but it also creates them in a genuinely confusing ratio. [p. 92]

While science and technology may cause a sense of unease, especially when we view the thickened air of our cities around the world, and while science and technology have contributed to the speed, precision, and mindlessness with which we kill each other with pollutants and in military combat, the attack on science is risky. As Lessing (1971) maintains in his chronicle:

> But science is indivisible, a seamless web of accumulated knowledge, and to destroy a part would rip the whole fabric. The beneficial and pleasing effects of science cannot really be separated from the potential harms. No drug to save lives can be secured, for instance, that is entirely without risks or side effects, for all drugs are by nature toxic agents and therefore subject to misuse. Every discovery or invention of man has this dual aspect. And it does no good to try to retreat to the nineteenth century or the sixth. Konrad Lorenz, the famed naturalist and animal behaviorist, has been going about warning hostile student audiences that if they tear down man's store of knowledge to start afresh, they will backslide not a few centuries but two hundred thousand years. "Watch out!" he says. "If you make a clean sweep of things, you won't go back to the Stone Age, because you're there already, but to well before the Stone Age." [pp. 90-91]*

Harsh words have been directed at science and at technology, and equally harsh words have been used in their defense. The debate, the battle, may be with us for some time before it fades away, perhaps to return again in another twenty or one hundred years. In the meantime change will continue. It has continued now for centuries; but the change is so great, so widespread, so often ignored, overlooked, or unknown and unrecognized by so many among us, it may seem a pseudo-problem (Westman and Gifford, 1973).

The matter of change in our environ-ment is a very real problem to Nicolas Charney (1972) who wrote these words:

> The process of change, which is to a great extent the historical process, heretofore has been largely controlled by ruling elites. But great numbers of Americans have now gone far enough toward solving the basic problems of security, food, and shelter to begin thinking about the next step—participation in shaping their lives and their society. With our enormous resources, this seems an eminently reasonable expectation. Even so, most of us paradoxically feel as if we are the subjects of change rather than its masters, and the rigidity of the very institutions that have generated these resources has become one of the problems to be solved. [p. 29]*

We shall return to the idea of the rigidity of institutions, but for the moment, something may be gained by looking into Charney's phrase, "most of us paradoxically feel as if we are the subjects of change rather than its masters."

It is common for people who are involved in their own psychotherapies to peel back the onion layers of feelings in a concerted effort to become acquainted with themselves. It is common, that is, among these individuals who strive for a more intensive and extensive development of a sense of personal identity than may be achieved in the routine of daily living. In the process of getting to know themselves and their strengths in a more definite way, a shift occurs. It is difficult to describe the shift, the change, as it takes place. In the beginning of psychotherapy, they may often say in different ways that they feel owned by the feelings they have, especially the feelings of discomfort such as anger, fear, and anxiety. As they progress, however, and as the shift takes place, a reversal can be seen. They no longer feel owned by the feelings; they recognize *they* own the feelings. After the shift, the change in perspective, they are better equipped to do something about their feelings rather than

---

*Courtesy Fortune Magazine.

*Copyright 1972 by Saturday Review Co. First appeared in Saturday Review Sept. 12, 1972. Used with permission.

simply to experience and react to them. A world of choices opens up.

Perhaps a similar change can take place between man and the science and technology he has developed. Neither owns man, although man may stand in awe or anger over what he himself has done, and as Charney points out, it seems reasonable to consider the idea that we can shape our own lives. We have the abilities to bring under control those factors that have damaged our planet and that continually seem to damage the internal psychological environment of many of us (Adler, 1970).

The literature of our times is loaded with dismal prophecies for the future of mankind. It seems the dreams of a better world constantly elude us (Sommer, 1969), but it is the only world we have. No matter how technologically skilled we may be, no matter how intriguing it may be to consider communicating with living things on a distant planet, we cannot leave Earth to seek refuge and a better home elsewhere. Not, at least, in the twentieth century. And so we are forced back to Toffler's (1970) comments on the magnitude and inevitability of change within our own environment, which lead to changes within ourselves. And, as Reich (1970) has pointed out:

Of all the changes that have happened to man, perhaps the deepest and least understood is his loss of the land, of weather, of growing things, and of his body that these things give. [p. 188]

Ehrlich and Ehrlich (1970) maintain that:

Some biologists feel that mankind's evolutionary history has been such that the present environments to which he is subjecting himself are essentially asking him to "fly with one wing." [p. 204]

and they quote three biologists from the University of Wisconsin* who have expressed the idea "that mankind's genetic endowment has been shaped by evolution to require 'natural' surroundings for opti-

---

*H. H. Iltes, P. Andrews, and O. L. Loucks.

mum mental health" (p. 204). Richard Sommer (1969) points out that beneficial environments can be built for specific individuals and for specific groups (the mentally ill, the aged), but changing and improving the environment in which we all live calls for a great deal of planning. However, Spilhaus (1972) has said:

In the United States, planning is suspect, the reaction from "liberals" to long-range, far-reaching plans is to label them demagogic or autocratic. On the other hand, the reaction of some "conservatives" to the same plans is to label them wild-eyed, idealistic, or socialistic. [p. 714]

Planning, long-range planning, and cooperation among the members of mankind take place when there is a need to avoid or recover from catastrophies. Catastrophies are typically obvious, and they typically involve so many of us that cooperative planning becomes more than sensible: it becomes necessary. Because we have injured our own planet to a point approaching catastrophe, we humans face what has been described by Barry Commoner (1972) as a common problem of global survival. He quotes U Thant as saying:

Perhaps it is the collective menaces arising from the world's scientific and technological strides and from their mass consequences, which will bind together nations, enhance peaceful cooperation and surmount, in the face of physical danger, the political obstacles to mankind's unity. [p. 49]

Eric Hoffer (1963) has expressed the idea that humans unite in a swift and sure way when they are confronted by real or imagined dangers. The individual human instantaneously uses strategies of defense when confronted by real or imagined dangers to the psychological self. But what are the dangers? For mankind in general, global pollution, overpopulation, and the constant risk of nuclear war appear to be obvious dangers. And for the individual human, what are the dangers?

When the individual is considered, the specific psychological dangers are difficult to define. Psychological dangers are based on the quality of the reactions we have to problems—societal, moral, and ethical. And, in many instances, the problem is not the problem. The solution is.

Solving problems in an adequate fashion is often difficult because there seem to be too many solutions, too many ways of reacting. If you have a problem at school or at work or at home, you can find yourself in great difficulty because there are so many available ways of solving a problem.

We are surrounded with solutions to problems. You can stroll around outside and pick solutions up off the ground. If you do not see any on the ground, look up. You are bound to see some solutions flying around, or hanging from trees, or stuck to the sides of buildings. Solutions are everywhere, and they are normally free. They do not cost anything, usually, because they are often worthless. A large number of people seem highly skilled at solving problems with a quick answer seemingly loaded with expertise. The question is there, rarely asked, and sometimes simply ignored: if there are so many expert solvers of problems, why are there still so many problems? Perhaps something has been overlooked in the busy search for easy solutions. It may be useful here to consider one of the central ideas from the realm of science and the field of technology: define the problem with great care (Platt, 1973).

To define the problem, to make the diagnosis, to arrow in to the heart of a difficult and intricate circumstance requires skill. The effort to define the problem usually takes more knowledge and brainpower than finding a solution. Perhaps because of that we humans prefer the quickly defined solution rather than the carefully defined problem, but the result is that many problems remain genuinely unsolved. Could we admit to this if we were to communicate with creatures on some distant planet? Perhaps not, for it seems difficult to face the matter when we try to communicate with each other. Yet, as Kenneth Boulding (1964) suggests, the human family has the capacity to resolve problems which face us. He says, "A large part of the solution of any problem is the identification of the system where the problem lies" (p. 101). He goes on to comment that mankind has an extensive body of knowledge but our system of knowledge is not always useful because:

We believe too many things which are not true. We do not know things that are true, and we have values . . . which are inconsistent with the successful management of conflict or the process of human development. [p. 102]

Boulding maintains, however, that more humans know more about more than at any other time in the history of man. And the knowledge can be directed and channeled, first into the matter of defining what our problems are and then into doing something about them.

It may seem out of balance to wonder about the nature of the problems and to hear a comment about defining the problems we have, for they have seemingly been defined by an array of poets, politicians, scholars, and philosophers. What has usually been defined are not the problems but the symptoms of problems or the results of problems. The global pollution, overpopulation, the constant and almost self-perpetuating risk of nuclear war are, on the surface, obvious conditions that have developed because of some of man's ways. Are man's ways the problem? Part of the problem? Perhaps. While Arthur Clarke (1968) may eloquently state, "for every man who has ever lived, in this Universe there shines a star" (p. 7), we must attend to our own Earth, for as Boulding (1964) points out:

> Our precious little planet, this blue-green cradle of life with its rosy mantle, is in one of its most critical stages, perhaps the most critical stage, of its whole existence. It is in a position of immense danger and immense potentiality. [p. 192]

Perhaps we could transmit those words to the distant beings of another planet, and perhaps they would understand. They could not, however, travel from wherever they are to wherever we are in this great galaxy for purposes of rescue. There is not enough time. We must rescue ourselves.

1 DEVELOPMENT

This chapter contains a brief review of a limited number of factors that contribute to the development of the human individual. The chapter is designed as a base or a foundation of sorts for the rest of the book. There are several ideas that may be useful to keep in mind while reading. Anne Anastasi (1972) has called these ideas *orienting concepts;* they are well established and thoroughly supported by research, and they form anchor points for anyone who wants to know about human behavior.

The first orienting concept defined in this chapter and the one that forms the base for the last chapter is modifiability. *Modifiability,* in psychological terms, means the individual can change. There is little doubt that an individual changes as he or she grows from infancy to adulthood. He or she is changed through experiencing the environment and experiencing the self. He or she is changed through learning, and as Anastasi states it, "Modifiability is manifested not only in what is learned but also in the ability to learn" (p. 1097).

The ability to learn is ultimately based upon what has been inherited. What has been inherited, however, is an extraordinarily broad spectrum of potentials, which will be mentioned in this chapter. The potentials any one of us may have do

not, however, mean very much without the existence of a second orienting concept called *interaction.* In this chapter some mention is made of the interaction between what is inherited and what is experienced. At the center of the concept, however, is the fundamental idea that it is impossible to clearly identify just what is that it is experienced (via interaction) which leads to a specific behavior. A single and perhaps obvious event in anyone's experience does not lead to behavior that can be attributed only to that single event. Another but less accurate way of expressing the meaning of interaction is to state that everything is related to everything else. An individual human can be viewed as a gigantic three-dimensional web. If one strand of the web is touched, that one strand will quiver in response; so will the rest of the web. And, perhaps, a strand on the far side of the web, out of sight and unnoticed, breaks.

The personal web of the human consists of a blend of inherited factors and experiences, and except for the obvious, it is often difficult to separate the inherited from the experienced. When an individual interacts with his environment, he is influenced by that environment in a great many ways. The environmental influences are often unrecognized or unknown. At the same time, the individual influences his own environment in a multitude of ways that, again, may often be unknown or unrecognized. What is called behavior is the result of the ebb and flow of a multitude of mutual but not necessarily equal influences. What is called behavior is based upon what Anastasi calls a *multiplicity of variables.* Any real-life situation involves a multiplicity of causes, of effects, of influences, of environmental factors, and of inherited aspects of the individual human. In the language of the orienting concepts, human behavior is modifiable, in part, because of the interactions of a multiplicity of variables.

ZERO POINTS AND DEFINITIONS

A sperm cell penetrates an egg. They merge to form a single cell called a zygote, and something new begins. We know the sperm is male, the egg female, and that each carries twenty-three pairs of chromosomes. When blended in the zygote, they form forty-six pairs. The chromosomes carry thousands of genes, and we know each gene is a molecule composed mainly of deoxyribonucleic acid (DNA), and we have discovered that DNA molecules produce complex chemical substances called enzymes. These enzymes control the formation of the vitally necessary proteins within each cell, and because of their control, genes are able to determine the kinds of tissues that make a body. What we do not know is the answer to the question: when does a person become a person?

We can measure the wind and know the speed of light and unravel some of the mysteries of the surface of the moon. We have partially analyzed our sun and accurately calculated the trajectories of the planets. We have great libraries filled with poetry, prose, and songs about man's ways, but we cannot mark the precise moment when a human becomes a human. As Jerome Lejeune (1970) has said:

"When does man begin? The information is spread out . . . but it can be summarized under the two headings defining an individual, that is, unity and uniqueness. It is impossible to state at what time these two qualities appear, although we know that it is after fertilization. [p. 11]

We cannot name that point in time when we each begin to exist as unique individuals, different from all others, functioning with a physical and psychological unity that makes us human. Because of that, we must invent a moment, a time of beginning, a zero point. We can, in this book, call it birth.

The term *development* takes into account the many factors that contribute to an individual's personality. Human development consists of steps or phases through which an individual passes, collecting and retaining a large number of attributes and characteristics. To use a rough analogy: a pearl develops, building layer upon layer, becoming larger, but remaining always a pearl. The pearl does not change into something else, and development, in this book, does not mean change, although change can contribute to development.

Development is the ongoing, continuous process. Change may affect and influence that process. For example, changes in body chemistry mark the beginnings of adolescence, and adolescence is one phase in the continuous development of a human. Changes in the level of an individual's stamina and response speed can be found in humans as they advance into the middle and old age years. And it is change within the individual, as well as changes in the environment, that requires adaptations and adjustments. One of the main characteristics of adequate development is the increasing skillfulness with which an individual can adapt and adjust.

The unique and special ways in which an individual adjusts to his inner environment and to his external environment is called that individual's *personality.* In a broader meaning, the term personality refers to the ways in which an individual behaves, the manner in which he or she functions with other people, and the typical ways in which the person relates to the overall surrounding environment. Personality is a composite of what has been inherited (relatively fixed and unchangeable components) and what has been learned (relatively changeable, somewhat fluid, and sometimes malleable components). The primary focus in the book will be on those aspects of personality that are learned.

Learning is any relatively stable or sometimes even a permanent change in behavior based on (1) experience and (2) practice. Experience can often be a passive learning style; practice usually involves some measure of active participation in the process of learning.

While development of personality is mainly a psychological process that leans heavily upon different aspects of learning, maturation does not. *Maturation* refers to organic, bodily, physical growth. It is impossible for a human to walk, no matter how much he may try, before his physical development (maturation) has reached a point where it is possible for his body to function in a walking way. The physical process of maturation is obviously based upon hereditary factors, although some environmental influences can alter maturation. Two environmental influences capable of altering the maturation process are malnutrition and early (infantile) emotional deprivation (Tanner, 1973).

The word development has a broad, general meaning, which includes the psychological aspects of the individual as he stands alone, as he exists in relationships with other people, and as he exists within the total environment. *Socialization,* on the other hand, is a term that defines a narrower spectrum of behavior. Socialization refers to the learning of behaviors that are acceptable and customary as defined by the group to which the individual may belong. It is possible to consider socialization as an important ingredient of psychological development because both involve learning behavior, particularly the learning of language. *Language* is made up not only of the spoken and the written word but also of facial expression and the tone of the voice, as well as of gestures of the hands and movements of the whole body.

Environment has no fixed definition. There is the physical environment made up of rocks and trees and asphalt, which we can see, but there are gamma rays, x-rays, and television antenna emissions, which are as invisible to us as the lines of force associated with a magnet. We cannot see the wind, but we see what the wind does. Sunlight is unseen by us unless we look at the source of that light or at the surfaces upon which that light falls—the surface of a lake, a leaf, a speck of dust—and then sometimes we can only know sunlight if it exists next to an opposite, a shadow. Which affects us more, the light or the shadow?

There is, according to Amos Hawley (1973), an uncertainty about what environment really is. But then, most of the certainties we live by are the ones we invent. As a result, we can uncertainly call the environment anything (1) that is external to the individual and (2) that has an influence or a potential influence upon the person. Within a very short time after birth, however, an increasing number of things are no longer external to the individual. They have been internalized, and they then become a part of the internal environment, the intrapersonal or, to use another term, the intrapsychic environment of ideas, impulses, feelings, hopes, intentions, attitudes, and opinions.

PRECONDITIONS AND POTENTIALS FOR DEVELOPMENT

We are, at birth, alive. We have, at birth, physical equipment that has genetically endured through thousands of generations and that we use in developing from infant to child to adolescent to adult. At the core we have a brain and a spinal cord, the human central nervous system (CNS), which weighs, at birth, about 12 ounces. It grows during the years of growing, and when it is fully matured (physically), it weighs slightly more than 3 pounds (Asimov, 1964). The brain and spinal cord we inherit maintain control over other inherited equipment. One of the results of that control is the learning of a code that helps us to learn another code. The first code is called language. Language helps us to learn the second code, which can be called the code of behavior and which anthropologists label as culture (Alland, 1967).

The inherited equipment that seems necessary for learning a code of behavior consists of the following:

1. Eyes that can see objects close at hand, far away, and in the middle distances
2. The physical equipment that allows us to speak (lips, tongue, soft and hard palates, glottis, vocal cords, nasal airways)
3. Feet and legs that permit walking in an upright position
4. Arms and hands, especially hands equipped with thumbs and fingers that allow us to hold things such as food, firewood, or tools
5. A digestive system (and related systems) that calls for a varied diet but that requires protein for survival
6. A cerebral cortex within the CNS that can function to control thinking behavior and sexual behavior

We can, when infancy is past, walk and talk and grab for food with our hands while looking around at our world and the people in it with stereoscopic color vision. Our bodies do not require gigantic amounts of grass and hay for survival the way cows and elephants do. And we have the capacity for thinking and for the control of that intricate and complex behavior called mating and sexual behavior.

Thinking is of course an invaluable human characteristic and so too, perhaps, is the control of mating that led, in our long past, to the founding of small organizations called families and larger organizations known as tribes and nations.

The preconditions mentioned above are genetically determined. Their combination sets humans apart from other organisms. Eagles and hawks have better eyes, but they cannot talk or think in complex ways. Kangaroos may have superior feet and legs, but their arms and hands are weak and crude compared to human equipment, and their brains are smaller and less well developed. Dolphins may have a relatively large brain, an ability to talk, and a need for protein in their diet, but they are enough different from humans in other ways to have, perhaps, developed their own code of behavior, but that remains to be shown by further research and study.

Overall, these preconditions of behavior form a unique combination of characteristics; they form the basis for what can be called the potentials we all have for development. We are, at birth, alive. Being alive is an actual condition, a reality. A number of other conditions are, at the moment of birth, merely potentials; they are realities of the future for an individual. No newly born human can stand in the sand at the edge of the sea watching the gulls circling over the water. They may have only the potential for growth and development to a point where that is an actuality.

At birth no human can sense the grit of ghetto brick or the majesty of a Canadian lake, but the potentials are there, built into the person. The potentials are inherited. Whether (and how) the potentials become actualized depends upon the interaction between those potentials and an array of environmental factors.

The potentials for development that are typically present at birth and that most directly apply to the ideas contained in this book are named and described in the following paragraphs.

1. **Action:** The potential for action is inherited. We inherit bodies that are able to move, awkwardly and ineptly at first, but with a growing and developing smoothness and skill as the years pass. Actions are observable behaviors such as dancing, laughing, talking, simply sitting in a chair, or pole vaulting. Actions are sometimes referred to as *conative behavior,* which can include a great variety of automatic behaviors such as walking and habits such as smoking or repeatedly wiggling a foot while sitting in a chair.

2. **Perceiving:** The equipment of perception is a part of all we inherit from our biological parents. Most of us inherit ears and eyes that work, tongues that are able to taste, noses that can sniff and smell a great variety of aromas, and nerve endings in the skin that help us to know when we touch or are touched. Perceiving is an intricate behavior that has a clear biological base, the base of sensing. We must sense sounds, odors, pressures, tastes, warmth, and coolth before they can be perceived.

3. **Learning:** The central nervous system, the brain and the spinal cord, is an inherited collection of billions of cells that form the biological base for what is learned. What is learned by any individual is or can be fantastically intricate, but the potential for learning is, at the core, a matter of inheritance.

4. **Thinking:** This at-birth potential is often referred to as *cognitive behavior.* Cognition, as in the words recognize and recognition, has to do with intellect, the "use of the mind," whether it is logical or illogical. Thinking is not directly observable, although an individual human may experience within himself what is called thinking.

5. **Feeling:** This genetically based potential is sometimes called *affective behavior,* and it has to do with a wide variety of behavior ranging from sadness and depression through happiness and ecstatic joy. Feelings are not directly observable, although they often may be expressed through action.

6. **Striving:** Purposeful, goal-directed behavior is genetically built into each individual. Soon after birth it shows itself in what is called *the primal dialogue* between mother and infant (see Chapter 4). Later in life it takes the form of making plans often concerned with what to do and sometimes concerned with "how to be."

7. **Defending:** The behavioral potential labeled here is described in some detail in Chapters 7 and 8. It refers to protecting oneself psychologically against a multitude of real and imagined psychological assaults.

8. **Repairing:** In a very real sense, repairing refers to the rescue of oneself in one manner or another. When all else fails, the infant may have a temper tantrum, and if that does not bring needed attention or relieve tension in an adequate way, the infant may withdraw and slide into a state of decline (see Chapter 4). Overall, however, repairing and self-rescue can involve beating on a pillow (instead of another person), yelling, crying, talking things over with a close friend, and active participation in one or a variety of psychotherapies that are described near the end of this book. Repairs are often necessary because defending does not always work.

9. **Creating:** The potential for being creative is not limited to a few brilliant individuals. To complete old and familiar tasks in new and different ways or to invent are possibilities well within the reach of almost anyone, if they can allow themselves some degree of psychological freedom.

These behavior potentials are the main factors that form the psychological beginnings of a person. They are the psychological aspects of what has been biologically transmitted. These potentials for growth have existed for mankind for thousands of generations, and if they change biologically, they change in a leisurely way, in a slow, evolutionary manner and at such a gradual pace the changes from one generation to the next cannot be recognized.

We are, all of us, made up of some hereditary factors, and we are all endowed with a purpose or a project, according to Jacques Monod (1971) a French molecular biologist and Nobel Prize winner. He has named this characteristic of living things, the endowment, *teleonomy.* He is, of course, speaking from the viewpoint of biological science, and when he talks of purpose, he means a biological (or teleonomy) rather than a psychological purpose,

There are two other factors that Monod says are characteristics of living things: (1) autonomous morphogenesis and (2) reproductive invariance. *Autonomous morphogenesis,* in its most lean and stripped-down definition simply means that living things are capable of self-construction. Living things are not yet assembled in a shop or turned out on some factory production line. Living things produce living things. Onion plants will produce, by way of their own seeds, other onion plants. Humans will produce humans. There is no known recorded evidence in all of man's history to indicate that onions have produced humans or that humans have given birth to onions. And that idea moves us into what Monod labels reproductive invariance.

Reproductive invariance, from the standpoint of humans, means that people always produce other people, and the genetic changes from one generation to the next are basically nonexistent. If by chance there are genetic changes from one generation to the next, they are either labeled as transitory mutations or they cannot be detected by any method, machine, or technique now known.

Stability and invariability are strange factors to consider if, at the same time, we consider the idea of change, of evolution according to Charles Darwin (1936). Yet, genetic stability and invariability exist. For example, Monod says there is a living thing, known as the *Lingula,* that has remained genetically unchanged for 450 million years. He also mentions another living thing, the oyster, that has not changed genetically (or, perhaps, in the way it tastes) for the past 150 million years. Then Monod adds:

Lastly, one may estimate that the present-day cell, characterized by its invariant basic chemical organization . . . has been in existence for from two to three billion years. [p. 122]

Leaving lingulas, oysters, and single-celled living things behind, let us move back to man. Considering the idea of reproductive invariance in humans, it seems reasonable to assume that humans who lived 5,000 or 6,000 years ago were not genetically different from their descendants today.

To take it one step further: the people who built the Pyramids, who handcrafted Stonehenge, and who cooked the food for those who made the Great Wall of China looked the way we look, except for the matter of clothing. They may even have behaved (in at least a few ways) like the people who now build our freeways and skyscrapers and who use microwave ovens to prepare meals. According to the *constitutionalist* ideas of human behavior, the personality of an individual is a matter of heredity. In contrast, *environmentalists* maintain personality is developed, shaped, molded only by the individual's surroundings, the environment. Moving off those extremes, however, are those who maintain personality is the result of interactions between that which is inherited and that which results from environmental experiences. For an example, Dobzhansky (1972) has stated:

Species other than man become adapted by changing their genes to fit their environments. . . . Man, by means of his culture and technology, changes his environments to fit his genes. [p. 528]

He goes on to say:

All bodily structures and functions, without exception, are products of heredity realized in some sequence of environments. So also are all forms of behavior, also without exception. Nothing can arise in any organism unless its potentiality is within the realm of possibilities of the genetic endowment. [p. 530]

For a different kind of example of the thinking of those who believe personality is based on interactions between hereditary factors and environmental influences, we can turn to the work of Alexander Thomas, Stella Chess, and Herbert G.

Birch (1970). These three designed a research study that took into account the observation that children differ in temperment from the moment of birth. To begin, they collected data on the behavior of a large number of infants. They then analyzed the data and identified nine characteristics of behavior:

1. The level and extent of motor activity.
2. The degree of regularity in eating, elimination, and the asleep-awake cycle
3. Acceptance or withdrawal from a new experience
4. Behavioral adaptiveness to changes in the environment
5. Sensitivity (threshold) to stimuli
6. Response intensity
7. General mood (cheerful, crying, friendly, unfriendly)
8. Degree of distractibility
9. Span of attention; persistence

Each of these nine characteristics could be rated as high, medium, or low, and the researchers found they could define behavior in infants as young as 2 months old with this scale. The rating scale was tested on a variety of infants. Some were mentally retarded, some were middle-class children, some Puerto Rican, and there were a number of premature babies. When these behavioral scientists were satisfied with their rating scale, they began to use it in a long-term study of 141 children from eighty-five families in which the parents were highly educated.

The study began over sixteen years ago, and during those years the researchers were gradually able to identify four types of children. The types are shown in Table 1.

In addition, Thomas, Chess, and Birch found a substantial consistency in behavior from age 2 months through 10 years. For example, in the first of the nine categories listed (level and extent of motor activity), they found that an infant rated as having a high level of activity will show that high level as he moves ahead in years.

Table 1. Some typologies of childhood behavior

Type	Percent	Characteristics of behavior
Easy	40%	High degree of regularity, acceptance of new experiences, high behavioral adaptiveness, positive general mood
Slow to warm up	15%	Initial withdrawal from new experiences, slow behavioral adaptiveness, mild response intensity, slightly negative general mood
Difficult	10%	High degree of irregularity, withdrawal from new experiences, slow behavioral adaptiveness, high level or response intensity, negative general mood
Mixed	35%	No specific behavioral trends identified

At 2 months: when diaper is changed, infant wriggles; during sleep there is a high frequency of bodily movement.
At 5 years: runs instead of walking; often leaves the table during meals.
At 10 years: cannot sit still long enough to do homework; engages in a variety of sports that require a high activity level.

In contrast, a child rated as having a low level of activity will show these behaviors:

At 2 months: rarely moves during sleep; immobile while being dressed.
At 5 years: sits quietly even during long ride in a car; takes a long time to get dressed.
At 10 years: eats slowly; likes to read and play chess.

There is, for most of us, a consistency to our behavior. That consistency, whether it is in the level of activity we maintain or in any other variable, may exist to such a degree that it remains unnoticed. Inconsistencies can often be more easily recognized. Both the consistencies and the inconsistencies we exhibit may be based not only upon a combination of hereditary potentials and environmental effects but also upon what we ourselves decide to do with ourselves. But that brings into view the third main influence upon behavior, the self. A review and discussion of the influence of the self will be postponed at this point so we can more quickly move into reviews of development.

REALIZATION OF POTENTIALS

For a few pages, let us take a look at an overall picture of a lifetime. We shall use as our vantage point the overall view presented by Erik Erikson (1963, 1968), who was born over seventy years ago in Frankfurt, Germany, but who became an American citizen in 1939 (Maier, 1965).

According to Erikson, there are eight main stages of development (see Table 2). We will move through these eight stages in a few pages.

Infancy

A newly born human is a supreme example of an unfinished product. When a baby is born, he is uncivilized, illiterate, and physically incomplete. Beginning at the

zero point called birth, the baby must live for months before the realization comes that he is an individual. At the zero point he has zero experiences in sensing the separateness that exists between himself, all other people, and things in his environment. The blanket he clutches is as much a part of him as his hand, and his mother is not another person but a part of him as he was a part of her for almost a year. He may not sense much about his own physical uniqueness or develop much awareness of his own body until almost two years have passed. And at the end of two years he will be aware of much more than simple feelings of physical comfort or discomfort. As the infant develops physically in some incredibly intricate ways, he also develops psychologically.

It may be that during the first two years of life the most important, most vital psychological development is the development of a sense of trust. *Trust* is a sensing, a

Table 2. Erikson's stages of development (1968)

Stage	Ages	Label
1	0-1+	Infancy
2	2-3	Early childhood
3	4-6	Childhood
4	7-11	School age
5	12-20	Adolescence
6	21-34	Young adulthood
7	35-65	Middle age
8	Over 65	Old age

H. Armstrong Roberts

feeling, that at least some important sectors of the world are dependable and that some of the people in the world (the infant's world) are warm, caring, available, and friendly.

The idea of trust, as well as some closely related aspects of human behavior, will come up again in later pages of this book. At this point, however, it is time to move on to the next state of development.

Early childhood

The second and third years of a lifetime are usually marked by the development of a sense of autonomy. *Autonomy* involves some strivings toward personal independence and the *beginnings* of an extraordinarily important part of adult living called approval of oneself.

During the time labeled early childhood the child optimally should come to feel he is an accepted, an approved human, sometimes self-reliant and sometimes able to use the help and guidance of adults who are important to him.*

If, in infancy, the small-sized human has developed some sense of trust, he begins to assert himself in early childhood. He typically will begin to insist that he can make his own decisions about sleeping or not sleeping, eating or not eating. Inevitably, as his physical ability increases, he normally develops an increasing independence. There are times when parents interpret the rising sense of independence (autonomy) as rebellion. A genuinely and totally independent child who is free of all restrictions is something of a savage. Families usually have a low level of tolerance for savages in their midst, and so the

child must endure (and sometimes enjoy) what is called the civilizing or the socializing process.

The civilizing process involves a curtailment of independence. The child must, if he is to somehow make his way in a relatively peaceful manner, accept and conform to many of the demands the parents put on him. One of these demands involves the development of control of bladder and bowel.

Childhood

During the fourth, fifth, and sixth years of his lifetime the child moves well beyond the world as he knew it during infancy and early childhood. He can walk and run with greater ease; he can talk skillfully, and he has by now an increasingly certain idea of who he is, who mother is, and with a growing importance, who father is.

To continue his development toward an appropriate and satisfying level of maturity the individual child must during these years develop a sense of initiative. The sense of initiative can form the base for a realistic sense of ambition and purpose.

Human initiative is typically guided, controlled, directed, facilitated, and inhibited by what can be called conscience. Having a conscience is not simply a matter of having some sort of inner voice telling the person "don't." A conscience is not simply inhibitory with its messages that say "don't cheat" and "don't kill" and "don't be late." A conscience can also send telegrams that say "do." The "do" factors may range from "do be free" to "you must graduate" to "do trust another person." The development of a conscience is a major factor in the overall development of a person from the savage infant to the civilized adult. And it is during the stage of childhood that a person's conscience begins to grow.

At about the same time the individual begins to develop a conscience, he may begin to develop what is commonly known

*To a child the most important adults are usually his parents. If the child has no parents or if the parents are not a part of his immediate surroundings, other adults swiftly become parent-substitutes. In some families, older brothers and sisters are more truly parents to a child than the biological mother and father.

as self-defeating behavior, a learned behavior. Self-defeating behavior is so widespread, so common, so often a part of the behavior of humans past the ages of 4, 5, and 6 that it can almost be called normal.

That which is called normal is not usually that which is ideal or that which is hoped for. Normal behavior is behavior that is the most frequent, the most typical, the most abundantly seen. Under the umbrella of this definition, normal behavior can be adequate and positive or it can be inadequate and negative. Normal does not refer to the quality ("good" or "bad") but the frequency of behavior. Within the framework of this concept of normality, it is possible to view self-defeating behavior as normal, inadequate, negative, and perhaps, "bad" for the individual.

There will be more about self-defeating behavior in future chapters. For now, it may be enough to point out that self-defeating behavior is directly connected with the child's growing awareness of who mother is and who father is.

School age

The fourth stage of behavior is called school age, partly because school and all the people and activities connected with school come to be important to the person who falls within the age range from 7 to 11 years. At school, at home, and in the neighborhood the person who is in the school age stage develops and extends his conscience. He also typically works toward the major developmental achievement of this age group: a sense of industriousness.

The school age stage with its development of a sense of industriousness means that the person produces. He may build model airplanes, construct tree houses, dig caves in vacant lots, write short and sometimes fantastic poems, collect stamps, compound gunpowder, sew, knit, proudly memorize the multiplication table, learn how to cook, and work hard at becoming an accepted member of a gang. Girls prefer the company of girls and there are girl gangs. Boys run with boys in gangs. It is a period of normal homosexuality. It is also period of relative serenity.

The school age years are also called the *latency period.* The aspects of behavior that are latent are directly related to behavior begun in childhood: the growing awareness of who mother is and who father is.

Adolescence

During this fifth stage of development the individual moves through life's hurricane season. The years from ages 12 through 20 are marked by physical changes and often by emotional storms of high intensity.

The physical changes that take place during adolescence include not only increased growth but also bodily changes connected with sexual functions. For girls there is the beginning of menstruation, the development of the breasts, and the appearance of pubic hair. For boys there is the descending of the testicles from the torso into the scrotum, the appearance of pubic hair and whiskers, and the deepening of the voice. Beyond these and many other physical changes there are psychological changes and developments of great magnitude. The most central of these psychological developments is labeled the development of a sense of identity.

During adolescence the individual must begin to learn how to identify himself. The first step involves the realization there is such a question as "Who am I?" The second step is to become aware that it is possible to answer that question. And it is the adolescent who must begin to answer that question with at least some accuracy some of the time.

If the adolescent is to be successful in eventually knowing "This is who I am," he must wrestle with two psychological competitors. One of these competitors is in the form of other people who will tell him who he is, sometimes with great inac-

Dan O'Neill/Editorial Photocolor Archives

curacy. The other competitor in the wrestling match is his own conscience (Josselyn, 1952; Maier, 1965). His conscience may forcefully tell him what and who and how he ought to be, but his conscience can be as inaccurate as the people around him.

There are other conflicts that the adolescent faces. He may strive to reach ahead to future time and try to be an adult while longing for the remembered serenity of the school age years. He may want to break loose from his family, to cut the connections with his parents, yet he may feel anxious and fearful and even abandoned if his parents do not sometimes stand in his way. He may spend great energies in trying to belong to a group, but he may often feel a strong need to be alone, away from the storm.

To be alone can be, for the adolescent, a matter of finding an island of sanity in a crazy world. When he is alone, the adolescent person may spiral upward into daydreams that may sometimes be glorious and sometimes fearful. Alone, the adolescent may listen to the radio, watch television, masturbate, read books, write in a diary, and slowly, gradually become a person who can put together some of the pieces of the puzzle of identity. As John Aldridge (1969) states:

> To define himself, to become aware of himself at all as an individual human being, a person needs to acquire what Henry James called the prespective of "otherness." This can only be acquired if he has the opportunity to be physically alone in the sense that he is deprived of the usual social distractions and soporifics and therefore is forced to turn inward and seek satisfaction in the consciousness of his own powers, the cultivation of his own unique perceptions. In time, if the isolation is prolonged, a person will develop a powerful awareness of his own identity and a correspondingly powerful awareness of the very different identities of other people. [p. 103]

Young adulthood

From about the age of 21 to around age 34, the young adult moves from the identity problems of adolescence to a sector of potential pleasure called intimacy.

Intimacy is an aspect of human behavior that involves a limited number a significant fellow travelers on the time line we call a lifetime. Intimacy is an intricate aspect of life, an aspect that calls for some courage, some elements of honesty, a measure of trust and initiative, and a large amount of the awareness of one's own identity.

Middle age

The central factor, the main developmental achievement, of middle age has been given the eriksonian label of generativity. *Generativity* refers to a matter of generating life: it refers to the idea of older people living in and through younger people, sometimes hoping for some manner or measure of immortality by way of their generative efforts.

Old age

The eighth and last state of development begins at age 65 and ends at death. Old age is a time of decline. It is also a time when the individual can develop a sense of completeness. A sense of completeness seems to exist behind the words of Ilya Ehrenburg quoted in Chapter 6 of this book. A sense of completeness can be seen in these words by an old person, "Well, I did alright. It wasn't such a bad life." A sense of completeness may also be found in this description (Poland and Sanford, 1971):

> When he was seventy years old, his son gave a birthday party for him. His wife went with him and they held each others' hand as the cake was brought in, and everyone sang the birthday song. He blew out the candles with two breaths and then he looked around the room at the people there. . . . Everything was fine, he thought. Everyone was getting along all right, better than he had hoped, and he felt within himself a serene sense of completeness. He kissed his wife lightly and wondered which one of them would live on, alone. He felt at peace, even with that thought on his mind. [p. 44]

REVIEW QUESTIONS

1. Give real-life examples of Anastasi's orienting concepts. Which is the most difficult to describe?
2. When do *you* think a human becomes a human?

3. What is the difference between learning and maturation?

4. Which one of the preconditions has the greatest influence upon the potentials for development?

5. In addition to the nine potentials for development listed in Chapter 1, can more be named? What are they?

6. Does Monod believe in evolution?

7. During which stage of development does an individual's conscience begin to show itself?

8. What does John Aldridge say about the need for adolescent isolation from other people?

9. What is the primary psychological event in young adulthood?

10. During which developmental stage is trust an important and leading factor?

11. How do constitutionalists and environmentalists differ?

12. What is meant by autonomous morphogenesis?

2
TIME AND CHANGE

North Vietnam has been visited by Americans. Some have gone voluntarily for personal or military reasons, while others have been temporary residents forcibly held there as prisoners of war. This is, obviously, recent history that goes back only a couple of decades. But we can go back further in the history of that distant land. We can go back to 40,000 B.C., according to Wilhelm G. Solheim II of the University of Hawaii (1972). He and a colleague, Chester F. Gorman (both are anthropologists), assembled data from what they had pieced together after exploring and digging up ancient burial sites. Solheim, with substantial help from Gorman, has concluded that the citizens of ancient Southeast Asia developed a culture including a technology that roughly parallels what was developed in areas of the world such as the Middle East.

What happened to man and what man caused to happen in North Vietnam and in Thailand, Burma, the Phillipines, in Indonesia, on Formosa, and in the southern part of China is separate from but sometimes interestingly similar to what happened in Egypt, in Asia Minor, and, perhaps, on the island of Crete. Civilization began, not in 40,000 B.C., however, for civilizations do not instantly appear out of nowhere. As far as can be determined,

there has never been a commitee of cavemen who sat down around a campfire somewhere grunting back and forth deciding it was time to be civilized. Instead, the activities of man—ancient man—seem to have been loaded with a snail-paced movement and a development so slow it seems impossible today. Life was the same for one generation after another after another after another after another—until it seems a blur, an almost unbelievable slowness, not in the activities of individuals but in the thrust of what we now call progress.

For ancient man there was no such thing as progress as we know it today. There was, instead, survival. And survival was based (1) on cerebral control of impulses and urges, perhaps centrally upon the control of sexual urges and impulses (Alland, 1967) and (2) on the development of technology. Technology has a starting point somewhere. It may be that technology began when one of our forefathers decided to sleep in a cave rather than on the bare ground. Perhaps technology started when an early human discovered the meat of a deer tasted better after it had been roasted on a small forest fire. No one can tell yet when technology began, but it seems certain that technology began as an effort to insure survival. At the core,

23

at the most basic level, survival depends upon getting enough to eat. Getting enough food and getting that food in a predictable and controlled way is called agriculture. We will never know who planted the first seeds, but whoever it was, they planted something more than could be grown during a summer season. They planted civilization.

Technology and civilization are intertwined aspects of the human condition. But the human condition is not now what it once was. The slow development of early technology and the seemingly sudden rise of civilization has evolved into an accelerated technology and what is viewed by some as a decline in what we call our civilization (Marx, 1964; Mumford, 1967; Michener, 1970). Nevertheless, civilization is our environment, and whenever we consider environment, we must consider the orienting concepts of modifiability, interaction, and the multiplicity of variables.

Humans are, of course, modifiable. They can and do change, and the history of man's ways indicates the change or the potential for tolerating changes is high. It seems that what we inherit is a broad enough spectrum of potentials to insure not mere survival but growth—beneficial growth—in a variety of directions. In effect, our interactions with our environment and with each other have developed a civilization so loaded with a multiplicity of variables it seems almost strange sometimes to be concerned about the limitations imposed upon humans by what is inherited. Some of those limitations are real and perhaps penalizing. We humans have only so much strength, only so much dexterity, only so much speed, and no more. But in spite of these and some other limitations imposed by hereditary factors, we learn. And, as has been mentioned earlier, we forget. We are forced to relearn, to rediscover, or sometimes to reinvent. We also reappraise. It seems time now to reappraise our technology and our science as

Rickover (1972) has done. Neither one is an irresistible force. Both are tools. That is part of what this second chapter is about.

CHANGES IN LIFETIME STYLES

We all measure things. When we take advantage of gravity, we have measurements we call ounces, pounds, and tons. We measure by using space, and we have millimeters, inches, square feet, and cubic yards. We mark the measure of things with dimes and dollars, angles and azimuths, inclines, declines, synclines, and time. We have seconds and minutes and hours. We have waltz time, geologic time, and lifetime. We measure things by happenings, experiences, and events. The Wright brothers' first flight was an event, and so was World War II, the invention of the transistor, and the development of a polio vaccine.

Birth is an event. So is death.* The interval between birth and death is a lifetime.

According to Fred Borsch (1967) and Alvin Toffler (1970) the existence of man on Earth can be measured by 800 lifetimes laid end to end. The first 650 lifetimes of man's existence were spent in roaming across the lands or living in caves. Writing was developed about seventy lifetimes ago. Printing was invented eight lifetimes back, and man could measure heat and cold with at least some precision only five lifetimes into the past. Railroads have been around for three lifetimes. Electric motors have been used for the last two lifetimes, and transistors have existed for less than half a lifetime. The first man-made earth satellite was launched about a quarter of a lifetime ago. Each invention, each new machine, is a symptom of change.

Man's existence on Earth can be measured by change. Kenneth Boulding states that there have been as many changes

_____
*On a later page, death is viewed from another perspective.

during his own lifetime as there were between the birth of Julius Caesar and his own year of birth, 1910.* He adds, "I was born in the middle of human history, to date, roughly. Almost as much has happened since I was born as happened before" (Toffler, 1970, p. 15). That takes into account a lot of happenings. And happenings happen so rapidly now, it is sometimes a wonder anyone is able to adjust, to cope. Some among us adjust and cope well; others do not. The differences between the two are sometimes slight. But then differences mean comparisons of one sort of another; differences imply measurements, and ideas of measurement usually bring up the matter of zero points and base lines.

Earlier we arbitrarily selected a zero point called birth. There are zero points on thermometers, wind speed indicators, and automobile speedometers. These zero points or base lines are useful in establishing different kinds of measurements, but there is no clear base point for the crisp measurement of adjustment behavior. The sentence "Some of us adjust and cope well; others do not " indicates some rough level, an approximation, a general concept about the goodness or the badness of adjusting and coping behavior because human functioning can be viewed as taking place within a variety of *systems* (Sanford, 1966). Not only are there school systems, neighborhood systems, and gang or social club systems, but also are always, or almost always, systems of belief, family systems, social systems, economic systems, and delusional systems in which bias, prejudice, and personal and nonobjective certainties play a large part. To phrase matters in a slightly different form: it is careless to merely talk of "the adjusted individual"; the base point and the system must also be considered.

---

*Jacques Monod and Fred Borsch were also born in 1910.

Adjustment of any kind is a matter of (1) degree and (2) relativity. As for the matter of degree, adjustment can be talked about as "better than" or "worse than" some sort of average, but what is the relationship with average? Psychological adjustment may be, for any one human, fine at school but poor at home, excellent at the coffee break but miserable on the job, superb at age 5 but disastrous at age 19. A person who moves through life is not a well-wrapped package sent through the mails, inert and passive. A living person experiences the systems, adds to and subtracts from those systems; he experiences them and they experience him. No matter where we walk, we all leave footprints.

We are all a part of different social systems, and the systems—large and small—have a history; most of them existed before we hit our individual and personal zero points; many will probably exist after we are gone from the scene. And so let us look briefly at some systems, one of which can be labeled as time. Others will be discussed later in the text.

There are people alive today who can remember the days before television. There are people who can recall the way things were before cellophane tape, ballpoint pens, and nylon. Those were the "way back" days when all the swimming suits were made out of wool that smelled funny when it got wet. John Barrymore was a big star then, and no one had even heard of Doris Day. Maybe you know some people who remember rumble seats, the NRA, CCC camps, and WPA projects. Bread cost a nickel a loaf. Calves' liver was free, and hamburger cost ten cents a pound. That was a mere forty nostalgic years ago. There are a few genuinely ancient people around, alive and well, who can remember when someone down the block bought the first radio in the neighborhood. They can recall going to church in a wagon pulled by an old horse. They will tell you that when they were young, the only things that moved in the skies were clouds, birds, kites, and balloons. It is not that way now.

Now almost everything has changed. The signs and symptoms of change can be found in each invention, each new machine that is added to the environment in which we live (Fuller, 1973).

Evidence for change in the environment can be found in the records of the United States Patent Office. The first U. S. patent was issued to Samuel Hopkins in 1790. It was, according to the laws of the nation, signed by three officials of the government of the United States: George Washington, Edmund Randolph, and Thomas Jefferson. In the first year of its existence, 1790, the patent office issued only three patents. In 1890, one hundred years after it began, the patent office issued slightly more than 25,-000 patents. Now, in the 1970s, that office awards almost 70,000 patents a year (Hollomon, 1967). Each patent is a symptom of at least a small change in our environment. And we all are, in part, products of our environment.

The inventions and discoveries recorded by the patent office form a year-by-year diary of the changes in our environment. That leads us to a well-documented, thoroughly supported, and carefully (sometimes) researched idea: when the environment is changed, people change. There is another factor that may account for changes in humans over a period of time. The other factor is called heredity. In humans the inherited, genetically based factors change, if they change at all, in an extremely slow manner. They may change at such a slow pace they cannot be recognized unless you consider vast reaches of time going back one hundred (200?) lifetimes before we kept records of our own activities.

A review and an examination of the records man has kept about himself is known as the study of history. As Kenneth Clark has said, "History is ourselves"

(1969, p. 347). The story of mankind is, in some respects, the story of large groups of men, women, and children lurching and staggering along from one crisis to the next. Except for the ice ages and perhaps some of the great plagues and famines, most of the large-scale crises seem to be man made. Revolution and warfare, episodes of economic depression, widespread poverty and starvation, civil unrest, and reigns of terror mark our history. Historically we humans have been a part of these crises just as much as we are all a part of the present crisis of change. We are all a part, however remote, of the business conducted at the U. S. Patent Office. We are a part of that business because we use many of the devices that are patented. It is unavoidable; we are all participants in our own technology, whether we invent or merely use the inventions. For example, we can turn to a brief comment by John Updike. He has written of his participation in the technology of hydraulics and plastics in this piece of light verse called "To a Waterbed" (Cole, 1972, p. 66).

No Frog Prince ever had a pond
So faithful, murmurous, and fond.
Amniotically it sings
Of broken dreams and hidden springs,
Automatically it laves
My mind in secondary waves
That answer motions of my own,
However mild—my amnion.
Fond underbubble, warm and deep,
I love you so much I can't sleep.*

For a brief list of other inventions that we may use and that have changed our environment, see Table 3.

People who are now past the midpoint of Erikson's middle age group were born before the first television inventions were put together, but half the present population of the United States was born after television moved from the laboratory to the living rooms of almost every family in the land.

---

*Copyright © 1972 by Harper's Magazine.

Table 3. A list of some inventions*

Invention	Date	Inventor
Safety pin	1849	Walter Hunt
Color photog- raphy	1881	Frederick Ives
Zipper	1893	Whitcomb L. Judson
Air conditioning	1911	Willis H. Carrier
Automobile self- starter	1911	Charles F. Kettering
Television icono- scope scanner	1923	Vladimer K. Zworykin
Television image pick-up tube	1928	Philo T. Farnsworth
Electric shaver	1928	Jacob Schick
Polaroid glass	1932	Edwin H. Land
Electronic computer	1946	J. P. Eckert and J. W. Mauchly
Transistor	1948	J. Bardeen, W. H. Brattain, and W. Shockley

*Adapted from Harth, M., editor: The New York Times encyclopedic almanac, New York, 1971, The New York Times Co.

To bring the matter to a more useful level: adolescents and young adults of the present day grew up with television sets in their houses. Their parents did not. That makes a difference of not small importance, for the change is a matter of an alteration in the family environment. Alterations in the great and general system called the environment cause alterations, changes, in the people who inhabit that environment.*

While man's genetic base may remain invariant, his environmental system base has changed and continues to change, but as Amasa Ford (1970) has pointed out, "Rapid technological change has become

*George Gerbner (1972) states there have been only three major changes in communications technology in the whole of man's history. The first was the invention of writing; the second was the invention of printing; the third was electronic communications, which includes television. Each resulted in drastic environmental alterations, with the last bringing about the greatest change in the shortest time.

so familiar in developed countries over the past 20 years as to blunt our perception of what is happening" (p. 257). The changes in the environment lead inevitably to changes in behavior, or at the minimum, to changes in some behavior that may trigger a chain reaction leading to more changes.

The changes in our environment, based as they may be in a growing, blossoming, often enriching, increasingly widespread, and frequently destructive technology, can become so pervasive, so subtle sometimes, and as Ford states, so familiar that we may often overlook what the changes do to us as humans. Robert Morison (1967) has pointed out:

It is hard to see how enriching the environment and increasing the contacts of young children can do other than increase their capacity for intelligent choices later in life and thus free them from both external and internal constraints that normally limit personal freedom. [p. 432]

There is an optimistic ring to Morison's words, but what is the result of "enriching the environment and increasing the contacts of young children"? To develop an answer or a part of an answer to that question, we must look again at man's history.

While there may be historical dates to remember in connection with inventions, there is no such invention date for schools. School systems, or the idea of schooling, developed within the family before there was any writing. Perhaps they developed within the family of the caveman. Dressed in animal skins and covered with insect bites and thorn scratches, the cave-dwelling father may have grunted instructions to his son in the art of stealing honey from the bees or showed the boy where to find wild duck eggs or how to catch fish with his bare hands.

Moving ahead thousands upon thousands of years, we find that schooling was still part of the activity of the family. Fathers taught their own sons how to work at a trade, and because of that effort, families often became known and named according to the work they did. Anyone whose name is Smith has a line of blacksmiths somewhere in the history of his family. The same can be said for those whose names are Cooper and Baker and Cook. The Carpenters among us have ancestors who worked with wood, and anyone named Currier has forefathers who cared for (and curried) horses. The craftsmen of centuries ago taught their crafts to their sons. Mothers taught their daughters how to cook and sew and how to bear children, how to be midwives, and how to keep the fire in the family hearth alive. But because of the increase in the level of technology, those teaching activities moved out of the family and into the schools three or four lifetimes ago.

As Morison (1967) points out, "Survival in the modern world depends on the rapid mastery of new knowledge" (p. 430). New knowledge is not transmitted from father to son or from mother to daughter. Old knowledge is. The old knowledge can be useful; some of it can also be obsolete. Some of the knowledge transmitted from one generation to the next may simply involve an effort at trying to figure out and to know what life in this world is all about.

What causes something to happen, something such as human behavior, is a central, immensely important factor in knowing, in making sense out of whatever happens. Francis Bacon (Kahn, 1954) said that ignorance of causes leads to inevitable failure, especially in the realm of knowing. B. F. Skinner (1971), in writing about the causes of behavior, looked at ancient history and stated:

Man's first experience with causes probably came from his own behavior: things moved because he moved them. If other things moved, it was because someone else was moving them; if the mover could not be seen, it was because he was invisible. Gods and demons served in this way as causes of physical phenomena. [p. 38]

Invisible spirits, demons, wraiths, phantoms, and a crowd of gods and goddesses were parts or facets of systems invented by early man to explain what he did not understand. Believing in these inventions helped to make the world more sensible, more predictable, more personal, and less awesome. Inventing the spirits and the demons and believing in them formed a base, a springboard, a launching platform for a further evolution and development of what is usually called culture.

The evolution and development of culture seems to move in spurts. Kenneth Clark (1969) has described these spurts. He maintains the first took place about 3000 B.C. "when quite suddenly civilization appeared, not only in Egypt and Mesopotamia but in the Indus Valley . . . " (p. 23). The second great burst of activity occurred in Ionia, Greece, and India around 500 B.C.; the third came about A.D. 1100 and is still with us, affecting the whole world. These three great episodes in man's history are known as times of change, times when intellect and energy were poured into a variety of areas, including an effort to find an increased measure of sense, order, and predictability.

The Egyptians did more than fight wars, worship cats, form a nation, and build pyramids. They kept records. They made observations and kept precise records of the Nile River flood cycle. They also produced, hand written and on papyrus, what is either the first book or the oldest known book. The book is titled *The Precepts of Ptah-Hotep,* and it is over fifty-three centuries old. It contains ideas such as:

Be not arrogant because of that which thou knowest; deal with the ignorant as with the learned; for the barriers of art are not closed, no artist being in possession of the perfection to which he should aspire. [Garnett, 1899, p. 104]

The Egyptians of 3000 B.C. formed the first cities the world had ever known. They built a nation and made observations of events and causes. They were involved with a variety of engineering efforts, but more importantly, they invented writing. Their achievements (many are not included here) were based upon the centralized control of power (Cottrell, 1957). They had a highly organized, disciplined form of government. That at least tells something about how they managed to do all that they did. Why they did what they did is another matter.

For 1,000 years before and for more time than that after 3000 B.C., the Egyptians had a system of religion so filled with gods and goddesses it "must have been as bewildering to the mass of the Ancient Egyptians as it is to us" (Cottrell, 1957, p. 21). They had over 2,000 deities at one time or another, and all had to be somehow taken care of. There was, for the Egyptians, a close connection between taking care of their religious beings, which usually included the king, and getting taken care of. Their religion and their great technological accomplishments were developed and designed to make their world more sensible, orderly, predictable, and systematic.

By 500 B.C., plus or minus a century, the Greeks had a variety of gods and goddesses they could call their own. They had Hercules and Zeus and many others in their heavens. They had people walking on the land who were known by the names of Pythagoras, Aristophanes, Sappho, Plato, and Aristotle, a man of immense influence in his own time and for centuries beyond into our time. His name and his influence will, perhaps, still be felt hundreds of years beyond today.

It was Aristotle who observed, "Man is by nature a political animal" (Cohen and Cohen, 1960, p. 10). Aristotle, it seems, was by nature an animal loaded with curiosity. He was driven to find out, to know, to organize and make sense and order out of all he touched and talked about. What he wrote was used, together with the Christian Bible, as the prime source of authority during the Middle Ages (Kahn, 1954). Unfortunately, his writings were used in a way that might have saddened him. They were used, not as a launching point for new thinking, but as a prison of the intellect, a jail cell for what is called "the truth." New ideas during the Middle Ages were dismissed, thrown out, ignored, or penalized if they disagreed with the Bible or with Aristotle's writings.

A span of fourteen centuries is needed to bridge the gap that exists between the death of Aristotle and the birth of Peter Abelard. Aristotle was one of the last of the great Greeks. Abelard represents the first of a new breed of thinkers, men who wanted to shake off the intellectually suffocating era known as the Dark Ages or the Middle Ages. Abelard's ways mark the start of the third great episode in man's cultural evolution. He said, in A.D. 1122, "By doubting we come to questioning, and by questioning we perceive the truth" (Clark, 1969, p. 44). One hundred and fifty years later Roger Bacon insisted that statements "of fact" must be based on observation and backed by data (Kahn, 1954). The words seem out of place, as though no one knew the Egyptians had made observations and collected data about the Nile flood cycle more than 4,000 years earlier. Yet, because Bacon said what he said, he was called a heretic, a man linked with Satan, dedicated to the destruction of the word of God. He was arrested and put in jail in 1277. Slightly more than 200 years later Columbus said that the earth was round. Many thought he was mad, but Pythagoras had said the same thing 2,000 years before. Copernicus believed the earth revolved around the sun, and this observation, backed with data, was quietly published in 1543. Fifty years later Galileo talked openly about the findings of Copernicus and was jailed. No one remembered, perhaps, that Aristarchus had concluded, 1,700 years before

Galileo was born, that the earth moved around the sun (Kahn, 1954.)

The struggle continued, a grim sort of war between familiar systems of established doctrine and what has come to be known as the systems of science and technology. Both sides were immersed in sometimes separate and distinct efforts to make sense out of the world, to find and to identify an apparently necessary form of order and predictability.

The struggle continues, but the balance of power and influence has changed in the past century. As Gunther Stent (1972), a professor of molecular biology, points out:

> Common sense tells man that he is the center of the universe. Onward from the first days of his infancy, he perceives the world in an expanding series of concentric spheres—his own person, his family, his neighborhood, his town, his province, his nation —within which, with increasing distance from him, events assume an ever diminishing emotional significance. His own toothache causes him more pain than the broken leg of his brother, which in turn causes him more pain than the death of a neighbor, of a dozen strangers, of a hundred foreigners. It is hardly surprising therefore that the traditional beliefs of nearly all peoples incorporated this man-centered view, to which the unfolding of modern science has done ever increasing violence. Since the Copernican revolution of the sixteenth century, astronomy has taught that not only does the Earth revolve around the Sun but that the Sun, hundreds of thousands of times bigger than our Earth, is itself but a tiny speck in our galaxy, which is itself only one of a myriad of other galaxies lost in an immensity of space. And since the Darwinian revolution of the nineteenth century, biology has taught that even in the history of our own astronomically utterly insignificant Earth, man figures only in the very last of many epochs, not the product of a special act of divine creation but evolutionary descendant of and close relative to lower forms of life. No wonder that for the past century belief in God, that source of law and order in the man-centered universe, has waned as these scientific notions gained wider and wider currency. [p. 125]*

Stent's comment leads to an obvious

---

*From Stent, G.: An ode to objectivity, The Atlantic, Nov., 1971. Copyright © 1971, by The Atlantic Monthly Co., Boston, Mass. Reprinted by permission.

question: is science now the source of law and order? It is not, or at least it should not be, according to Theodore Roszak (Wade, 1972). Roszak has been called the foremost spokesman of antiscience, yet Roszak denies the label. He would rather be known and remembered as someone who preferred that science be equalized with such disparate sectors of the environment as mysticism, the occult, and a humanistic view of mankind.

Perhaps what Roszak prefers is ambitious, for our history is loaded with opposing long-term trends defined by Ernst Mayr (1972) and Amos Hawley (1973). Mayr has traced the impact of the work of Charles Darwin upon the ideas man has had about himself and about the world in which he lives. Prior to Darwin, a good many people believed the earth was created approximately 6,000 years ago. Darwin and several others suggested the earth was ancient, and since then, radioactive carbon dating and a newer dating technique called "D-form" indicate our planet to be old (Henahan, 1972). That the world was not created 6,000 years ago conflicted with the old and often treasured ideas of Adam and Eve in the Garden. The conflict ended for science in the rejection of creationism, and this apparently required that most people seek out a new concept of God and a new basis for religion. What Darwin did, what he started, is only one aspect of what has gone in the long-term trends that make Roszak's ambitions seem high. What Darwin did may be viewed as enormous and profound; whether it is viewed as good or bad seems to depend on the viewer.

"Enormous" and "profound" can be brought into play as words to describe Hawley's ideas of the results of *organizational expansion.* The expansion of organizations refers to the three-century trend in the development of gigantic urban environments. These environments are diffuse, and while they may overlap one another, they are organized to some degree.

The organizational expansion of our urban environment has led to the following:

1. A dependence upon other localities for food, which therefore, along with other materials, must be trucked, trained, or flown in
2. A great rise in housekeeping problems concerned with the efforts to somehow take care of garbage, which is on the land, in the air, and in the waters in and around the urban environment
3. A change in energy sources from wood and coal to petroleum products and atomic power
4. A general decline in the awareness of the genuine, "real" surface conditions of the planet
5. A similarity between many aspects of many urban environments, a similarity that seems to be approaching standardization

With regard to the interlocking aspects of these results of organizational expansion, it is possible in every city in the land of more than a few hundred thousand citizens to buy a hamburger that (1) has the same amount of meat in it (brought from somewhere else), (2) has been cooked the same length of time (using piped-in fuel), (3) is covered with the same pickles and sauces (grown and bottled elsewhere), (4) enclosed in the same kind of bun (baked in a factory), (5) wrapped in the same sort of paper (manufactured in another place), and (6) served by the same sort of harried but sometimes smiling person behind the counter who (7) wears the same kind of apron and paper hat. The hamburger is, in this instance, a monument to standardization and technology.

But to return to an item: the general decline in the awareness of the genuine, "real" surface conditions of the planet. A part of our "real" surface conditions is the weather surrounding us. The weather has been a legitimate subject of scientific and technological study for a long time. We cannot yet order the weather we want, but how we react to weather conditions is another matter. A small slice of our reactions has been studied, and some of these findings hark back to the question of whether science is now the source of law and order. Perhaps a part of an answer to that question may be found if we briefly review some research in a limited area of human behavior—reactions to the threat of tornadoes.

Slightly more than thirty-five years ago, a California businessman searched across the nation and gathered together as many talented midgets as his budget would allow. The midgets were given special training and provided with splendid costumes. They worked under bright lights and in front of cameras. Eventually they appeared in a movie. In that movie the midgets were called Munchkins, citizens of Munchkinland, and they were on hand to greet Dorothy (played by Judy Garland), whose house had been transported to their locale by a Kansas tornado. As John Sims and Duane Baumann (1972) have pointed out:

> Fortunately for the majority of Americans, their most vivid image of tornadoes derives from their memory of the dark twister weaving across the plains of Kansas in the film *The Wizard of Oz.* But unfortunately for those living in certain areas of the North and South, the awesome force of the tornado is a very real presence. In these locations, the announcement of the tornado watch or the tornado warning are familiar spring messages. [p. 1386]

A tornado watch is a technologically based statement of probability, a notice prepared by the National Weather Service and broadcast on radio and television stating that weather conditions are such that a tornado may develop in six hours or more. A tornado warning is an urgent message, radioed and televised, that a tornado is going to strike at any moment. People are advised they should prepare to take cover immediately. Both the watch and the warning tell of potential threat, for a tornado is a violent storm that can rip buildings apart, lift massive trucks off the highway, peel orchards and wheat fields away from the land, and kill people.

Each year, on the average, 119 people are killed by 649 tornadoes in the United States (Harth, 1971). It seems reasonable to expect most tornado-caused deaths will take place where are the largest numbers of people exposed to the greatest numbers of tornadoes. It seems reasonable, but it is wrong. What makes it wrong has perhaps been identified by Sims and Baumann, a psychiatrist and a geographer. They combined their talents in a project to research human reactions to the threat of tornadoes.

A heavily populated area with a high frequency of tornadoes is said to have a high casualty potential. The highest casualty potential from tornadoes exists in a zone that runs from Dallas through Topeka, Kansas, to Chicago and on to Detroit. That is the strip in which the most tornado-caused deaths can be *expected*. The *actual* number of deaths is highest in the deep South. The difference between potential and actual is not based upon violence of tornadoes, or upon differences in the strength of buildings, or upon the average duration of a tornado. Instead, the difference is based upon psychological reactions, at least according to what Sims and Baumann found. Their research involved white, female adult citizens in four counties in Illinois (North) and four counties in Alabama (South). All the counties had a similar history of tornadoes, and the people who were studied were similar in age, education and income. And yet, with all these similarities, there were sharp differences in actual casualty rates. The proportion of deaths in Alabama was twice that in Illinois. The researchers suggested the difference is based on a psychological dimension: the extent or degree to which an individual believes he can control his own life. As they concluded:

Persons like the respondents from Illinois, who believe they direct their own lives, who believe that what they do affects their futures, go about confronting the possibility of a tornado in characteristic style. They use their heads and the technology of their society, and they take action. In the aftermath of a tornado, they would indeed see those who had escaped as "lucky" (in the sense of random, not destined), go about helping the needy, and occasionally pause to observe themselves and their fellowmen as fascinating creatures.

Persons like the respondents from Alabama, who believe that God (or fate or luck) controls their lives, who have less confidence in their own ability to have an impact on reality, to effect change, also confront a tornado in a manner that is consistent with their attitudes. They place less trust in man's communal knowledge and control systems; they await the fated onslaught, watchful but passive. In the tornado's aftermath, they feel with the victims (there but for the grace of God . . .) and then recover to perform good works.

Although admittedly based upon only a small sampling of behavior of a small number of respondents, these findings and interpretations may be relevant to the disproportionately higher death rate from tornadoes in the South. Fatalism, passivity, and perhaps most important, lack of trust in and inattention to society's organized systems of warning constitute a weak defense against the terrible strike of the tornado. [p.1391]*

Sims and Baumann used questionnaires to explore internal versus external levels of control. An example of internal control is found in the statement: "What I know, how I am, and what happens to me is under my control." For an example of external control, we can use this statement: "What I know, how I am, and what happens to me is a matter of luck or fate." While both statements imply a measure of trust, in which direction is the trust aimed? Sims and Baumann suggest those who are like the respondents from Illinois place their trust in technology and its scientific underpinings and in themselves. It is, perhaps, not too great a stretch of logic to consider that those from Illinois (and people similar to them) find some sense

*From Sims, J., and Baumann, D.: The tornado threat: coping styles of the North and South, Science, vol. 176, pp. 1386-1391, June 30, 1972. Copyright © 1972 by the American Association for the Advancement of Science.

of law and order in the distant system of science, in the immediate and pervasive system of technology and in themselves.

Of all man's developments, none influences our times and our lives more than the systems of science and technology. Both have contributed heavily to the changes that go on around us, changes we can often ignore or overlook but that affect us all.

SCIENCE AND TECHNOLOGY—TWO SYSTEMS

There are some among us, members of the larger human family, who say we must dispense with science and return to the bucolic life. We must, they say, develop a love of nature. Alan Watts (1958) has a brief commentary about that:

> We know that the "love of nature" is a sentimental fascination with surfaces—that the gulls do not float in the sky for delight but in watchful hunger for fish, that the golden bees do not dream in the lilies but call as routinely for honey as collection agents for rent, and that the squirrels romping, as it seems, freely and joyously through the branches, are just frustrated little balls of appetite and fear. [p. 1]

But Eric Hoffer (1968) has made this statement concerning man and nature:

> You can count on the fingers of one hand unequivocal expressions of the eternal enmity between man and nature. I can think only of Hardy's "Man begins where nature ends; nature and man can never be friends." Thoreau, who sided with nature, recognized that "you cannot have a deep sympathy with both man and nature," and admitted "I love nature because she is not man but a retreat from him." [pp. 166-167]

Yet science, one of humankind's most intricate developments, has as its primary thrust the study of nature, including man by man. Pause for a moment to consider Paul Doty's (1971) brief definition:

> Science is understanding, primarily of the physical and biological worlds, but also, to the extent that it is possible, of the more complex domain of human behavior. [p. 998]

In a different style, Alan Watts (1951) presents this definition:

> The true splendor of science is not so much that it names and classifies, records and predicts, but that it observes and desires to know the facts, whatever they may turn out to be. [p. 127]

Science as the pursuit of understanding, as an effort designed to get at the facts, is sometimes confused with technology. The two are not the same. As Doty (1971) points out, "Technology is simply the multiplicity of ways in which human groups go about satisfying their physical needs" (p. 998). Doty could have added to or amended his definition to include psychological needs.

In societies that have a high level of technological development (as in Japan, Canada, the United States, and much of Europe), technology is used not only in the production of food, clothing, and shelter, but also in the production of toys. It forms the base for the manufacture of ski boots, surf boards, electric guitars, strobe lights, motion pictures, and dune buggies. At times science and technology are tightly linked. For instance, the hydrogen bomb is a technological device that is a direct descendant of scientific research, as is the cellulose content of throwaway, disposable baby diapers. The same can be said for such technological devices as solar batteries, nylon backpacks, polio vaccine, plastic contact lenses, football helmets, and shoes made of Corfam. Humans, though, use a variety of technological devices that have not originated in the scientific laboratory.

The first technology existed without any sort of link with science. The first technology was agriculture (Frankfort, 1954). The Dutch depended upon technological trial and error, not on scientific research when they built their first windmills (White, 1970). Technology and not science has spawned such items as ice skates, ashtrays, bicycles, knives, diving boards, and lawn mowers. As it is now though much of our newer technology is the result of science. Scientists do research. They run experiments and work to get at the facts, at understanding. What is uncovered or discovered by the scientists is, when possible, applied by technologists.

Technologists may be engineers, dieticians, nurses, physicians, computer designers, test pilots, teachers, zoo keepers —millions of people in thousands of occupations—all of whom circulate in our society as typical or near-typical citizens. Scientists, in contrast, are supremely specialized, uncommon people who work with a precision and care more rigorous, more orderly, and more tightly controlled than almost any nonscientist can imagine. Scientists develop, use, and produce science.

In the hazy distant past, man believed in spirits and demons and the magic and witchcraft his own mind had conjured up in order to make the world (as he knew it then) a more sensible, more predictable, and less awesome place in which to live. The belief in systems of magic and witchcraft faded as humans gradually grasped the idea that there may be some greater force than humans could exert, a force controlling the movements of stars, the growth of plants, the birth of babies. The idea can be expressed in a number of ways. It can be said that man developed religion, that man invented gods, or that God revealed Himself to man. In any case, magic and witchcraft faded, although not totally, and what is called religion received more attention.

Man's belief in gods or a God or in some unknowable but powerful force has, in its turn, slowly faded since the end of the Middle Ages, and a belief in science *and* technology has come to the fore. While there has been a recent and noisy surge of barbs and challenges aimed at science and technology,* large numbers of people maintain a fervent belief in both. Many people believe science will eventually uncover and organize all that is to be understood and identify all the facts we need to know. Many believe technology

---

* See Prologue.

Daniel Brody/Editorial Photocolor Archives

will design and build the machines that will repair, renovate, and preserve our damaged planet.

Many people believe science and technology will provide us with solutions to the problems we have. On a more basic and personal level, the belief that science will find all the answers is similar to the belief small children have: parents will take care of everything. The belief that science will take care of everything and eventually solve all problems may be similar to a dependence on other people rather than an appropriate level of dependence on oneself.

At the other extreme is the scientist or technologist who wants to take charge of the solving of problems. As George P. Elliott (1971) has pointed out:

One who imposes the values of science upon the moral and social life is likely, if he is of an emotional nature and has much spleen, to be in a state of chronic restlessness. The usual form this takes is rebelliousness and hostility toward those who are not with him. Rapid and extreme social change becomes for him a necessity, without regard to the anxiety which such change generates in ordinary people and to their reactive cruelty because of that anxiety. [p. 107]

The scientist or the technologist who wishes to take charge, who wants to impose the values of science upon moral and social life, acts as a parent who will take care of everything. But as David Bakan (1972) has pointed out:

It would be wrong to reject the scientific model in its entirety; to dismiss the grand history of science and its role in increasing man's understanding of himself and his environment; or to disparage the potential of science to change man's future. [p. 88]

Very few of us can be called scientists, but we all experience the results of the scientific endeavor. We all participate in our own technology. One of the results of that increasingly complex technology is the development of a distance, a gap between generations. As Morison (1967) has pointed out:

The family, which is a fine mechanism for transmitting conventional wisdom in a static society, is relatively poor at assimilating and transmitting new knowledge essential to survival in a rapidly moving world. [p. 430]

Considering the incredible level of change going on around us, it is possible to conclude that the family, as it has existed for a long span of man's history, is now an obsolete institution. It no longer functions as it once did as the main source of moral and social values. Nor does religion, according to the comments of Gunther Stent and others (Kahn, 1954; Booth, 1964; Graham, 1971). With the influence of the old and classic family structure on the decline and considering the idea that religion has lost its centuries-old hold on man, the question arises once more: is science now the source of law and order?

REVIEW QUESTIONS

1. In what ways are mere primitive survival and living within a civilized society different? How are they the same?
2. How does technology help humans overcome their inherited limitations?
3. What is time?
4. What name is given to the records man has kept about himself?
5. What are the three major changes in communications technology?
6. What does John Updike try to communicate in his poem "To a Waterbed"?
7. What technological advances have been made in your lifetime? Which has affected your life the most?
8. What was it that both Aristarchus and Copernicus believed in?
9. What is organizational expansion? What are its consequences?
10. John Sims, Duane Baumann, and Judy Garland and *The Wizard of Oz* are all interconnected. How?
11. What is the essential difference between science and technology?
12. Is science now the source of law and order?

3

STABILITY AND BALANCE

Octavio Paz is a philosopher, a poet, a writer, and a former member of the Mexican diplomatic service; he was Mexico's ambassador to India for six years. Now he spends much of his time traveling. A short time ago he was interviewed by Rita Guibert (1972). She asked him what plans he had for the future; he replied he would like to abolish it. What Paz did not like about the future has been briefly described in the example of the standardized hamburger given in Chapter 2. While Hawley refers to urban environments' approaching a similarity, regardless of where they may be, that nears standardization, Paz calls it a matter of progress toward uniformity. It is a movement, an evolution toward sameness.

We are surrounded by change, by progress of some sort, by evolutions, revolutions, and convolutions in our environment; we are, at the same time, immersed in similarities, standardizations, and uniformities. But to understand one side, we must sometimes be aware of the other. Sunlight is more real because of shadow, and days mean more because we have nights. There are limits, though, to this matter of understanding through contrasts. It is doubtful whether anyone can understand the very rich by being very

poor or whether a human can know of sex by way of absolute celibacy. Still, we all seem to live face to face with two central and undeniable aspects of life that in themselves are contrasts: stability and change.

Edward Spicer (1971), the anthropologist, has written of persistence, of stability in the face of change. In his work he refers to the persistence of group behavior, persistence in the old and familiar ways of behaving even when members of the group are surrounded by an environment filled with a multiplicity of variables that spell change. To Spicer, a group does not mean a student body or a nation or an empire; instead he refers to nonpersistent empires such as the Spanish Empire, which disintegrated into a variety of nations, one of them being Octavio Paz's Mexico. There is also the British Empire, more recently disintegrated into Ghana, Burma, Tanzania, Nigeria, and other nations, including India. These disintegrations are matters of change. As for stability, it may exist and persist through times of change because of what Spicer calls the *identity system*. An identity system is not some aspect of an empire or a nation. It is not based upon a political, governmental system. Instead, according to Spicer, it refers to "a people's" belief in (1) certain symbols and (2) what the symbols stand for. A symbol may be a word printed on a sweatshirt, a flag, a trademark, or a crucifix.

Identity systems, which involve a group or a people, have a set of *identity symbols* that may be reasonably permanent fixtures of the history of the group. The identity symbols that provide the foundation for a stability or a persistence of identity for a people are (1) the land, (2) language, (3) music, (4) dances, and (5) heroes. These symbols have a greater meaning and a greater unifying force if there are pressures to compromise or to abandon them.

The Jews, for example, had only the memory of a land that was once theirs, but the symbol of that land acted as part of the glue holding them together through centuries of dismal treatment in Europe and other places of the world. They had their Israel in their hearts long before it was firmly under their feet, and they had their own language, music, dances, and heroes. American Indians had their land too, something they regarded as the most important thing in their lives. They had languages and dances and music and heroes, but after the end of their eminence on the American continent, the symbols they had began to fall apart. Dee Brown (1970) has described their decline, and a part of that decline can be identified by an 1890 change in their dance, which was called the "Dance of the Ghosts." The "Dance of the Ghosts" consisted of some that was old and some that was new—the new being a part of the white man's ways. The old was the dance itself, but the new consisted of dancing under the direction of the Christian Christ. The old symbol of the dance was compromised by a newer symbol, Christ, and this compromise spelled change and instability rather than a genuine persistence. Yet what the Indians hoped for was a persistence of their ways, for the purpose behind the dance was to

abolish the white man and to bring back the great herds of buffalo and horses to their land, where only Indians would live. But as a group, as a people, the various tribes declined; they were pushed into decline by the insistence of the cavalry, the pioneers, the gold seekers, and the railroads, perhaps all banded together and motivated by another kind of symbol, the dollar sign.

At one time the dollar sign was a greater symbol of stability and permanence than it is now. More durable than the dollar, the ruble, and other monies are ideas. And one of the ideas in this chapter has to do with the persistent importance of reputation and self-esteem. There appears to be a great striving on the part of individuals to stabilize and maintain their own levels of reputation and self-esteem. There are many among us—individuals rather than groups—who spend energy to function persistently at a level that may often be uncomfortable. The persistence, the consistency, the stability seem to be of more value, or less awesome, than the possibility of change in which the individual moves out of a life dominated by discomfort. It is, for these individuals, a matter of sameness at all costs. The tangible and intangible symbols of a personal identity are used to maintain old ways, old discomforts. In contrast, however, many among us use these same but still personal symbols of identity as tools for change. Part of this chapter illustrates that contrast.

CHANGE, STABILITY, AND CHAOS

If you are ever seriously injured or sick and cannot or should not move or if you become old and feeble and your body begins wearing out, a nurse may put a thin, flexible tube into your urethra and slide it up to your bladder. Your urine will then drain out of you, traveling down the tube to a plastic bag attached to the side of the bed. You may, if you are conscious, think about one of the mechanisms of your own stability, urination. On a related track: you can take a shower in the morning and anoint your body with sprays and lotions that in hot weather may last until mid-afternoon; but then the natural body odors may prove too powerful for the chemicals, and for those concerned about such matters, it is time to shower again, to anoint the body again, to become "civilized" once more.

The sweat we produce and the urine we excrete form part of a chain of events, all of which are involved in stability. Sweat and urine were at one time the water in a glass of water, the water in watermelon, the water in a potato or a hamburger or a bowl of cherries. It is necessary that we take the water in—necessary for life—and it is necessary that to continue with life, we expel it in one way or another. We also take in food and expel the waste. We breathe in air, use some of it, and expel the rest, all in the name of stability. We all are involved with the matter of stability all of the time. Our bodies require it for survival. So do our minds.

Stability is necessary for life, but one of the most obvious characteristics about a lifetime is the opposite of stability, and that is called change. Babies are born; they grow and develop and move along the time line through ages and stages toward the inevitable decline of old age and the personal ending of death. For an observer, a spectator, the changes that take place in another person are often obvious.

One of the least obvious characteristics about living is change within ourselves. We each move slowly from a burbling, mumbling, cooing person to someone who can talk, but who among us can remember learning how to talk? We grow physically, but who can recall the physical sense of growing? Our eyes change over time and our ears change too, but the normal changes that happen in a day or in two days or even in a month are too small to

be noticed, especially by the person to whom and within whom the changes happen.

The sweep of lifetime changes can be recorded in photographs and home movies, but they are usually so gradual that they are only dimly known, if at all, by the person experiencing them. A boy does not get up one morning and simply begin decades of shaving. The appearance of a beard is a gradual matter, triggered by a genetic process that begins well before he is born. Girls are born with eggs in a ready position, but it may take ten or twelve or fourteen years for an egg to be brought physically to the place where its fertility is beyond doubting. The development of the menstrual cycle is as gradual a process as the appearance of whiskers, and both describe an evolving change in the person.

We are all involved with changes all the time; we are all involved with stability all the time. Achieving a balance between the two is known as the process of *homeostasis.* As Maslow (1943) points out:

Homeostasis refers to the body's automatic efforts to maintain a constant, normal state of the blood stream. Cannon [1932] has described this process for 1) the water content of the blood; 2) salt content; 3) sugar content; 4) protein content; 5) fat content; 6) calcium content; 7) oxygen content; 8) constant hydrogen-ion level (acid-base balance); and 9) constant temperature of the blood. Obviously, this list can be extended to include other minerals, the hormones, vitamins, etc. [p. 374]

And, according to Noyes and Kolb (1963):

There are those forms of activity which are directed essentially to maintaining the biological needs of the individual: for food, water, oxygen, warmth, and elimination of waste products and protection against attack. These may be classified as:
1. Ingestive,
2. Eliminative,
3. Shelter-seeking, and
4. Agonistic patterns of behavior,
the latter being any activity resulting in contact or contest, whether it results in fighting or flight.

These biological needs, these physiological motivating conditions are stacked or put in an orderly arrangement that leads us to more complex types of behavior. Noyes and Kolb (1963) continue:

> The other forms of behavior are concerned with the procreative and social existence of species, the identifiable activities of which are
>
> 5. Sexual and mating,
> 6. Care-giving and care-taking,
> 7. Mimetic and communicative, and
> 8. Exploratory or investigative. [pp. 12-13]

This stack of eight can be simplified. The first layers are the physiological motivating conditions. The next layers consist of factors relating to personal safety while the top, most complicated, layers are made up of *interpersonal* and *intrapersonal* factors. That is, the interpersonal involve people in face-to-face (or phone-to-phone) situations; the intrapersonal involve a person alone, dealing with his internal psychological environment, his thoughts, and feelings. The intrapersonal can extend to a person's being concerned about the feelings he has about the feelings he has, but more of that later.

To briefly summarize at this point: we are, as living things, constantly spending our energies in trying to maintain our own stability and balance. The most routine (and also the most necessary to life) efforts at maintaining personal stability are ingestive and eliminative. The most routine are physiological; the most complex efforts are psychological.

Valerie

Valerie was 20 years old, chronically aloof, friendless, and 100 pounds overweight. She rarely took a bath; her hair hung in lank, oily strands over her face, and the clothes she wore were smudged with dirt and lightly covered with cat hair.

Valerie lived alone in a small room containing an old bed, a small sink, and three cats. The room was on the second floor of an old house owned by her parents. Her parents lived in the house, and sometimes she could hear them, but she never saw them. Every morning her mother left a small sack of food on the floor outside her door and took away the sack she

had left there the day before. The sack her mother brought contained Valerie's food, some cat food, a new can of Sterno, and a book. When she was sure no one was in the hallway, Valerie opened her door and swiftly grabbed the sack, pulling it into the room. She fed her cats first and then herself, warming the food over the blue Sterno flames. Then she sat on the floor to read the book her mother left her.

When twilight came and the room darkened, Valerie closed the book, finished with it whether she had read all the way through or not. She cleaned out the cats' sandbox, put the empty cat food cans and other garbage in the paper sack, and put the sack in the hall outside her door. She held the door open, listened, and then ran down the hallway to the bathroom, where she hurriedly relieved herself. She ran back to her room, shut the door, and went to bed with her clothes on, the three cats curling up silently and close to her fat body.

Life had been an uninterrupted haze for Valerie for more than three years. Her daily routine was undisturbed. She had read at least the first half of more than 1,000 books but had talked with no one, an isolated island of a person watching the seasons change on the other side of her one window, reading, sleeping, and eating the time away until, on a weekend afternoon, both her parents were killed in an automobile accident.

The police extracted the wallet from her father's body and got the home address. Within an hour after the accident a police car pulled up in front of Valerie's home. The house was dark and no one answered the knock on the door. It was well past twilight and Valerie was asleep with her silent cats.

The next morning there was no sack of food and a book by Valerie's door. She was bewildered and frightened by this interruption in the routine. Throughout the day, Valerie fidgeted and looked out the window at the green leaves on a tree, at the green grass, at the roof of a neighboring house, and at the sky. When sunset came again, she ran to the bathroom, evacuated her bowel and bladder, and sped back to the safety of her room.

There was no sack the next morning. Valerie was terrified. She slammed the bedroom door and turned to the dirty bed. She pulled at the bedspread, tore it off the bed, and began ripping the fabric with her hands. She screamed and kicked at the cats, which ran under the bed. She beat her fists against the bedroom door and urinated at the same time. And then, exhaused, she knelt on the floor, put her forehead against the door, and wept.

There was no sack by her door the next morning. She stared at the floor for a long moment, dimly recalling the stairs that led down to the hallway on the first floor. She remembered the kitchen and the food that was there. She closed her bedroom door and sat on the floor trying to remember what the kitchen was like. There were cupboards and counters. Was there Sterno in the kitchen? Where was the cat food? She sat on the floor dazed until early afternoon, and then slowly she opened the door to her room and crawled on her hands and knees down the hallway to the top of the stairs. Behind her, the cats huddled close to each other in the doorway of her room, watching Valerie as she went out of sight down the stairway.

She was still crawling when she reached the kitchen. From the distant reaches of old memories, she recalled bread in a metal box on one of the counters, and she stood up to look. It was there. She fumbled at first but eventually opened the bread box and grabbed at some slices of stale white bread, which she stuffed in her mouth as the doorbell rang. She froze for a moment, then ran from the kitchen. Within fifteen seconds she was back in her room, out of breath but holding a half dozen slices of bread in one hand. The doorbell sounded again, then again, and then everything in the house was silent once more.

Valerie sat down on the floor and gave some of the bread to the three cats. She kept the rest for herself, slowly chewing and wondering what had happened to change her life. She finished eating the bread just before sunset and went to sleep once more with the cats huddled against her.

When she woke up, it was late morning and she felt enormously hungry. She sat up in bed and edged her feet across the mattress and onto the floor. She stood up slowly, went to the door, opened it, walked down the hall, down the stairs, and out the front door. She walked down the steps to the street. She walked into the middle of the street and sat down. For half an hour each car that went by slowed down and curved around her. At noon the police came in a black-and-white car and took her to the medical school at the university. She was admitted to the psychiatric wing and was briefly interviewed and given some medications. Two practical nurses gave her a bath, braided her hair, and gently put her to bed.

The next morning she was given a large breakfast and was interviewed by a psychologist. Later she was seen by a psychiatric social worker, who pieced together Valerie's recent experiences after several lengthy interviews. A week later Valerie was taken to the state mental hospital, where she now lives.

The struggle to maintain stability and balance is largely a struggle to get whatever it is one needs. We need air (oxygen) and so we breathe. We need water and we drink. And if what we need is taken care of, we do not struggle at that level; we move on to the next level. If we have enough air and water and if when hunger moves in on us, we eat, then we can become concerned about shelter and warmth; and if these in turn are achieved, then we can move up the line of conditions and work at taking care of our needs for safety from angry animals, predatory humans, and other dangers. And if all these physiological and safety needs are somehow fulfilled, it is possible to move on to the needs for an adequate level of self-esteem, an appropriate sort of reputation, and finally on toward the matter of self-actualization.

Maslow (1943) turns the matter around and looks at the other side of the coin:

> If all the needs are unsatisfied, and the organism is then dominated by the physiological needs, all other needs become simply nonexistent or are pushed into the background. It is then fair to characterize the organism by saying simply that it is hungry, for consciousness is almost completely preempted by hunger. All capacities are put into the service of hunger-satisfaction, and the organization of these capacities is almost entirely determined by the one purpose of satisfying hunger. The receptors and effectors, the intelligence, memory, habits, all may now be defined simply as hunger-gratifying tools. [p. 374]

It is difficult for genuinely hungry children and adults to eat a meal and, at the same time, watch their table manners. It is also difficult for the well-nourished businessman, the swift-minded disc jockey, or the welfare worker with a steady job to fully comprehend hunger and poverty unless they themselves have had direct and personal experience with those conditions.

But along this line of thought, in *Lady Windermere's Fan,* Oscar Wilde has said, "In this world there are only two tragedies. One is not getting what one wants, and the other is getting it. The last is the real tragedy." Perhaps Wilde was not writing about the physiological. He may have penned the words as he thought of psychological needs. That was evidently what was on George Bernard Shaw's mind when he wrote these lines from *Man and Superman,* "There are only two tragedies in life. One is to lose your hearts desire. The other is to gain it." And along that track, here is a fragment of free-form verse (Laing, 1970, p. 38):

I want what I can't get
because
what I can't get *is* what I want.
I don't want what I can get
because
what I can get *is* what I don't want.
I never get what I want
I never want what I get.*

That is how it can be in the realm of experiencing one's own psychological needs—confusing and conflicting. Yet the psychological needs we have can be condensed and capsuled into four categories:

1. Psychological needs that are related to the need to belong to some kind of group or to others; these are the needs for *social interaction.*
2. Psychological needs that relate to one's own *reputation.* These include needs for recognition and status, for

appreciation, for the earned and deserved respect of other humans.
3. Psychological needs that relate to one's own *self-esteem,* which may include such facets as self-respect and self-confidence, achievement needs, and needs for autonomy, for knowledge, for competence.
4. Psychological needs that relate to one's own strivings for *self-actualization.* These can include the need to be creative in the broadest sense, the needs connected with efforts to improve oneself, to become more able, more capable, to actualize and realize to a higher degree many of the potentials for development mentioned in Chapter 1.

Whether or not you are "self-actualized" (or try to be), it will be useful while reading this book to keep in mind this sector of human behavior: there is a part of each one of us that welcomes prestige and respect. Each person needs the nod of approval, the smile of acceptance. We seek applause and strive for status and work to earn the esteem of companions and strangers. In so doing, we sometimes risk a treasure called freedom. There is a line between the light of approval and the shadow of slavery. We can work for esteem and respect from others and achieve great things in the process. But when what we do is governed by the level of approval we may get, we can become slaves to that approval. We can become owned by other people, those who give or withhold acceptance, applause, and respect. It is a risky piece of business, finding the balance between earning approval and being owned.

There are words people use to describe their own private slaveries. Sometimes the words are "What will the neighbors think?" (Perhaps they do not care.) At other times the words might be "If I did that, some people might laugh at me," or "Maybe she'll get mad if . . . ." We often think those words. There are times when

---

*From Laing, R. D.: Knots. Copyright © 1970 by Pantheon Books, a division of Random House, Inc.

we say them out loud. When we do, are we being civilized and well mannered? Or are we really losing a piece of personal freedom we do not have to give away? There may be something more worthwhile than the approval of others. It is called approval of oneself.

Approval of oneself forms a base that leads to living up to one's own genuine potential. In the words of A. H. Maslow (1943), "A musician must make music, an artist must paint, a poet must write, if he is to be ultimately happy. What a man can be, he must be. This need we may call self-actualization" (p. 379). Yet, there are pressures that operate against attempts at self-actualization. These same pressures may interfere with the development of an adequate degree of self-esteem. They are pressures for maintaining and sometimes enhancing one's own level of reputation.

We are, according to some who have looked into the matter (A. Freud, 1946; Brown, 1959), almost constantly at work trying to maintain and to improve our reputations. There are some humans who spend great energies in trying to establish and develop a "good" reputation with a variety of other people. Success is rare in this effort; it is too simple, too easy to appear and to be genuinely insincere to some of that variety. As a compromise, we may try to maintain and improve a reputation with a select few whose views we believe to be worth more than others.

The very young are deeply involved in establishing or trying to establish reputations as good children, adequate children, newcomers welcomed by their parents, especially by mother. Within a few years the child moves beyond the front door and mixes with other children in the neighborhood, and the matter of establishing, maintaining, and improving a reputation becomes increasingly more complex. By the time the child has moved from childhood to the school age years, his main concerns about his own reputation are usually centered on the gang he is connected with. He is also still involved with his own parents and often with the parents of friends. As he moves into adolescence, he must take heed of this reputation with people of the opposite sex. By the time he is an adult, he may have to care for his reputation in relationships with the boss at work, with a representative of a loan company or a bank, with the landlord, the gas station mechanic, bartenders, waitresses, friends, and companions.

In this gradually more complex set of circumstances connected with reputation, the need for a "good" reputation may come into conflict with the need for a "good" level of self-esteem. Stanley Coopersmith (1968), in writing about the matter of self-esteem, maintains:

One of the more significant concerns of modern society is how to produce competent and self-respecting citizens. . . . Philosophers from time immemorial have recognized that the feeling of personal worth plays a crucial role in human happiness and effectiveness. . . . Although the importance of self-esteem in influencing behavior is widely appreciated, most of the ideas and evidence on the subject remain rather vague and intuitive. Clinicians are well aware in a general way that many of the disturbed patients who come to them for treatment feel themselves to be incompetent and socially rejected. [p. 96]

The last sentence of the quotation from Coopersmith brings us to Paul. Paul found his own personal level of stability by accepting the reputation his parents had built for him. While that reputation could not be called positive, since it seriously hindered his development of an adequate level of self-esteem, it was stable and predictable. Because of this, his needs for self-actualization were unmet, unfulfilled.

Paul

Paul was a college sophomore. When he came into the office, he sat down in the chair and stared first at the ceiling, then at the floor. When he was offered a cup of coffee, he quickly shook his head, indicating no, and began to tap his fingertips rapidly on the arm of the chair. He cleared his throat and looked back up to the ceiling. He said, "A friend of mine thought I should come and see you."

"Oh?"

"Yeah." And then a long silence. Paul cleared his throat again and said, "Well, I'm here. I mean I made it this far."

"Yes, you made it this far. Can you tell me some things about yourself?"

"Well, yeah, I mean I guess so. I go to college." Another silence. "I don't know about college," he continued. "I mean I don't know if I should be there. You know what I mean?"

"Not exactly."

"Well, I don't know—I'm not sure I can make it. I mean, well, do you know what I mean? No, I bet you don't. I have a hard time talking sometimes. I mean I have a hard time explaining things to people."

"It sounds like you mean everybody."

"Well, yeah, just about. Yeah, I guess it is everybody I know, except for Allison maybe. Sometimes it's really hard to talk with her."

"And sometimes it's easier."

"Sometimes it is. Yeah sometimes. I mean, if we're talking about school it's easy, but, well, you know, she's pretty nice to me."

"Is that all right with you?"

"Oh, yeah, I mean yes. Yes, it is. Sometimes I get a little nervous about it. I mean, well, you know."

"No."

"Well, I get nervous when she's nice. Not all the time, though. I'm not that screwed up. I mean I'm not that bad off, but a friend said I should come and see you."

By the end of that first hour, Paul was able to make a few more statements about Allison and, in his halting and tentative way, describe himself as often feeling "like a little boy. You know, a little kid."

He came back two days later, again talking about Allison and himself and school. He was failing in school, he said, because he could not study very well and, besides, everyone else in all his courses was brighter. As he put it: "You know, it's like they got something I haven't got. I guess you'd call it brains." He was given an intelligence test during his third visit—the Wechsler tests—and the scores were computed while he sat in his chair, looking at the floor and rapidly tapping his fingers on the arm of the chair. After the scores were figured, Paul

was presented with the results: full scale I. Q., 131.

When he was given the results of the tests and the interpretation of those results, Paul asked, "Are those tests any good?"

"They're useful."

"Well, I mean—I don't think that's right. Well, maybe it is. But you *know* I'm dumb."

"No, I don't know that."

"Well, I don't have the brains the other people have, I told you that."

"Yes, you told me."

"Well, umm, well—don't you believe me?"

"Believe that you're dumb?"

"Yeah."

"No."

Any person's attitude toward himself is initially rooted in the rocky soil of the attitudes the parents (or their substitutes) have toward him. Growing up within a family structure, the child will *introject* the attitude; that is, the child will experience his parent's attitudes and feelings about him; he will take them in and not only accept them but also make them, eventually, his own attitudes about himself. It is a learning process that begins before the learning of language. It is a learning process that often does not need a spoken language, for the attitudes and feelings the parents have can often be expressed in actions, in the movements and gestures, in the quality of the touching and handling by the parents of the infant and child. This learning process is a part of the general area of behavioral activity called socialization.

Socialization is the transmitting of human culture. All human infants and children, and to a lesser extent, adolescents and young adults, are socialized in human culture. As Elkin (1960) has pointed out, "We may define socialization as the process by which someone learns the ways of a given society or social group so that he may function with it" (p. 4). How does a young person learn the ways of *this* society? First, and most obviously, he must associate with, interact with, and be included in special groups. The first interaction and association are with the parents; the child learns how to be a child, and in this society that can mean learning how to be at least mildly inadequate. The child can learn at home and at school that there are rewards for not being too self-sufficient, too independent, too competent. As a result he may learn (1) that modesty, and sometimes self-derogation, is rewarded, as in Paul's case, and (2) that expressions of self-approval or self-praise go unrewarded or punished, also as in Paul's case.

In the daily process of living, these two related factors of socialization in this culture can be described (in a tightly limited way) by the manner in which individuals may handle compliments. Take, as an example, the young adult male who is a genuine, unadulterated "jock." He may spend a couple of hours each day doing push-ups, lifting weights, practicing his tennis, or jogging at dawn in the park or across the campus; in the classroom or even while waiting for the bus, he may quietly do his isometric exercises. His muscles ripple and bulge, and he looks like a Greek god or Michelangelo's marble statue of *David*. Somehow or other, for reasons that may be conscious or unconscious, he spends time around a swimming pool acquiring a tan. If a woman were to say to him, "You have a beautiful body," the probability is low that he would be honest and say, "Yes, I have." The chances are much higher he would say something like, "Aw, my legs are too thin."

We can, to develop another example, describe this practice of socialized dishonesty by giving an example that involves women. Some women spend a substantial amount of time and money in getting ready for an evening's entertainment. They may buy a new frock together with matching shoes and colorful undergarments. They may also purchase a small supply of an exotic perfume. After that

they have their hair done by the hairdresser, go home, bathe, and spend at least an hour putting on facial makeup with the patience, precision, and skill of an artist. When the man comes to pick them up, he may gallantly and honestly say "You look beautiful." The reply may be "Oh, but my eyes are so bloodshot."

These are, of course, two examples of a small fraction of the total realm of human behavior. The examples, however, connect to what Coopersmith had to say about self-esteem and what Silvano Arieti has said about some of the negative factors that children face in growing up within the family structure. Arieti (1955) maintains:

> His strivings toward self-esteem and self-realization are thwarted by the destructive influences that the surrounding adults have upon him. His security is attacked and anxiety originates. Inasmuch as he needs these adults in order to survive, he has to accept their destructive influences, which he may take for granted and consider necessary.
>
> If the parents are hostile and disparaging, the child will acquire the same attitude toward himself and toward society. Disapproval brings about discomfort, fear of punishment, anxiety. Anticipation of disapproval engenders further anxiety. [pp. 45 and 46.]

The second quoted paragraph from Arieti describes what Paul was eventually to describe about himself. He grew up in a family setting in which the parents disliked him. Mother love and father love are not instinctual. His father rarely spoke to Paul, and if he did, it was usually to criticize or to demand. The father was a brilliant, highly paid corporation lawyer noted for his lack of humility. He was, as a psychiatric social worker said, "arrogant in a way that only a woman could appreciate." Paul's mother was petite, a middle-aged woman who dressed in expensive clothes, played bridge three afternoons a week, and quietly despised her husband and all other males, including her son.

The son, Paul, knew it and from an early age learned how to despise himself. He disliked himself so firmly that he found it difficult to tolerate Allison's friendly ways.

Her views and comments disagreed with his ideas about himself, and they were either dismissed or denied, buried, or caused him to feel anxious and ill at ease. Allison liked him, and that liking collided with his dislike for himself and interfered with the stability and balance he had achieved and tried to maintain. Paul's self-esteem was low. At the same time he worked at maintaining a low level of reputation, not only with his parents but also with Allison and with the faculty of the school he attended.

Allan

Allan was 20 years old. He came to the office motivated by his lawyer and a judge who wanted to collect some information about his "sanity" before deciding whether to bring him to trial for destruction of property. When Allan came in for his first interview, he shook hands in a hearty way, sat down, and began talking about himself without any hesitation. He unreeled the history of his life, often with great detail. He was able to name every teacher he had had in elementary school. They had all liked him, he recalled.

Allan had lived a quiet life. He was born and grew up in a small midwestern town. In high school he had worked every Saturday in his uncle's hardware store on the main street. The hardware store was located next door to one of the three movie theaters in the town, and when he was finished with a Saturday's work, he usually walked next door to see the movie before going home. On Sunday he sometimes went to church with his parents, but more often he preferred to find a friend and drive around the town and the countryside all day. He preferred the countryside, he said, because it was more peaceful, and he and a friend could drive for miles on gravel roads under the blue summer skies gazing over the great fields of wheat and corn. He remembered the long drives as times of contentment and peace.

When he graduated from high school, Allan spent the summer working in the hardware store. In the fall he packed up his clothing and moved eighty miles away to a junior college. By the middle of the second semester he was flunking all his courses, so he dropped out of school and went back home to live with his parents. He began once again to work in his uncle's store, selling hammers and nails, tractor parts, and electrical wire. After a few months summer came again and Allan grew restless. He wanted to do something different, something that had some action in it. He applied for a job with the local fire department. He was given a series of tests, was interviewed by the town fire chief, and was accepted for training.

The training began with familiarization with fire-fighting equipment. He was taught how to connect a hose to a hydrant and, when the proper signal was given, how to turn the valve on the hydrant so the water would be released to rush through the hose to its destination—the flames. Allan was also required to take a course in first aid and to learn how to drive the fire truck. The training progressed well. Allan was, for the first time in his life, he said, really interested in what he was doing. He also believed other people had more respect for him.

Late in the summer a traveling carnival came to town on its annual circuit of the Midwest. The people from the carnival set up their tents and booths, their sideshows, the ferris wheel, a small portable roller coaster, and several other rides in a field near town. Allan went there the first night. He bought some popcorn and strolled around the carnival grounds. He pitched baseballs at milk bottles, but he did not hit anything. He threw darts at a dart board and won a small paper Japanese fan. He walked by one of the sideshows and stopped to watch a woman in a bikini play with a big snake. At ten o'clock he was tired, so he went home to his parent's house, went to bed, and slept. He woke up the next morning, had breakfast, and walked to the fire station for more training and, as he said, "to joke around with the other guys there."

His shift at the fire house ended at eight that evening, and when he got off work, he went out to the carnival again. This time, he headed directly for the sideshow to watch the woman in the bikini and her snake. He watched four shows in succession. He would have watched four more, he said, but the show closed down for the night. Allan walked around the carnival grounds for half an hour and returned to the site of the sideshow. He went inside the tent, empty now and dark. He walked up the steps to the stage where he had seen the snake charmer. He walked across the stage and down some other steps and out the back of the tent.

"The snake charmer lady was there," he said "just standin' there drinkin' beer out of a bottle. She was suprised to see me come out of that tent, but when she got used to me bein' there, she got friendly. She even asked me if I wanted a beer. I told her no, but she kept on talkin' and askin' a lot of questions. She wanted to know who I was and where I worked and all that kind of stuff. She said she liked my muscles too. Anyway, that's how it got started."

Within fifteen minutes Allan was in a trailer with the snake charmer, and eventually they had sexual intercourse. It was his first experience. "I'd heard about it, like everybody does, and I made jokes about it, but that was the first time ever."

Allan walked home and went to bed. He did not, though, go to sleep. He thought about what had happened to him. He thought and thought about it, and then he began to worry. He worried about what his mother might think if she found out what he had done. He worried about his father. He wondered and worried about venereal disease, and he got up and went into the bathroom to look at himself. He took a shower and went back to bed, worrying.

He leaned forward in his chair and said, "By the time the sun came up, I didn't know how to do anything but sweat. I mean to tell you I was worried sick." He sighed and sat back in his chair, "I thought maybe I had the clap or somethin' worse." He sighed again.

"I thought maybe she was pregnant. I thought about that idea for a long time, about how she might show up someday and point at me and tell everybody what I did." He paused, frowning. "Well, anyway," he went on, "I got up and took another shower and shaved and got all ready to go down to the fire station."

He did not eat breakfast. He told his mother he had a touch of the flu. She thought he had better stay at home, but he said no, he did not want the chief mad at him. Allan went outside and walked down the street to the station. When he got there, he polished a big brass hose nozzle and picked pebbles out of the treads of the tires on the fire truck until nine o'clock. Then it was time for another lecture on first aid. He walked into the classroom in the back of the fire station, sat down in a chair, and

waited. Within a few minutes several other firemen-students came into the room and sat in other chairs. Then the fire chief came into the room with Dr. Drake.

"He's the family doctor and everybody in town knows him. Anyways, he's a good doctor but real stern. He's one of the elders in the church. I don't think I ever seen him smile but don't get me wrong, he's a real good doctor."

The fire chief introduced the physician and said, "Dr. Drake's here to teach you some things you might have to know someday. Firemen have to be ready for any kind of emergency, and what he's got to say will come in handy sometime or other. I want you men to pay attention."

The physician told the small group of firemen-students that they might have to deliver a baby in the line of duty. He drew some diagrams on a blackboard, showing the birth canal. Allan sat in his chair, fascinated and frightened. He thought about the night before. He thought about the snake charmer coming into the room and pointing at him.

"Godamighty, it was terrible," he said. "I thought I was gonna bust like a dropped watermelon."

As the lecture progressed, Allan writhed in his chair. He could feel the sweat run down inside his arms, and he started to choke. He bent down in his chair and began to retch, and in a sudden burst he ran out of the room, sprinting for the fire truck. He jumped up into the driver's seat, turned the ignition key, started the engine, and roared out of the fire house.

"I tore outa that place like a dog gone crazy."

He drove the big fire truck down main street and out of town. He careened along the highway and then turned off on a gravel road. He drove at high speed in the heavy truck, leaving behind a great cloud of dust that hung in the still air. He drove the truck as fast as it would go, and then he lost control of the steering. The truck veered off the road, ripped through a fence, and cut a swath 10 feet wide through the trees of an apple orchard.

"I couldn't stop. I couldn't let go of that steering wheel or get my foot off the gas pedal. I just plowed right through those little trees and then through another fence and that's when I hit those two horses."

When the truck hit the horses, the impact jolted the truck and jolted Allan back to reality.

He stepped on the brakes, stopped the truck, and quickly turned off the engine. Allan got out of the fire truck, walked slowly over to one of the dead horses, and sat down on the ground next to it. He began to cry, and in talking about it, he began to cry again.

"Those were prize horses. They were really good horses, real beauties. And I killed 'em." He cried some more and then wiped at his eyes with the back of his hand. "I didn't mean to do it. Honest. But I did it. Everybody knows I did it, but I didn't mean to. It's just that somethin' came over me, like a spell."

Allan went on trial for destruction of property. The apple trees were valued at fifteen thousand dollars. The two horses were estimated to be worth over a hundred thousand dollars, and at the end of the trial Allan was given a sentence of three years. The sentence was suspended, though, on the condition that Allan get professional help for his emotional problems.

SOME CONCLUSIONS

Allan's emotional problems can be tightly defined with the sharp-edged technical words known by any clinical psychologist or psychiatrist. His emotional problems can be labeled with a diagnostic label, but the label and the definition leave out a central feature: Allan's balance of self-esteem and reputation. When he ran from the classroom to the fire truck and roared out of town, Allan was a moving example of an agonistic pattern of behavior, one of "those forms of activity which are directed essentially to maintaining . . . protection against attack" (Noyes and Kolb, 1963, p. 12).

His agonistic pattern of behavior resulted in flight, and for the moment any thoughts of self-esteem and reputation were irrelevant to him. He had to run to protect himself from an imagined, anticipated attack and to protect himself from his own overwhelming sense of guilt. Guilt, in the behavior of humans, is an elusive factor. It is possible for individuals to commit crimes and feel no guilt. It is also possible for an individual to feel guilty even though he has done no wrong. The

differentiation is between *being* guilty and *feeling* guilty. If a person *feels* guilty, he may sense a lowering of his own self-esteem. He may also have to contend with an imagined sense of having a lowered level of reputation.

In the small town where he had grown up, Allan had a reputation for being a peaceful person, a quiet lad who had some slight sense of initiative, a cooperative individual who troubled no one, a person who had lived most of his life as a silent bystander. He was concerned about his reputation, so concerned that he refused to live in his home town after the trial was over. His concerns about reputation weighed heavily on him; they overshadowed and outranked his sense of self-esteem. He had lived much of his life in a quiet and invisible prison, a victim of his own self-imposed form of slavery. When he thought—imagined—his reputation was in danger of being demolished by the pointing finger of the woman from the carnival, he swiftly slid into a panic state from which he had to escape. His escape, which surprised everyone in the small town, brought him to trial. The judge was more forgiving and more understanding of Allan than he was of himself. And in time the judge proved to be correct. Allan followed the edict of the court and sought psychotherapy (not with the author). He was seen two years later for a reevaluation, and it was obvious at that time that he had matured in a substantial way. He owned himself with a definite sureness.

In the meantime, and in sharp contrast to Allan's growth toward a mature self-ownership, Paul refused the idea of psychotherapy. He decided to accept his grim situation; he remained stabilized at a massively uncomfortable level, a silent, frightened, and bitter bystander. Paul's decision was self-defeating, yet what he did was understandable. He preferred stability to what he feared would become chaos if he explored his life and tried to change it. It was not that he loved his life. He hated it, hated himself, but that was life to him, and he wanted no part in any surprises.

There are few surprises that are welcomed. Surprise parties and unexpected gifts are fine. Once in awhile someone wins something in a contest or a drawing, and that is an acceptable surprise. Beyond those and perhaps a few other examples, most surprises seem to come in the form of bad news. There are surprise pregnancies, earthquakes, flash floods, and unexpected sudden deaths to contend with. There are quick and surprising riots, robberies, and surprise visits from bill collectors. There are political coups and palace revolts, insurrections and revolutions that are surprising to us, for we prefer to live in a world in which most matters are predictable. Christmas comes but once a year, and so do birthdays, anniversaries, most vacations, and many other celebrations. The sun comes up each day, each day is twenty-four hours long, and the year lasts for twelve months. We depend upon these predictables; we organize our lives around them.

It is not enough that we have twenty-four hours and twelve months. We also make plans, pass laws, develop public and private rituals, and put people (including ourselves) into named categories. We use words such as good and bad, black and white, right and wrong, introvert and extrovert in an effort to make life more predictable, seemingly more under control. Paul believed, although he did not directly admit to it, that if he were to learn more about himself, his life would get out of his control, that he would quickly slide into chaos. As he said, "Yeah. I know, um, I guess I know that I'm hanging on to my hang-ups. But, you know, that's me."

Paul was not his own person. He was his parent's person. They owned him in open and subtle ways, and he accepted that ownership. What they saw was not Paul but their image or fabrication of Paul. For reasons that remain unknown, no real or consistent contact was possible with the parents. Because of that (and because of their probable fear of psychology), it was impossible to develop a meaningful and comprehensive view of the intermixture of the relationships within the family. Yet Paul, it seemed clear, introjected the views of his parents; he saw himself as they saw him: inadequate, insufficient, and helpless. In essence the parents were incapable or unwilling to connect with Paul as a legitimate functioning, live, viable, searching human being. Instead of forming a relationship with their son, they chose to relate to what they believed and needed him to be. He existed, for them, not as a person but as a vague and elusive representation of an object caught in their critical and demeaning searchlight, which probed and penetrated not his strengths but his inevitable, human weaknesses. As a result, Paul responded not to himself as a solid, physically intact person but as the shadow of himself created by the luminous and hostile eyes of his parents.

Klein (1963) has a comment that relates to Paul's pain. In a speech Klein said:

> May I finish with a story by the German biologist, Von Uexkull, about a man who discovered his own shadow. This man came to believe that his shadow was a living thing. At first he imagined his shadow to be his servant, because it copied all his movements; but he gradually began to doubt this and to believe he was imitating the shadow. Thereafter he showed more and more consideration for his shadow, allowing it to have his seat or bed while he himself remained uncomfortably to one side. This man was eventually reduced to being the shadow of his shadow. Perhaps we also are too conscious of our shadows and forget that we are ourselves. [p. 288]

REVIEW QUESTIONS

1. Why did Paul choose to remain as he was?
2. Why does Octavio Paz want to abolish the future?
3. What is change?
4. What did George Bernard Shaw have to say about psychological needs?
5. What is an identity system? What are the identity symbols?
6. Can you briefly describe Allan?
7. In which ways were Paul and Allan similar?
8. What is agonistic behavior?
9. Can you distinguish between interpersonal and intrapersonal?
10. What is self-actualization? Why is it so difficult to define?
11. What did Stanley Coopersmith have to say about self-esteem?
12. Why did Allan not go to jail?

4

THE EARLY YEARS

Bees sting. They have a reputation for being slightly dangerous living things. They also have a reputation for being busy. They make honey and wax and they dance. There is probably no playfulness in their dancing, according to Karl von Frisch who spent half a century studying the behavior of bees (Krogh, 1948). The circling dance, *Rundtanz,* and the wagging dance, *Schwanzeltanz,* are the principal means by which bees communicate with one another. Now this is the sort of information that is easily dismissed as being merely mildly interesting but of little real relevance. For von Frisch, however, this information and his knowledge of other aspects of bee behavior probably saved his life and certainly earned him an enormous admiration.

Von Frisch began his work with bees in Austria well before World War II. When the Nazis moved in and took over the government of Austria, they threatened either to toss von Frisch out of the country or to toss him into a concentration camp where few people survived. His work, however, was considered so important by the Austrian food supply ministry that he was allowed to continue. During the war his laboratory was severely damaged in air raids, and his house was completely destroyed by bombs. In the midst of wartime

destruction he studied a part of life. His research earned him the admiration of his fellow scientists, and one of them, George Simpson (1969), believed the interpretation and understanding of the dance of bees required substantially more ingenuity and creativity than the splitting of the atom. Simpson also wrote of man and of life. He believed that many who study life see man as an animal living in a world populated with a great variety of other animals. They forget, he said, that man is a unique animal, gifted in ways that clearly distinguish him from all other organisms.

One of the primary gifted ways of humans is the use of written and spoken words—a central feature of what is known as language. With the written and spoken word, people try to make sense out of the world around them and try to communicate what sense they make of the world to each other. It is an infinitely more complex style of communication than bees use. Because of that complexity, though, the understanding of language is clouded. Most of us learn to read and to write in school, but we learn how to speak without any formal training. The average or normal child requires no tutor to teach him to talk, yet within a few years after birth children can speak in complex ways, forming long sentences (perhaps as long as this one is) to communicate. Noam Chomsky (1969) has pointed out that the language a child speaks is the language he hears, but the capacity for language is based upon what has been inherited. As Eisenberg (1972) has put it:

Languages, insofar as they have been studied, appear to share fundamental structural characteristics, a universality that argues for an as-yet-to-be-identified basis in common structures in the central nervous system. [p. 126]

Once more we arrive at the point of interaction between what has been inherited and what has been experienced. Again, it seems that what has been inherited forms a base so broad as not to be particularly limiting. In this chapter about the early years a thin sliver of human experience or possible experience is covered. Undergirding that which is experienced, however, is that which has been inherited, and in reading this brief chapter it seems appropriate to keep in mind that humans inherit such a broad spectrum of potentials no environment can challenge all of them to their limit. This may be especially the case in the early years of living.

TRUST AND MISTRUST

Arthur Clarke is a scuba diver. He likes to put on a rubberized suit, swim fins, a face mask and a steel tank loaded with compressed air. He likes to dive deep into warm water trailing a stream of bubbles behind him as he searches. When he is not on one of his searching dives, he writes. So far he has written more than forty books. Most of them have been searching books based on outer-space science fiction and science fact. When he is not diving or writing, he travels. And when he travels, he likes to visit with people and have quiet conversations with them.

If you were to talk with him, he would look at you through rimless bifocals, and you would look back at a thin, balding man who might remind you of Alec Guiness playing the part of a British businessman. You will know, however, that Clarke (1968) is not playing when he writes such passages as the following:

Behind every man now alive stand thirty ghosts, for that is the ratio by which the dead outnumber the living. Since the dawn of time, roughly a hundred billion human beings have walked the planet Earth. Now this is an interesting number, for by a curious coincidence there are approximately a hundred billion stars in our local Universe, the Milky Way. So for every man who has ever lived, in this Universe there shines a star. [p. 7]

The quotation is from one of Clarke's books, *2001: A Space Odyssey,* which, when it was made into a motion picture, ended with an ancient astronaut being reborn, perhaps with a different genetic base than humans usually have. If you were to ask Clarke what the ending of the movie meant, he might shrug and say, "It means whatever you want it to mean." If you were to ask him the same question in a slightly different way, he might smile and say, "It could be about time. It could be about time and humans." And after that, you might sit back in your chair to think about time and its passing.

Calendars and clocks tell us of the passage of time. So do tree rings, antique shops, and the tolling of bells. Time is measured in enormous quantities by geologists and in extremely small units by electronic engineers. Time is an important factor in football games, airline schedules, music, pregnancy, and cooking. Time cannot be seen or heard. It cannot be weighed or painted or photographed. It can, though, be experienced, learned about, known.

Small children learn about time when they hear their mothers say "Wait a minute," or "You can do that tomorrow." When they are older, children can reach ahead and look back over time, talking about last summer and next year and "When I grow up. . . ." By the time we are grown up, each one of us has our own special and private sense of time that may be difficult to put into words. Numbers help. The numbers we use are labeled with words like "minute" and "hour," but the numbers and their labels are inventions. We have other inventions connected with time. We have hourglasses, wristwatches, and high precision atomic clocks, but no matter how elegant and sophisticated they may be, they do not organize time; they merely organize our ideas of what time may be.

The invented minutes and hours sum up to become days, months, and years, and the years can be put together and sometimes given another label: a lifetime. Erikson has thought and written about lifetimes, but he has not organized them. He has, however, organized some ideas of what a lifetime may be.

In Chapter 1 we briefly put a toe in to test the water in Erikson's version of the moving stream of life. Erikson (1968), you will recall, divided a lifetime into eight stages. In this chapter we will take a longer and deeper look into his ideas and the ideas of several other thinkers and concentrate upon the first three of those stages of development.

The probability is high that during the first two years of life the most important, the most vital, psychological development is the development of a sense of trust. *Trust* is a sensing, a feeling, that at least

some sectors of the infant's world are dependable, that some of the people in that narrow and understandably circumscribed world are warm, caring, available, and friendly. Before trust can develop to any extent, the infant must survive. Survival, in this context, is both physical and psychological, and it has been described in words and on film by Rene Spitz (1965), a research-minded physician. He spent a lifetime specializing in studies of infants. According to Dr. Spitz, when a baby is 7 or 8 days old, he begins to show an important behavior, the *rooting response.*

Changing the baby's body position, sometimes merely by picking him up, causes the inner ear balance mechanism to be tipped in a new and different direction. The slight and temporary disturbance of the inner ear is one of the factors that brings about this complex rooting response. Rooting takes place when the infant, searching for nourishment, turns his head to one side and snaps his lips open and shut. When the infant finds the nipple and begins to suck, he can feel the breast against his face. He experiences the sense of contact. It is a physical response—a complex, reflexive behavioral pattern that can be seen in every human infant in all parts of the world.

The rooting response is physical, but it has great psychological importance. It sets in motion a two-way contact: the infant has a relationship with his mother, and the mother has a relationship with her infant. Dr. Spitz calls this reciprocal contact the *primal dialogue.* The dialogue becomes as necessary to the life of the infant as food. To stress the point: the infant must have food or he will starve to death. The infant must also experience the primal dialogue or he may die. (Spitz, 1965; Elkind and Hamsher, 1972) The primal dialogue involves not only the nursing of an infant but also the touching, handling, and fondling of the infant in gentle and comforting ways. Touching and moving and making

Table 4. Erikson's first three developmental stages (1968)

Stage	Ages	Label	Major development
1	0-1+	Infancy	A sense of trust
2	2-3	Early child-hood	Autonomy, independence
3	4-6	Childhood	Initiative

sounds the infant can hear is called *infant stimulation,* and if the newly born person experiences the touch and sound of a mother or her substitute, he may more surely move toward the development of some sense of trust.

The primal dialogue and infant stimulation describe a reciprocal relationship between mother and infant and the attachment of the infant to his mother. Detachment is also of importance.

The human infant . . . separates himself from his mother at the first moment any mode of locomotion is possible. He does not wait until he can creep or walk efficiently. The separation, once effected, increases in distance and duration over the life of the individual. [Rheingold and Eckerman, 1970, p. 83]

The quality of the infant's attachment to the mother may help to develop the beginnings of trust that, in turn, may make detachment more comfortable for the infant. If the infant can detach and then reattach with ease, the infant slowly learns mother is dependable, that he can go away

H. Armstrong Roberts

from her, and when he comes back, she will still be there. And then Rheingold and Eckerman add:

> In time he walks out of the house, plays in the yard all morning, goes to school, goes still farther away to high school, then to college and to work. He crosses the country, and now he may go even to the moon. [p. 78]

Moving out into the yard or the neighborhood street is a part of the development of autonomy and of independence, factors mentioned by Erikson as central to the second stage of behavior, early childhood.

Moving out into the yard or the neighborhood or to the moon and beyond is based on many aspects of trust combined, sooner or later, with aspects of mistrust. Total and absolute trust may be appropriate for the infant in the crib cared for by an extraordinarily attentive mother, but for the person moving around the house and into the yard, the neighborhood, and on to the moon, total and absolute trust can lead to an imbalance; mistrust is often a necessary ingredient for survival.

Mistrust may show itself in an appropriately cautious exploration, and the mistrust that develops in infancy and that hopefully curbs a blind, total level of trust extends to the adult world and can be seen in curious and common circumstances. For instance, to have an absolute and all-encompassing level of trust in the goodness and benevolence of all other drivers on a freeway is naive. To put great, absolute, and enduring trust in the messages contained in radio and television commercials is also naive.

There is a futuristic example of a balance between trust and mistrust in a brief article published by Carl and Linda Sagan and Frank Drake (1972). Their article, titled "A Message from Earth," was concerned with *Pioneer 10,* the first spacecraft to travel beyond our solar system. As they pointed out:

> It seemed to us appropriate that this spacecraft, the first man-made object to leave the solar system, should carry some indication of the locale, epoch, and nature of its builders.
>
> It appears possible that some civilizations technologically much more advanced than ours have the means of detecting an object such as Pioneer 10 in interstellar space, distinguishing it from other objects of comparable size but not of artificial origin, and then intercepting and acquiring the spacecraft.
>
> But if the intercepting civilization is not within the immediate solar neighborhood, the epoch of such an interception can only be in the very distant future. Accordingly, we cannot see any conceivable danger in indicating our position in the Galaxy, even in the eventuality which we consider highly unlikely, that such advanced societies would be hostile. [p. 881]*

The idea that there may be hostile beings in distant civilizations is an indication of some mistrust.

The ability to move beyond the immediate vicinity of mother or her substitute is again based upon trust, which because the world is not totally benevolent, requires the balancing component of some mistrust. It may be possible to easily imagine the development of trust in an infant who is fortunate enough to experience the affections and attentions of a mother who has nothing else to do but care for her baby. Mothers do not often have that kind of time available to them; other matters must be attended to, and one of them may be the father.

There are fathers who, having sired a child, may grow to detest him. They see their partner focus attention upon the infant, attention they once had for themselves. It need not be an obvious process; young adult males rarely say out loud, "I am jealous of that infant," but the sense of jealousy, of rivalry, can be there, affecting the interchange of ideas and feelings between the two parents and influencing the infant in ways that are difficult to identify with sureness.

The mother may have a close bond with the infant, may need the infant as much

*From Sagan, C., Sagan, L. S., and Drake, F.: A message from earth, Science, vol. 175, pp. 881-884, Feb. 25, 1972. Copyright © 1972 by the American Association for the Advancement of Science.

as the infant needs her, and may be able to take care of her husband in a more or less adequate manner, as well as keep on top of such household tasks as preparing meals, shopping, and washing clothes. But it is within this complex setting that the mother must find ways to take care of herself.

While it is useful and often important for the mother to take care of herself, not only in a physical but also in an emotional way, she is faced with an infant whose needs are primarily physical. There are of course the needs for air and for warmth, but the central need for the new infant is the repeated need to be fed. It is a primitive and vital aspect; it is the physiological need-satisfaction system in its most basic form. Self-esteem and reputation seem a long way off. They may not be so distant, though, for as Stone and Church (1964) have stated:

> Early in infancy, the baby comes fully awake only at times of crisis, such as hunger. At these times he is on the verge of what the adult would call panic; the baby has no time perspective, for him the crisis drags on interminably, and he is helpless to do anything about it. If relief is delayed, he becomes even more upset or exhausts himself with crying; already a tiny seed of distrust has been planted, and the next time the panic is a little closer, the crisis more exigent. Eventually, of course, he is always fed. His panic subsides, but it leaves a residue of suspicion and distrust. . . . If his equilibrium is promptly restored, on the other hand, his existence is secure. [p. 59]

If the child's existence is secure, he may more easily develop a sense of trust, which Erikson has likened to the idea of faith, the idea or feeling that sooner or later (but the sooner the better) everything will be better and that the world, for the most part, is not a bad place.

Many things may be better for the infant as he moves beyond the stage of infancy if his early trust is firmly developed. This trust, to be firm, is not limited to trust in mother or in whomever takes care of him. For the trust to be firm the infant must trust himself, trust in his own rightness to

be alive, to detach himself legitimately from mother, to move well beyond her sight and the sound of her voice.

If the element of basic trust is impaired, and if basic mistrust is the most prevalent, Erikson (1968) says it will be:

> expressed in a particular form of severe estrangement which characterizes individuals who withdraw into themselves when at odds with themselves and with others. Such withdrawal is most strikingly displayed by individuals who regress into psychotic states in which they sometimes close up, refusing food and comfort and becoming oblivious to companionship. What is most radically missing in them can be seen from the fact that as we attempt to assist them with psychotherapy, we must try to "reach" them with the specific intent of convincing them that they can trust us to trust them and that they can trust themselves. [p. 97]

AUTONOMY, SHAME, AND DOUBT

If the infant has managed to experience an environment that has led to the development of a genuine, basic trust, he may more easily move into the stage of early childhood. It is during those second and third years of life when the central development, if it takes place, is the development of a sense of autonomy.

The development of a sense of autonomy, of independence, of *freedom to do* does not mean the development of a lifetime style that can be seen in the lives of soldiers of fortune. That lifetime style develops later, if at all. In early childhood the person begins to assert himself. He can assert in a physical way with an increasing sureness, for his body reacts more surely to his own wishes. He not only has a gradually more certain command of his bowel and his bladder but also a greater control of the language. He can talk with his parents and with other children and if they are available, with a great mixture of other humans including the mailman, the trash hauler, grocery store clerks, policemen and the parents of his friends. He can talk to them, and he can talk back to them, showing a mixture of the savage and the civilized.

There is, in the development of a sense of autonomy, a matter of finding some balance between the savage and the civilized. The most extreme example of pure autonomy is the ultimate savage, a person responsible to no one for anything under any circumstances. It is impossible for such a human to exist in even a primitive society. As Eisenberg (1972) has stated, "Man is man only in society" (p. 126). It is usually inaccurate to label a member of a tribe in Borneo or Mindanao as a savage. They are civilized, but not often in ways we find easily familiar.

To exist in any kind of society, including the miniature society of the family, there must be some curtailment or dilution of the development of the sense of autonomy. If the curtailment or dilution is overly strong, effective in a negative way, and if it lasts for a long enough time, the growing child will experience feelings of shame and doubt. With the introduction of those feelings into a person's psychological life, growing up leaps to a level of greater complexity. For the infant there exists a balancing between trust and mistrust. For the person in early childhood the balancing is between autonomy on the one side and the development of shame and doubt on the other. For the most part, the parents own the scales. They can, if they choose, weight the scales heavily on the side of autonomy. If they are so inclined, however, they may load the scales on the side of shame and doubt. When they do, the child is on the road to becoming an overcivilized person. And that is a lifetime style quite different from the reasonable adventurer or the soldier of fortune.

Paul, who was discussed in Chapter 3, was an overcivilized person. His becoming overcivilized began at an early age; he had few freedoms, few available ways for creating his own satisfactions, and as an adult he needed to learn how to decivilize

himself. He had been so thoroughly oppressed that he carried a large component of mistrust around in his psychological luggage. Because of that, it is possible to assume his oppression started very early, perhaps in infancy, although that would be difficult to determine.

Jody

Paul was an example of an extremely overcivilized individual. A less extreme, and therefore more common, example of an overcivilized human is embodied in the person of Jody. Jody wore expensive clothes, elegant clothes, and as she sat down in the chair, she carefully placed her purse in her lap. She folded her hands and rested them lightly on top of the purse. She smiled in what seemed a careful way.

"It's really very hot outside."

"Yes."

"But it's cool in here. You have a very nice office. I certainly like that picture. It's a Picasso, isn't it?"

"No."

"Oh, I thought it was. I like it, though. It has good form. A very remarkable picture. Is it an original?"

"It's a print."

"Oh." (pause) "I hope you don't think I was being—um—condescending."

"Are you ever condescending?"

"Oh, my, no. At least I hope not. It's not proper."

"Proper?"

"No, it's not. I'm not supposed to—um—I'm not—um—I try not to be condescending. Sometimes I am, but not on purpose."

"By mistake."

"Yes, that's it."

She was able to admit to condescending behavior, but she said she never realized she was that way until after the fact. She went on to explain how she tried to be always pleasant. She worked at keeping her place, she said.

"And what is your place?"

"My place? To be a lady."

"That must be difficult, sometimes."

"Oh, my, no. Not now."

With that, she moved into a description of her family. Her father was a rancher, a large gruff man, a man who liked to swear and laugh and drink rye whiskey. He worked hard on the ranch, and it prospered. He built up a surplus of money and bought a small meat packing plant in town, and that became profitable, so he bought a trucking line. His three businesses eventually made him wealthy, and he hired his own managers and went into politics. He became a state senator.

"After that, I hardly ever saw daddy."

She had never seen him much before then either. She had been raised almost totally by her mother. Jody's mother came from a poor farm family in Iowa. She was born just before the Great Depression of the 1930s, and during the depression the family had been evicted from the farm because they could not keep up the mortgage payments. The family wandered westward, working their way toward Oregon. They got as far as Wyoming and settled in a small town. Within ten years World War II was in full swing. The father and two sons joined the Navy. Jody's mother remained in the small town, first in junior high school and then high school. She was in high school when word came that her father and a brother had been killed in the war. Suddenly there was a lot of money, insurance money, and Jody's mother was sent off to a small, private boarding school in northern California. She graduated with honors. Jody's mother moved on from the private school to a university, where she earned a degree in English. She entered graduate school and got a job as a teaching assistant. During her first year in graduate school, Jody's mother met Jody's father.

Referring to that time, Jody said, "Daddy always remembered when they met. He used to laugh about it. He'd laugh but he always seemed a little sad." Jody's parents were married in 1950. Jody was born a year later.

"Mother fussed over me. I really mean that. She fussed over me all the time. Why, the first thing I can remember is the fussing she did over me in a new dress. She kept trying to fix the little bow in the back. She wanted it to look just right. I remember that. It seems like it happened yesterday or just last week."

"What else do you remember about the fussing?"

"Oh, my. A lot. Mother fussed over my table manners. I learned, though. I've always had good manners. My mother taught me. She even taught me how to read. That was before I went to kindergarten." Jody smiled and again it seemed to be in a careful way.

"Do you remember playing with the other kids in the neighborhood?"

"Oh, there wasn't any neighborhood. We lived in the big house on the ranch."

"Do you remember playing?"

"Oh, my yes. I remember a lot of things about playing. I always played with mother."

"Always?"

"There wasn't anyone else around. That's not exactly true. There were the children who belonged to the hired hands. The cowboys' children."

"What about them?"

"Oh, my, let me think." (pause) "I saw them at church on Sunday."

"Did you ever play with them?"

"Oh, my no. Mother and I played. I never played with them. I played with mother. We had hundreds of tea parties. Just the two of us."

"Did you ever go anywhere?"

"Yes, yes. Many places. We went to Helena and Salt Lake City. We went to Chicago many times."

"You and your mother and your father?"

"Yes, sometimes. Mostly I went with mother. We always went to Chicago to shop for clothes."

"Where was your father?"

"Working. He worked all the time. He loved to ride the fence line. It took him a whole day on a horse."

"It's a big ranch, then?"

"Oh, my yes. But don't ask me how many acres. I never can remember."

"Is it a man's work to remember things like that?"

"Why, yes, it is. A lady has too many other things. . . ." Jody began to cry then. She opened the purse in her lap and pulled out a lace handkerchief. She dabbed at her eyes. "Oh, it's just terrible. It's awful."

"What's awful?"

"Me."

"Why is that?"

"I have this terrible thing."

"Oh?"

"Oh, my. I know it's such a disappointment to mother. It's embarrassing to be here. I feel so ashamed."

Jody said she felt deeply ashamed because

she had colitis. She had had colitis for several years, and the pain, she said, had increased, and her physician insisted she try psychotherapy before he considered surgery. She felt ashamed partly because of the location of the illness. She felt more ashamed because she had, she felt, disappointed her mother. She described herself as her mother's art work, and now that work of art was soiled, damaged, in need of cleansing and repair.

In the course of Jody's description of herself it became apparent she had a low level of autonomy and a high level of shame and self-doubt. She was not able to develop her own opportunities for satisfaction. Instead she had learned to depend upon her mother. And together, mother and daughter formed a relationship that excluded everyone else.

INITIATIVE AND GUILT

Jody's high level of shame and self-doubt began in early childhood. It interfered with her later childhood development of a sense of initiative. The sense of initiative can form the base for a realistic sense of ambition and purpose. Jody lacked a realistic sense of ambition; in her conversations she said she wanted to be a veterinarian, but later she admitted she disliked animals of all kinds. At one point she talked of becoming a beautician, an idea she gave up when she explained she had never learned how to take care of her own cosmetic needs. Her mother had always washed her hair, she said, and given her manicures while forbidding her to use makeup of any type. She had a small, faltering sense of purpose. Her verbal wanderings about an occupation meant little, she said much later, because her father had set up a trust fund in her name and as the only child she would eventually inherit his businesses. She did not want to get married. As she said, "Oh, why it would be like abandoning mother." But she was to change her mind about that matter.

When she first went into psychotherapy, she had little purpose in life beyond pleasing and being pleased by her mother. Her life was narrow. Although she traveled often to Chicago, Salt Lake City, and a variety of other places, she traveled as though sealed inside a stainless steel ball with a small built-in window. When she shopped in stores, she bought the clothes her mother liked. While visiting museums she exclaimed over exhibits her mother admired. But in her travels she could peer out the small window of her life and see other people. She watched them. She saw men embrace women at the airports. She witnessed arguments between people.

When she was eighteen, she began to read books her mother did not pick out. It was one of her first conscious movements toward a measure of autonomy, the first action she had taken on her own, beyond the power of her mother and outside the prescribed reading materials she had while going through school. Her conscience often tugged at her because she was doing a few things on her own. Yet she became intrigued by the world beyond the big ranch house and outside her private stainless steel capsule. She was, though, still her mother's prisoner until she could venture forth, take risks in living, and survive unscathed. Eventually she became a reasonable adventurer. During Jody's growing years she had been enclosed so much by the walls of the ranch house and her mother's watchful gaze, she failed to bring into full play what Erikson (1968) calls the intrusive mode of the childhood years.

> The *intrusive mode,* dominating much of the behavior of this stage, characterizes a variety of configurationally "similar" activities and fantasies. These include (1) the intrusion into space by vigorous locomotion; (2) the intrusion into the unknown by consuming curiosity; (3) the intrusion into other people's ears and minds by the aggressive voice; (4) the intrusion upon or into other bodies by physical attack; (5) and, often most frighteningly, the thought of the phallus intruding the female body. [p. 116]

In part because of the intrusive mode a child's world expands. In the beginning he has only one environment—mother and home. During the fourth, fifth, and sixth years of life the child adds another environment to his life—the neighborhood. As the child's activities expand his environment, he typically comes in contact with more and more people. He begins to develop an increasingly certain idea of who he is. Little boys become gradually more certain that being a boy is different from being a girl. Girls begin to realize they are different from boys. And, on the part of both boys and girls, there is an increase in the awareness of genitals. The natural and predictable outcome is the discovery of pleasure through masturbation. There is also the discovery of pleasure in acting out masculine and feminine roles with parents as models. Some children, as they develop and use a sense of initiative, may be given a great range of secure freedom in which to function. Other children may be almost completely ignored by their parents, and that may be considered freedom of another sort. In both instances, however, a freedom to explore, intrude, investigate, discover, and learn with few restrictions can foster the development of what may be called the soldier of fortune.

We have, within the human family, some members who are genuine soldiers of fortune. They follow the scent of adventure the way a leopard tracks a rabbit. They move swiftly along the trail with great skill, and at the end of the chase there is a decision. Does the leopard play with the rabbit or does it kill? Or is it the leopard who seeks death? So it is, sometimes, with the human soldiers of fortune. The soldiers of fortune among us cannot be defined a clean and precise way. A soldier of fortune may be a Portugese mercenary fighting for pay in someone else's war. A soldier of fortune may make beaded leather belts she can sell to tourists in San Francisco. A soldier of fortune may be a Formula 1 racing driver after the big win at the Grand Prix or a woman with a pair of skis streaking through the slalom gates at Aspen for the prestige and the money of first place.

Soldiers of fortune are after the quick killing, which can be in the form of real blood (for the military mercenary), or real gold (for the 49ers of California history), or real death (for the race car driver). Whether it is someone else's blood or nature's gold or their own death, soldiers of fortune move into and out of adventure, searching, sometimes finding, often flamboyant, always noticed, inevitably visible but transitory heroes.

There are others in the large human family who seem to move not at all. They sit by the side of the road, seemingly watching—never in the parade, rarely among the cheering throng of spectators, content to watch as though simply being there is enough. They live out their lives never intruding on anyone's territory, rarely noticed, nearly invisible. If they are seen at all, they usually fade from memory in a rapid way, lost in a haze of other memories and never recalled. But somewhere along the scale between the soldier of fortune and the anonymous bystander, there exists the reasonable adventurer. He or she can seem to be ordinary, "normal," but as Roy Heath (1964) has pointed out, "The principal characteristic of the Reasonable Adventurer is his ability to create his own opportunities for satisfaction" (p. 30).

This may be a simple comment, but it forms the beginning of a tour through alternatives that begin here and are continued in a later chapter in this book. Alternatives exist for all of us. We can choose, if we choose to choose, among a variety of lifetime styles. We can, if we choose, live the life of the soldier of fortune. We can be leopards in the rain forest on the prowl through sun-filled clearings and dark, shadowed places, stalking something, anything. We can move with silence on padded paws, going for the kill, whether it happens to the rabbit or to us.

We can be silent bystanders, waiting for a bus that never comes, the help that does not arrive, left alone to enjoy the warmth of sunlight, the rustle and movement of life around us, sensing the flow of time as it slides by. And we can be both, although not at the same time. We can shift from stalking leopard to silent bystander and then back again, dazzling any opponent or ally with our swift and fluid movements, and sometimes confusing even ourselves.

Once in a while a widely known human soldier of fortune collides with a silent bystander. The two quotations that follow are examples of this.

Some contend that certain personalities entertain an implicit death wish. These individuals are attracted to high-risk occupations. While politics does not compare to auto racing, it does represent a precarious calling and does prove attractive to adventuresome types. High-risk politicians are characterized by a willingness to extend themselves—actually overextend themselves—in seeking to advance their careers. They are willing to expose themselves to dangerous situations, possibly even subconsciously seek out such encounters, assuredly to satisfy internal psychological drives.

Robert Kennedy purportedly represents a prime example of this thesis. The senator's death wish, or at least his willingness to open himself to personal hurt, evidenced itself in private life in such treacherous pastimes as mountain climbing, navigating waterways such as the Amazon, and shooting dangerous rapids. [p. 20]*

And, to describe the silent bystander:

He was in real life withdrawing into a brooding isolation with a sense of personal failure and insignificance.

Working as an exercise boy, he dreamed of being a jockey, but an injury suffered by falling from a horse ended that hope. Later he bought a cheap pistol and slammed away, rapid fire, with hundreds of rounds on a target range. He fired each shot as if it would somehow make up for impotence. [Diamond, 1969, p. 50]

To mix the metaphor, a leopard, a

*From Crotty, W. S.: Presidential assassinations. Published by permission of Transaction, Inc., from Society, vol. 9, no. 7 (1972), copyright © 1972 by Transaction, Inc.

human soldier of fortune, was killed by a lonely and silent bystander. It could be called a collision of initiatives. The collision of initiatives is rarely as brutal an episode as the chance meeting between Robert Kennedy and his killer. Collisions are usually more benign.

During the third stage of development the child begins to acquire an increasingly certain idea of who he is, who mother is, and who father is. Slowly at first, and then with more and more gusto, the boy competes with his father for the mother's attention and affection. The boy may daydream about running away with his mother to some private place they can call their own. Many boys have daydreams about doing away with father so they can have mother all to themselves. Girls will often think about father the way boys think of mother. Girls may have daydreams about getting rid of mother. If these daydreams are fulfilled, trouble and turmoil develop. If these dreams and hopes come true, the boy would be without a father; he would be romantically involved with his own mother.

Sitting on the steps and looking at the car, he wanted his mother with him now. The car was parked not far away and he wanted to find the keys to the car and drive it away with his mother sitting next to him. He wanted to take her away somewhere so that they could go out to eat hamburgers and then get married and never come back. He worried about paying for the hamburgers because he didn't have any money. Worse still, he didn't know how to drive.

Waking with a start and sitting up in bed, he felt frightened at the dream he'd just had. In the dream, he was a lion, a strong and powerful lion. His father was a hunter looking for him. As a lion, he'd crept through the jungle quietly until he was within 10 feet of his father's back. He could see his father's shoulders and the back of his head. Leaping at his father he roared a lion's roar and extended his sharp claws. Abruptly, he woke up, feeling cold and afraid. [Poland and Sanford, 1971, pp. 16-17]

The idea of a boy doing away with his father and then living in a conjugal setting with his own mother is not new. The Greeks thought about it. Sophocles wrote a play based on the idea. That play was acted out on a stage 2,300 years ago. Near the end of the play the main character, King Oedipus, discovers he has unknowingly murdered his father and married his mother. He puts out his own eyes—blinds himself—and rages against his own life.

> So had I not come to shed my father's blood, nor been called among men the spouse of her from whom I sprang: but now I am forsaken of the gods, son of a defiled mother, successor to his bed who gave me mine wretched being: and if there be yet a woe surpassing woes, it hath become the portion of Oedipus. [Mullahy, 1948, p. 391]

The play is beyond doubt one of the ultimates in tragedy and forms a part of the historical treasures of mankind. ("History is ourselves." [Clark, 1969, p. 347]) At the same time, it describes an aspect of the history of each person. Intertwined within that personal history is the effort to avoid the tragedy. Avoidance in this instance leads to the beginnings of self-defeating behavior.

So that the boy's daydreams and hopes of having mother all to himself are not fulfilled, the boy can learn how to be self-defeating. He can learn to defeat himself, how not to be successful, how to lose. The learning may be appropriate in a narrow way during the third stage of development, but the effect can be felt long past the years of childhood. Here are two examples from Poland and Sanford (1971):

1.

> Fred was obviously intelligent. He talked with directness and a good knowledge of facts. He did well in high school and earned top grades during the first three years of college. In his senior year his grades began sliding downward. Eventually he flunked out. His friends were mystified and his parents were angry. Fred was not in trouble with a girl or in debt and he was not a campus activist. When people asked him what had happened, he merely shrugged his shoulders.

2.

> Pat saved money for two years. She wanted to go to Europe in grand style. She bought new clothes, a handsome set of matched luggage, and made reservations in first-class hotels. She bought a round-trip plane ticket and planned a two-month tour of the Continent. While she was standing in line at the counter at Kennedy International, she realized she did not have a passport. She walked to the observation deck to watch her plane take off. [p. 36]

The development of self-defeating behavior is reasonably understandable; its continuance is not. Yet self-defeating behavior is so widespread, so common, so often a part of the behavior of many humans past the ages of 4, 5, and 6 years, that it can very nearly be called normal.

Self-defeating activities may help to establish the lifetime style of the soldier of fortune. Such activities may form part of the core of behavior of the silent bystander. From time to time, self-defeating behavior can be seen in the life of the reasonable adventurer. Perhaps it is unavoidable. In any case it will compromise and dilute the impact of the behavior labeled initiative. When that takes place, the balancing scales may shift in the direction of a sense of guilt.

Feelings of guilt are linked with the development of initiative. As Erikson (1968) has pointed out, "The great governor of initiative is *conscience*" (p. 119). But conscience has two sides. To borrow a paragraph from Chapter 1:

Human initiative is guided, controlled, directed, facilitated, and inhibited by what can be called conscience. Having a conscience is not simply a matter of having some sort of inner voice telling the person "don't." A conscience is not only inhibitory with its messages that say "don't cheat" and "don't be late." A conscience can also send telegrams that say "do." The "do" factors may range from "do be free" to "you must graduate" to "do trust another person."

It will be useful to keep in mind the idea that a conscience is learned. The learning process may begin before the spoken language is learned: the language of words as well as the language of gestures facilitates the development of conscience, and each of us carries with us a large set of "do" and "don't" rules, many of which were learned as we learned to talk.

REVIEW QUESTIONS

1. How are autonomy, shame, and doubt interrelated?
2. Can you describe Jody's relationship with her father?
3. What is a *Rundtanz*?
4. Can you briefly describe the collision between a soldier of fortune and a silent bystander?
5. Who was Oedipus?
6. What part does the conscience play in human initiative?
7. What is the intrusive mode?
8. What is trust?
9. What is the principal characteristic of a reasonable adventurer?
10. Can you interpret the dream the boy had in which he saw himself as a lion?
11. How are guilt and initiative related?
12. What is the primal dialogue?

5
THE YEARS PRIOR TO ADULTHOOD

When we are very young, we are baffled and mystified by the person in the mirror who is "I" or "me." We may, when we are small, try to touch the "me" that is only a reflection. When we are older, we can lose ". . . this fresh and naive, direct way of looking at life" (Maslow, 1954, p. 228). Doris Lessing (1970) has captured a fragment of the sense of this loss and expressed it in these words about a girl and a room with a mirror in it.

It was a large room, built to the back of the house, lit by two tall candles, one on either side of a vast double bed spread with white. The windows were open on the veld, which was already greying to the dawn, and the moon had a pallid, exhausted look. A sheet of silver, inclining at the end of the room, took Martha's attention, and she looked again and saw it was a mirror. She had never been alone in a room with a full-length mirror before, and she stripped off her clothes and went to stand before it. It was as if she saw a vision of someone not herself; or rather, herself transfigured to the measure of a burningly insistent future. The white naked girl with high small breasts that leaned forward out of the mirror was like a girl from a legend; she put forward her hands to touch, then as they encountered the cold glass, she saw the naked arms of the girl slowly rise to fold defensively across those breasts. She did not know herself. [p. 78]*

There are sometimes long moments when we do not know ourselves, when we are without obvious and well-known feelings, when we exist as a day without weather or a flame without light. There are times when we are dedicated to the doing; being comes secondary. In human development these times are most clearly present during the years of apprenticeship that exist just before the lightning and thunder of adolescence.

This chapter consists of a review of some of the ways in which people past the age of 6 and under the age of 21 experience their world. What their world is like cannot be precisely known by anyone past that age range. It cannot be known with precision because memory is not a complete documentary film library. It cannot be known because of change; someone who is 7 years old right now lives in a world vastly different from the world of 7 as it was ten or twelve or fifteen years ago. And who past the age of 20 can describe in fine detail what it is like to be 15? The only real experts of the adolescent experience are the adolescents themselves, and they may not choose to describe their world with fluency and great detail. In a general sense we know their bodies change because inherited equipment triggers the flow of fluids and juices that produce bodily

Table 5. Erikson's fourth and fifth developmental stages (1968)

Stage	Ages	Label	Major development
4	7-11	School age	Industry
5	12-20	Adolescence	Sense of identity

changes. We also know, but with less sureness, that their minds change in such varied ways that adolescents are the mysterious and interesting neighbors who live next door to the place adults call home.

THE YEARS OF APPRENTICESHIP

According to Erikson's ideas of what a lifetime may be, the fourth and fifth stages cover thirteen years and several changes of great magnitude.

After the psychological turmoil of the years of childhood, the human child begins to settle into what could become a rut if it were not for the coming high winds of change that are a part of adolescence.

The school age years, compared to other times, are serene and peaceful, and they form what has been called "the years of apprenticeship" phase of life. As the person moves into the fourth stage of development, the powerful, sexually based feelings of childhood become hidden under the surface. They are not expressed in behavior; they become, according to many behavioral scientists, *latent;* that is, the sexually based feelings are not expressed by way of observable behavior.*

Yet there is some intellectual controversy and disagreement about what happens to the child's feelings about mother and father. As Joseph Cramer (1959) has pointed out:

> The period . . . has been called the period of psychosexual latency. As the term implies, this con-

—————————
* If feelings and emotions are expressed by some kind of observable behavior, they are said to be *manifested.*

cept stemmed originally from an idea that the sex impulses remained latent during this time. Subsequently, this notion was revised, for the study of neuroses in children of this age group indicated quite clearly that recession of sex (and other) impulses does not truly occur, but rather an increasing repression and renunciation of erotic activity of both an active and a fantasy nature. [p. 808]

At first glance this matter may seem to be a game with words, a semantic Cracker Jack puzzle. It is not.

If we take the more typical route and call this fourth stage of development the *latency period,* we label it as a time when psychosexual feelings are merely pushed off to one side, hidden but still felt beneath the surface and not shown in the behavior of the school age person. However, if we opt for Cramer's statement, we contend that the psychosexual feelings connected with mother and father are repressed, pushed out of conscious awareness to such a degree that they are not felt. They are then unconscious.

Because of later developments in a lifetime, especially during adolescence and early adulthood, it is more logical to opt for Cramer's idea of repression rather than accept the old and perhaps inaccurate idea that school age humans experience a decline or a recession in their psychosexual feelings. In reviewing the concept of repression, Mullahy (1948) has said:

> According to Freud, repression is the foundation upon which the whole structure of psychoanalysis rests. The essence of repression, he says "lies simply in the function of rejecting and keeping something out of consciousness." By and large its purpose is the avoidance of pain. [p. 9]

With the sexual storms of childhood held in check by repression, the person of the school age years can devote his attention and efforts to the development of a sense of industry, to the building of a previously unattainable industriousness.

The school age person is usually eager to make things—build models, sew, knit, compound gunpowder. The industrious activities are typically group activities devoted to play that resembles work. The play-work is a matter of apprenticeship, a preparation for real work that comes later. As Richard Quey (1971) maintains:

An important nonstructural reason for work groups lies in our basic human desire for protection from individual risk and external danger. All of us in varying degrees feel weak, anxious, and insecure, and we tend to equate safety with human companionship. To be alone or to act alone means to be unprotected and vulnerable. To act as part of a group is to have group insurance; the risks and penalties are spread over many persons with no single individual likely to suffer great hurt or loss. [p. 1078]

The groups can also be called gangs. During the school age years girls prefer the company of other girls, while boys run with boys in gangs. It is a time of normal homosexuality. Normal homosexuality means in part that boys prefer the companionship of other boys, and girls enjoy the company of other girls. There may be some physical , sexual playfulness between boys and between girls during this stage. There may also be some heterosexual activities that take place when a boy and a girl meet secretly, away from their respective gangs. During these usually brief en-

counters they may peek at each other's genitals. Then they return once again, each to the safety of the gang to which they belong, and resume the homosexual style of life that is a part of this developmental phase.

The normal homosexual style of life that forms a part of this stage of development can operate in ways that reassure the child. A boy can become more certain he is a boy. Girls can more surely identify themselves as girls. The identification of self more clearly in terms of gender is an apprenticeship factor that shows itself more sharply as the child moves along the time line toward adulthood.

During the school age stage of development boys and girls typically develop the art of persistence and patience. They learn how to adjust to the tools they use rather than to expect the tools to adjust to them, a behavior more common at an earlier age. Girls can learn how to use the tools necessary for taking care of their hair. They can also learn how to use tools in sewing, cooking, and putting on makeup. At this age some girls learn how to use tools and

Bruce Anspach/EPA Newsphoto

implements needed to take care of horses, to shampoo dogs, to mow lawns. Boys, if the opportunity exists, can learn to use hammers, saws, and screwdrivers in building huts, tree houses, and bookcases. It is a stage in life when there is a movement toward accepting, using, and becoming more familiar with the technology of the world. It is also a stage when the youngster gradually begins to realize the meaning of the color of his skin. At the same time he may come to realize the family background, which may include his father's occupation, plays a part in what he is allowed to do. In spite of his willingness to learn and to participate the child of this stage may find himself cut off from some activities and allowed to enter into other activities solely on the basis of factors over which he has no control—race and family lifestyle. The result can be the beginnings of a sense of inferiority.

At an earlier age the person who successfully developed a sense of autonomy was at the same time reasonably successful in keeping a sense of shame or doubt at a minimum. Moving forward in time the individual whose sense of initiative is blunted or compromised may experience a rise in the development of a sense of guilt. For the school age person a dilution or inhibition of the development of a sense of industry can result in the growth of a sense of inferiority.*

Blunting the development of a sense of industry can of course take place within the family. The parents play a part in this. Their part may be obvious; they may minimize and belittle the efforts and productions of the youngster. For instance, a girl may spend energy washing her own hair and then show her mother what she has done. The mother can respond with "I'm

really glad you can do that now," or the mother may say "You didn't get it clean." Or, more stressfully, the mother may tell her daughter, "You didn't do a very good job. Now I've got to wash it for you." Perhaps more injurious, though, is the mother or the father who simply ignores the youngster, who says nothing, who leaves the boy or girl standing alone. Parents who are passive at the moment their children expect even a small rewarding recognition are toxic at that moment. It is as though they inject the poison of feelings of inferiority into their children. Older brothers and sisters may perform in their own toxic ways with younger siblings who are moving through the school age years. What they do or what they may be allowed to do by the parents can result in as much blunting of industry as whatever the parents might do.

Schools offer a beautiful location for developing a sense of industry. There is an old adage connected with schools; the core philosophy of teaching is, according to Maier (1971), "Let those who know teach those who do not know" (p. 722). Yet, there remains an old saying attributed to George Bernard Shaw who stated, "Those who can, do, while those who cannot, teach." There may be more than a thin thread of truth running through Shaw's words. The school system in this nation of over 200 million is enormous. The large size of school systems in such places as New York City, New Orleans, Boston, Austin, and Phoenix requires an army of teachers, and in any sort of army there will be misfits, unhappy and psychologically injurious individuals. Some may delight in fostering a sense of inferiority in most of the students they supposedly teach. On the other hand there are large numbers of teachers who not only teach but also nourish their students. Many students may receive their only emotional nourishment from the school.

The school age phase covers a period of

---

*While the feelings of shame, guilt, and inferiority may develop well before the adult years, they do not usually fade with time. They remain and often play a part in the daily lives of many adults.

four years. In the middle of that time span endocrine changes begin to take place. These changes are the first quickening of the breeze that grows in force, leading into the storm years of adolescence. The endocrine changes are subtle at first, but they lead to an increase in the individual's general level of activity. A girl may play and work with increased vigor; a boy may become more energetic, and both may show an increase in stamina. However, neither will show an open increase of interest in the opposite sex (Maier, 1965).

The movement toward puberty usually proceeds at a rapid pace. The movement, though, is similar to the activities of a secret society. There are discussions between members of the same gang, conversations about sexual activities, furtive looks at nudie magazine covers on display at the store, quick glances at mother's bustline and father's clothed crotch. There may be an exchange of sexual jokes often poorly understood. The jokes, however, may be greeted with nearly endless giggles or uproarious laughter. When the giggles and the laughter subside, the youngster again sinks back into a sea of sexual wonderment. It is a time of stress.

It is a time of stress for the parents too. As the child moves closer to the years of adolescence, his parents may sense a growing concern about the youngster's sexual knowledge or lack of it. It seems there are several ways in which parents handle the matter. They can completely avoid any discussion of human sexual behavior; they can pretend it does not exist, or else they can hope the school system presents a program of some sort. Many schools do, but there is usually no coordination of what is taught at school and what the parents teach or do not teach at home.

If the parents have some small measure of courage about teaching a child something about sex, they may leave pamphlets or books around the house, located in places where the child can not possibly miss seeing them. If the parents have slightly more courage, they may read aloud to the child from a pamphlet or a book. With some additional bravery the mother or father may put the reading material down and talk face-to-face with his own offspring. The conversation is generally limited to the physiological aspects. Some parents, however, are able to discuss the psychological aspects of sexual behavior. They may talk about feelings and attitudes including aspects of pleasure, the excitement, and the emotional release of sexual activities. If such a discussion takes place, the child may be a member of a family that can help him to move more smoothly through the next stage of development, the stage of adolescence.

Sharon

Sharon married John on the last day of June. On the first day of July she came back to her parent's home. She said she was finished with John, finished with marriage, and more to the point, finished with men. She would not talk with her father or answer the telephone because she was sure John was calling. She was done with him. Her mother tried to find out what had happened, but Sharon refused to talk. Her father merely rattled his newspaper, grumbled a mumble, and puffed on his cigar.

The next day when she woke up, she put on a bathrobe and went into the kitchen hungry for breakfast. John was in the kitchen, and when she saw him, she screamed briefly and started to run toward her bedroom. John chased her, grabbed her around the waist, and picked her up off the floor. She kicked at him and screamed some more, and he chopped at her jaw—karate style—with the edge of his free hand. He carried her out the front door, down the sidewalk, and threw her into his car. She started to get out of the car, but he hit her again, and she collapsed on the car seat, crying. John jumped into the car, started the engine, and pulled away, speeding.

Within a few moments he was on the interstate highway leading out of town. He drove steadily for an hour, then pulled off the highway and stopped at a motel. He told Sharon they had reservations. He quickly checked in, got a room key, and drove the car around to a room on a side wing of the motel. When he stopped the car by their motel room door, Sharon began to swear at him, but he told her to shut up or he would hit her again. She quickly became quiet. He got out of the car, came around to the other side, and opened her door. Sullenly she got out of the car and spit in his face. He hit her once more, but not as sharply as before. She began to cry, and he grabbed her arm, pulling her across the sidewalk and into the motel room.

When they were both inside, he closed the door to the room, put the chain lock in place, and pushed Sharon into a chair. He told her they were married now and that made everything all right. He took off his clothes and stood in front of her. He shouted that what he wanted to do was legal now, permissible, not sinful, probably good for one's own health and well-being.

Sharon picked up a Bible from the motel desk and threw it at John. He dodged the book and chopped at her again, and once more she began to cry. With a great rage, John picked Sharon up out of the chair and threw her onto the bed. He reached down, ripped the bathrobe apart, tore her nightgown open, and then raped his wife. When he was finished, he lay on the bed next to her as she moaned and cried. After a time he got up, went to the telephone, and called room service. He ordered a large breakfast for two.

Fifteen minutes later the room service porter wheeled a cart full of food into the room; after he looked around quickly, he left in a hurry. Once again John locked the door securely and went to the laden cart. He poured coffee from the glass carafe and took a filled cup over to Sharon, now wrapped in an enclosing bedspread. Sharon silently took the cup from John, drank a sip, and stared at him with rounded and tear-filled eyes.

"Eat," he said. "And stop crying."

Sharon moved toward the cart, sniffling. She took a plate of food and a fork and retreated to the safety of the bed and ate silently. John scooped scrambled eggs into his mouth and almost breathed the coffee into his stomach. When they were finished with the meal, they sat for a long moment looking at each other silently.

Late in the morning John walked to a clothing store and bought some clothes for Sharon. He took them back to the motel, and quietly Sharon put them on and then went for a noon walk with John. At a roadside drive-in they ate chili dogs and milk shakes and walked around some more. Late in the afternoon they went into the clothing store, and Sharon picked out some additional clothing. Then they walked back to the motel.

Inside the privacy of their room, John took off his clothes, showered, and dried himself. He then sat in the chair by the desk and read the Bible to Sharon. He read about Adam and Eve and about the Nativity, and then he read some of the psalms to his wife. When he was finished, she was asleep, so he turned out the lights and went to bed next to her.

In the morning they checked out of the motel and drove back to the apartment they had rented. When they got inside the apartment, Sharon picked up the telephone and began to dial her parent's number. John clamped a hand over the phone and told Sharon to hang up. She did. Then he told her to try to think of him as the best friend she ever had.

That evening they ate dinner together, but they did not talk much. Later they watched a half hour of television, and then John thought it was time for bed. Sharon said no, she would rather watch some more television. John sighed, switched the set off, and said that was all they were going to watch tonight.

The next morning John called the psychology department of a junior college he had attended a year ago. He talked with an instructor he knew, asking the instructor where his wife could get some help with some problems she was having. The instructor told John whom to call, and then he assured John the man was a brother. John put down the phone, relieved that his wife would see a black psychotherapist.

They went together. At first Sharon could not or would not talk very much, so John gave the background reasons for their being there. He said that on their wedding night, his wife had locked herself in the hotel bathroom and refused to come out. He had broken the door in by using a small table as a battering ram, but the breakage made so much noise the hotel manager came up to the room and demanded to be let in. The manager told John he would have to pay for the damages and both of them should pack up and get out right now.

Sharon immediately put on some clothes and left the hotel. John packed up, checked out, and put the suitcases in the back of his car. He was not sure where Sharon had gone, was not certain of what he should do next, so he drove around town in his car for a couple of hours. At sunrise he called Sharon's parent's house, but no one answered the telephone.

He ate breakfast alone in a pancake restaurant, and when he went to his car to drive away, he looked in the backseat and realized someone had stolen the suitcases full of new clothes. He wondered about talking with the police, but he thought about the hotel manager; maybe the broken table and door had been reported and his name would be on a list of some kind.

John drove out of town, angry, feeling defeated, and alone. He stopped at a gas station and called Sharon's parent's home again. No answer. He got back into his car, swearing and beating his fist on the padded dash. He drove away from the gas station and pulled onto the highway with a roar, thinking of ways he could kill her.

He drove for over four hours, and by that time, he had traveled almost 300 miles, a streak of anger moving across the countryside and through a dozen small towns. At noon he ate a hamburger and drank a root beer at a drive-in on the edge of a town he had never seen before and did not want to see again. Then he headed his car back to where he had started.

It was night when he eased the car to the curb and parked half a block from Sharon's house. He got out and walked down the sidewalk past her house. A light was on in the living room. He saw her briefly through the window. It looked like she was watching television, but he could not be certain. John continued on down the sidewalk. He walked around the block back to his car. He got in, started the engine, and cruised down the street, staying close to the curb with his car lights turned off. He stopped the car in front of Sharon's house, turned the ignition off, and waited. He did not know what to do.

He sat there in his car for an hour before the light went off in the house. She's going to bed, he thought, going to bed in that bedroom up there, just like a good little girl in a good little family. He put his head back, resting it against the seat, and wondered if he could burn down the house. No, a door and a small table were enough for now. And then he slowly went to sleep.

When he woke up, the street was bright with early morning sunshine, and he quickly got out of the car and went up to the house. He walked around to the backyard and saw the kitchen window was open. He took the screen off and crawled through. As he stood up straight, he looked around and did not know what to do until Sharon walked into the kitchen. She screamed when she saw him and started to run toward her bedroom. John chased after her, grabbed her around the waist, and picked her up off the floor. She kicked at him and screamed some more.

"And then he hit me," Sharon said. "And he took me out to his car and threw me in. He *threw* me in."

"Then what happened?" asked the black therapist.

Sharon described the swift ride to the motel. "He told me we had reservations there. It was a plot. He kidnapped me. He had the reservations all made."

"I lied," said John. "I didn't have reservations anywhere. I just said that so you'd stay in the car."

"Where could I go? I was in my bathrobe!"

"Well, anyway, you didn't run away again."

The therapist wondered why Sharon would want to run away.

"I knew," she said. "I knew what he wanted to do."

The therapist pointed out to Sharon that what John wanted to do was a frequent activity in adult life. Hadn't Sharon known about that?

"Yes, I know people do that. People do it, but I don't."

"But you're married now."

"What difference does that make?"

John groaned.

The therapist organized a program that was to begin immediately. He introduced Sharon to a woman psychologist who took her to a separate office. In the office the psychologist talked with Sharon and discovered she knew almost nothing about sexual behavior. So the psychologist began to teach her, beginning with simple pictures of female and male genitalia. In the meantime the black therapist stayed with John, counseling him to slow down and not to expect his wife to be a sexual companion instantly.

ADOLESCENCE AND IDENTITY

The years of adolescence can be described as years of turmoil, a time of unrest, a hurricane season, a period of conflict and contention. It usually is, in this society; normally in the United States there are periods of great psychological discomfort for the adolescent and for the family of the adolescent. Margaret Mead (1928) has pointed out that in a more pastoral and more relaxed society, adolescents usually move through puberty and on toward the adult years without episodes of crisis or high levels of stress. Berelson and Steiner (1964), after reviewing a considerable amount of written material including research studies and descriptive essays on behavioral development, concluded:

> The evidence across cultures indicates that adolescence is a period of *Sturm und Drang** only in those societies that make it so . . . e.g., by putting severe limitations on sexual behavior, or by providing sharp breaks between dependent childhood and responsible maturity, or by demanding so fast a change that a large gulf opens between the generations. [p. 84]

Many American parents put severe limitations on the sexual behavior of their own children. Many develop family patterns that lead to and eventually create a sharp break between a dependent childhood and a responsible maturity. The language used within the family may sound familiar. "As long as you live in this house, you do as I say," and "When you get out of high school and get out of here, *then* you can call the shots. You'll be on your own then." It is as though some parents expect their offspring to become instant adults.

In contrast, Berelson and Steiner (1964) state:

> In some non-Western societies that take a relaxed attitude toward growing up, the adolescents do not

---

*Storm and stress.

suffer particularly from the stress and strains that seem to us a natural, even biological, accompaniment of adolescence. [p. 84]

Perhaps the stress and strains we may believe to be natural are based not on nature but on a pervasive ignorance of human development. In an extensive review of almost ninety research reports and published professional opinions concerned with the topic of child abuse, John Spinetta and David Rigler (1972) comment in part:

> The authors seem to agree that abusing parents lack appropriate knowledge of child rearing, and that their attitudes, expectations, and child-rearing techniques set them apart from nonabusive parents. The abusing parents implement culturally accepted norms for raising children with an exaggerated intensity at an inappropriately early age. [p. 299]

It may be useful at the moment to point to the findings of Steele and Pollock (1968) and the conclusions of Berelson and Steiner (1964). They all say parents usually raise their children the way they themselves were raised. This can be done unknowingly, unwittingly, unconsciously.*

Maria

Maria spoke English slowly and with a lilting accent. She spoke a mixture of Spanish and English with great speed and fluency. She was 19 years old, married, and the mother of three children. She was brought to the mental health center on a court order because of child abuse.

Maria, thin, tense, charged with an electric level of energy, was defiant during her first interview. She gave very little information about herself at that time; two days later during her second interview she said she thought she was going to be put in jail by the people at the mental health center. No one at the center, she was told, had any authority to put anyone in jail. She was only slightly reassured by that information, and on her third visit she disclosed more about herself.

---

*You can major in history, English, or psychology. You may choose to be trained in accounting, medicine, or engineering. You will, however, have great difficulty in finding a college or a university that offers a major in parenting.

Maria's parents had owned a small farm near Phoenix. They grew irrigated crops for a chain of supermarkets, and she had grown up knowing more about thinning carrots and radishes than how to read and write. When she was 10, her father sold the farm to a real estate company and moved his family to San Diego, where he bought a small restaurant. At first things seemed to go well, but after six years he was bankrupt.

Maria was pregnant. She had married her boyfriend when she was 16 years old and he was 18. They moved from San Diego to San Francisco, where her husband got a job as a bellhop in a large hotel. She gave birth to her first child and became pregnant again almost instantly. They moved once more, this time to Salt Lake City where they stayed for two months; after that, they lived in Boise for almost a year. When they moved from there to Denver, they had two children and Maria was pregnant again. In Denver her husband got a job in a car wash, and they lived in a small house with her husband's uncle; her third child was born in the living room of that house. Two weeks later her husband left a brief note for Maria, saying he was leaving her and would never come back. She cried, she said, for a half a day and then raged at her departed husband for the rest of the day and on into the night, hitting her two older children as she held the 2-week-old infant close to her. The uncle started yelling at her to shut up, to stop hitting the children, and she hollered back at him. She threw a shoe at him and then some wire coat hangers, and he walked out the front door and down the block to a bar on the corner.

The uncle stayed in the bar for an hour. He drank two beers slowly and then walked back to his house. Everything was quiet. Maria and her three children were asleep in their part of the house, and his own family was arranged on the couch and on the floor watching television. The next morning at breakfast the uncle told Maria she would have to leave. She immediately telephoned her parents in San Diego asking for money for the trip back to them. They agreed to send thirty dollars in the mail that same day; it was all they could afford. The uncle agreed to put up fifteen dollars.

Shortly before dawn three days later Maria and her three children got on a Greyhound bus in downtown Denver. The bus pulled out of the station and headed south. An hour later they were in Colorado Springs, and a half hour afterward they were in Pueblo. The bus stopped and all the passengers got off. Maria's oldest child, a 3-year-old boy, bounded off the bus and ran in circles for a moment, happy to be out of the cramped and crowded bus. Then, laughing, he ran in a straight line that took him into the middle of a busy intersection. Maria screamed and ran after him, carrying her baby. The boy ran through the intersection followed by his mother, and when he got to the far side, he jumped up on the curb and turned to watch her coming at him.

Maria ran up to her son and cuffed him on the head. He ran away from her, but she pursued him. Together they ran down the sidewalk, Maria hitting the boy over and over with one hand as she held the baby with the other. The boy stumbled and she began kicking him, but a man grabbed her around the waist and lifted her away from the boy. The boy stood up, crying, as the man shook Maria by the shoulders, telling her to shut up and calm down. At that moment a policeman came up to the man and told him to get his hands off Maria. The man was startled and let go of her, stepping back quickly. Everyone started to talk at once, but the policeman outshouted Maria and the man; he told them to come with him to the station, which was half a block away.

When they got to the station house, everyone went inside, but before they could talk with the desk sergeant, the boy collapsed, and his face turned blue immediately. Within ten minutes, he had been given artificial respiration, pure oxygen, and had been rushed to a nearby hospital emergency room. He was examined, but no one could diagnose what the problem was, although the boy still had great difficulty breathing. He was put in an oxygen tent and provided with constant nursing care, while his mother was booked for child abuse.

The boy was in the hospital for six weeks, and during that time his mother spent some of each day at the mental health center with her baby, learning infant stimulation techniques and attending classes in other mothering behaviors. She visited her son every afternoon. When he was released from the hospital, recovered as mysteriously as he had become ill, the judge who had issued the court order causing Maria to be brought to the mental health center told her to leave the state or consider the possibility of a jail sentence. She left the state with her three children.

When a person stands on his own private time line at a point that defines the end of the school age years and the front edge of adolescence, he or she can be called a *puber;* a puber is an individual at the onset of puberty. *Taber's Cyclopedic Medical Dictionary* (1960) defines puberty as the following:

> Period in life at which one of either sex becomes functionally capable of reproduction.
>
> A period of rapid change in boys and girls. It occurs in temperate climates between the ages of 13 and 16 in boys and 12 to 15 in girls, and ends in the attainment of sexual maturity.
>
> In the boy it is marked by appearances of hair on the face and chest, under the axilla, and on the pubes, change of voice, definite enlargement of the penis, and the appearance of erections and erotic dreams with ejaculation. Other physical and psychic disturbances are normal at this period, and end in the appearance of functional spermatazoa in the semen.
>
> In the girl menstruation begins, the breasts enlarge, and hair appears in axilla and on the pubes. [p. P-125]

Adolescence, biological adolescence, begins at puberty. And, as Leon Eisenberg (1970) has pointed out, *"biological* adolescence begins four years earlier than it did a century and a half ago, presumably because of improvements in nutrition and health" (p. 1689). Girls begin to menstruate and boys begin to have wet dreams, or as they have sometimes been called, "nocturnal emissions." Girls are often concerned about their supply of sanitary napkins or tampons; boys are sometimes concerned about what mother or an older sister will think when the bed sheets are taken away to be laundered. In both cases these concerns are only a small portion of the great kingdom of concerns boys and girls have in this society and at this time in their lives. The concerns are often great enough to interfere with a previously learned sense of industry. At school there

may be a quick decline in the industrious pursuit of academic activities; children in seventh and eighth grades frequently experience a drop in their grades. That drop is often caused by the concerns and worries of the early adolescent years (Branden, 1969; Josselyn, 1952).

The concerns of the adolescent in this society are incredibly varied. Many of the concerns, however, cluster around the central theme of developing a sense of identity. It is during adolescence that the individual must learn to identify himself to himself. There are several steps involved in this effort. The first step includes the realization that there is such a question as "Who am I?" The question does not leap suddenly into awareness; instead, it grows in a slow way. The adolescent boy may look in a mirror to see himself make faces. He may frown to see what he looks like when he frowns. He may smile in an effort to view what others see when they see him smile. Girls may arrange and rearrange their hair, watching themselves in a mirror. They may try on different combinations of clothes and the clothing of a friend, watching themselves seriously in a mirror as they do so.

In the continuing thrust toward realization of the question "Who am I?" the adolescent often seeks solitude. He wants to be alone. He needs to be alone—sometimes by himself, sometimes in a group—but existing apart from the group, watching, observing others, making mental notes of what he sees. As Aldridge (1969) says:

> He will take on the spectatorial attitude, the habit of seeing what is happening in the world of others as interesting or remarkable or preposterous just because it is happening to them and not to himself, because they are strangers or actors performing a play in which he has no part. [p. 103]

To be continually a spectator has its risks. The person may sometimes feel he is on the outside edge of life, looking in. He can evolve to seeing himself as a stranger, a trespasser on territory that always belongs to someone else, an alien, unwanted and unloved within his own family and sometimes even unwelcome in the gang of friends he once thoroughly belonged to.

As Linda put it, "There's nobody. I don't have any friends anywhere."

"None at all?"

"Not anybody. I pretend, though. Sometimes I can mess around and laugh and all that and fool other people, but I know I'm all alone. *I* know it."

"You're sure."

"Yes, I'm sure. Don't you believe me? Nobody calls me any more. I sit around the house, reading or just sitting there with acne all over my face and nobody calls on the telephone. They used to, but they don't any more."

"Do you ever call anyone?"

"Yeah. Sometimes. Well, not for a while, I guess."

"Why not?"

"They wouldn't want to talk with me."

In her own way, Linda was a silent bystander. She had withdrawn from most of the people around her; she was closed up, brooding, an unhappy spectator. But all that changed, as adolescents usually change as they move along their time lines.

There are two main phases of adolescence (Josselyn, 1952). *Phase 1* comes in a rush with the beginning of menstruation and wet dreams. The sexual tumult of the childhood years can no longer be easily repressed when the sexual development of one's own body becomes obvious. The adolescent may suddenly experience erotic impulses that can produce great surges of confusion together with sudden but transitory feelings of pleasure, followed by episodes of guilt feelings and a sense of shame and self-condemnation, almost all of which can be attributed to and based upon the ways in which this society contends with sexual matters.

Sarah*

In ninth grade a group of girls got close. We used to hug and kiss each other a lot and have slumber parties. Most of us had boyfriends, but we seemed very important to each other. Once in a while someone would say, "What are you, a homo?" and we'd laugh. It didn't mean anything and it didn't change our behavior in any way.

That's the only reference to homosexuality before college that I can remember. In college I got hit with Freud and latent homosexual tendencies. What did this mean for me, who had always been more emotionally attached to women than to men? In freshman year my roommate and I became very close and dependent on each other, but neither of us could handle the intensity; that happened to me a lot with female friends. In psychotherapy I asked (indirectly of course) if I had "those tendencies." After about fifteen minutes the therapist figured out the question and asked, "Are you wondering if you're a lesbian?" Me: "Not really—ahh, I'm just wondering what you think about those tendencies." "You've given no indications of that," he said. Phew! was my reaction, not knowing what those "indications" were! (That's the story of how expertise has power over people's lives.) So I didn't worry about being a lesbian, but continued to build close friendships with women; and the problems those emotional attachments brought weren't lessened.

After college I felt the sadness of women friends going in different directions without the question of sharing our lives, like there would be with boyfriends. I went with a guy for three years, but he was never more important to me than two of my female friends. That was to my liking, not his. He wanted to get married, but since marriage wasn't part of any world I could imagine for myself, he married another woman two months after we split up. Sometimes my friendships with women were threatened by their jealous boyfriends. With these feelings, I could no longer ignore the women's movement. I read something another

*From Boston Women's Health Book Collective, Inc.: Our bodies, ourselves. Copyright © 1971, 1973 by the Boston Women's Health Book Collective, Inc. Reprinted by permission of Simon & Schuster, Inc.

woman had written about her—and my—experiences. Fantastic! I wasn't alone. I began thinking that men didn't understand friendship, that they were sexual prowlers wanting all the attention focused on them; whereas my relationships with women seemed natural, exciting, and intense.

Working with Women's Liberation in Boston meant being with women all the time. A group of us who weren't really close but were friends would hang out together, circle-danced at a bar, played basketball. Diana was one of them. She and I found we could tune into each other's survival tactics: her piercing, allusive quips weren't offensive to me. What a relief. We could accept each other without many hurt feelings, we shared a lot of interests and criticisms of the women's movement. Eventually we slept together. That was over a year ago. [pp. 57-58.]

Phase 2 of the adolescent years comes on slowly as the person begins more surely to establish control over the erotic impulses.* The shift from phase 1 to phase 2 is as difficult to recall as learning how to talk. The shift may take place for the following reasons:

1. The individual may become more regular and experience more stability in his or her own physiological processes. That is, menstruation usually becomes more predictable or more acceptable or perhaps more psychologically comfortable after several years of experience. Wet dreams and masturbation may be accepted more as a normal process of life for boys.
2. Normally, there is an increase in the emotional detachment from the parents. Dating begins, and the parents may no longer be seen as the only real targets of affection, and anger, as they were during the years of childhood.
3. There may be a gradual mastery over what was once the kingdom of concerns. The varied concerns, some of which may have approached panic levels, can be more easily dealt with. The adolescent is often able not

only to leave many of the concerns behind but also to take up causes and become involved in movements or at least discuss issues and ideals in a near-adult manner.

In both phase 1 and phase 2, the adolescent may swiftly shift back and forth between episodes of seemingly disturbed, irrational, planless behavior and episodes of peacefulness and a quiet, rational contemplation of life. The shifting from one extreme to the other often exasperates, irritates, and sometimes bewilders parents.

As one father said, "I never know what to expect."

"Oh?"

"Yeah, it's driving me nutty. One minute she's sweet and ladylike and she reminds me a little of my wife. The next minute she's—well —crazy."

"You sound a little worried."

"Worried? Wouldn't you be? I never know what to expect. And her room. It looks like a pigpen. You should see it. A real mess."

"It's her room."

"But it's in *my* house. She keeps food in there and there's cookie crumbs all over the floor. I'm afraid we'll get mice or cockroaches."

"Does she ever clean it up?"

"Sure, but only after I've yelled at her a dozen times. I think she cleans it up about every three months."

"That's worth something."

"Maybe. But what about the way she acts? I mean what about all the different ways she acts? That really bothers me."

"Why?"

"Well, it doesn't seem right. People don't go around changing all the time like that."

"She does."

"Yes, she does, and I need to know why. What's wrong with her?"

"She's a teenager."

"That sounds like a pretty flippant answer to me. I'm serious. What's wrong with her?"

There *must* be something wrong, implies the father. There *must* be something wrong and his other theme, "I never know what to expect," contain the elements of a clash. The clash between

---

*You may recall that one of the preconditions mentioned in Chapter 1 was control of sexual behavior via the cerebral cortex.

parents and their adolescent children is based on a number of factors. Some of those factors are listed below:

1. The adolescent experiments with different ways of being, different modes of thinking, feeling, reacting. The experimentation is in this society an evidently necessary factor in working on the answer to the question of ''Who am I?''

2. Adolescent experimentation may be appreciated for what it actually is if the parents have been able to develop for themselves their own answers to the question ''Who am I?'' If, however, the parents have only a dim or hazy sense of identity, they may interpret the experimentation as a rebellion against them.

3. Both the parents and the adolescent are involved in the process of change in family relationships. The change is often great enough to reach the level of a crisis.

4. Because of the rapid environmental changes wrought by technology, the adolescent is an

Editorial Photocolor Archives

adolescent in a world enormously different from the world the parents knew when they themselves were adolescents.

These four factors that contribute to the clash between parent and adolescent are worth a few comments.

Adolescence as experimentation

In working with the question of "Who am I?" and in moving toward the answer "This is *me*," the adolescent will sometimes rip through a wide variety of behaviors at great speed. On Monday a girl can say a pale blue Corvette is the best car in the world, but when Wednesday comes, the best vehicle will be a rusty Jeep with a torn canvas top. On Saturday she may clean up her bedroom and observe impeccable manners at the dinner table. On Sunday morning she can be short tempered and sarcastic at breakfast. Money hoarded for a month will be deposited in a savings account on Tuesday, withdrawn on Friday, and spent on Saturday.

In February a boy may devote hours and days thinking about, daydreaming about, a girl who seems to him to be fantastically desirable. In March he cuts her off with a harsh look and a few hostile words, never to acknowledge her existence until May. In December he will plead for a tape recorder for Christmas, but beginning in January the recorder collects dust on the back of a closet shelf. In September he may make a solemn vow to study hard, complete all his homework assignments, and try for a listing on the honor roll, but by November he is so busy writing a novel he does not want to go to school.

After a couple of years of often tumultuous experimentation, many parents are generally wary of any promise or pleading or vow their child may make. The parents can comment about what they observe, and once in awhile the adolescent will agree. At other times, rarely predictable, the adolescent will make some comments back, using harsh words. As for his parents, the adolescent will sometimes tell them they talk too much, but three days later he may complain they do not talk enough. The contradicting phrases tumble out: "Mother, you just love to be a martyr" versus "You never think of anyone but yourself," and "You don't understand anything at all" versus "How did you ever get to know so much?"

The question soon develops: how does the adolescent really feel about anything? Some of the time the answer can be stated in one word—secretive (Josselyn, 1952). The adolescent keeps secret the feelings he has about himself, about other people, about life, and about the world in general. If he or she does burst forth with a barrage of words—revealing feelings and attitudes and conflicts—what is said may be on target, accurate, and relevant, but at the same time it may be limited and understandably lacking in a depth of understanding.

At other moments the answer can be stated with another word—confused (GAP, 1968). The adolescent in this society must take into account not only his own very real feelings and attitudes but also the feelings and attitudes other people tell him he has. Added to those two sources of information may be some ideal —some way he is supposed to feel according to religion or the gang he is in, the rules of the school, the ethics and morality of the times in which he lives, and a flurry of fads and fashions that exist in everyday life. It seems there is too much to take into account, too many sources of information and opinion; it is rare for an adolescent or, for that matter, most adults to select and to sort out only the relevant and the useful from the avalanche. A sense of overload is easily developed.

Another one-word answer to the question can be spelled out—conflicted (Glasser, 1972). The most hidden conflicts for the adolescent involve the clash between his surging, searing daydreams and impulses and the cold face of reality. A girl cannot possibly run off to a tropical island with Neil Diamond or Flip Wilson; instead, she must iron a dress and get ready for a date with John Anonymous. A boy will never actually win the big trophy at Daytona or Indianapolis, but he may scrape together enough money to buy a couple of gallons of gas for Saturday night cruising in a car. The chances of tearfully accepting an Academy Award are small, but the probability is high that tomorrow morning there will be another siege with acne. And so on it goes, the soaring, pleasurable larger-than-life daydreams versus a day-by-day existence. The gulf between the two can lead to a Grand Canyon filled to the rim with the debris of a thousand compromises with the real world. It is not much different for adults who cling to adolescence, no matter how old they may be.

There are other conflicts. A major one involves the person's conscience (Josselyn, 1952). The typical experimenting adolescent becomes involved in a contest with the conscience that was developed in childhood and during the school age years. It is an appropriate and necessary contest, for the adolescent is no longer a child, even though he may sometimes long to return to those years of serenity or to the years of early sexuality when the only close participants were the child and the parents. But the conscience developed during those times does not fit as well as it once did. Reality, the assassin of daydreams, becomes the adolescent's friend in the attempts to demolish those parts of the conscience that have now become obsolete. The girl can no longer be the good little girl. The son can no longer be the obedient, pliable, and often agreeable little boy. But how else can one be?

Experimentation with different ways of being helps the adolescent to find the road to how else.

Adolescent experimentation interpreted as rebellion

Adolescents experiment. It may exasperate the parents. It may also antagonize and frighten them. While the adolescent in this society may often be secretive, confused, and conflicted, he may also be trying to find out how to be a reasonable adventurer. His parents may not think so, however. He may try out different ways of being that are more different than mother and father can easily tolerate. For instance, a boy may tape center-fold pictures of nude women on the walls of his bedroom and then perhaps masturbate once in a while as he looks over his photographic gallery. Mother may not know or may unconsciously deny knowledge of the masturbation, but she may be offended by the pictures. She may be openly critical of their presence, and if her son refuses to take them down, mother will label his behavior as rebellious.

Another example is a girl who may buy and wear a thickly padded brassiere. Her father may see the dramatic change in her appearance and order her to take it off and throw it away. The girl may follow his command and then not wear a brassiere at all. Her father will notice *that* change, of course, and perhaps call it rebellious behavior.

There are other examples. A girl may attend a rally protesting abortion laws. The rally may be part of the evening television news program. Mother and father watch the news, see their daughter clearly and firmly fixed by the camera's eye, and they shudder. "What will the neighbors think?" A boy can try out for football, make the team, and then quit. The father prods him to return to the game, but the boy says no. Father says it is rebellion.

Rebellion means disagreement. Rebellion is a label used by parents and many others to describe behavior that disagrees with whatever the parents believe is right, proper, appropriate, or somehow necessary or traditional. The adolescent, in contrast, may not initially feel rebellious or improper, inappropriate or antitraditional. The adolescent may not feel these ways until the parents tell him that is how he feels. Then he may thrive on behavior in which he experiments at being improper, inappropriate, and against tradition.

Some parents may experience their own adolescent children as being almost continually rebellious. Other parents may sense more pleasure in the relationship they have with adolescents. The difference may be more a factor of parental behavior than adolescent behavior. If, for example, the mother and father have a psychologically and physically intimate relationship with each other,* and if they have in their own life histories managed to develop a reasonably certain idea of their own separate identities, they may more easily contend with, guide, and assist the adolescent in his movement toward maturity.

To stress the point: the quality of the relationship between the parents and their adolescent offspring is based upon the quality of the relationship between the parents.

Changes in family relationships

This third factor that contributes to the clash between parents and adolescents is founded on a simple idea. Almost every adolescent walks a path that leads out the front door, down the street, and away from the parents. For some parents this is intolerable.

In the Book of Genesis (2:24) these words appear, "Therefore shall a man leave his father and his mother, and shall cleave unto his wife: and they shall be one flesh." And in the New Testament, Matthew (19:5), it is written, "For this cause shall a man leave father and

mother, and shall cleave to his wife: and they twain shall be one flesh." In spite of a long tradition of children leaving home to make their own homes in the larger world, parents may look at their adolescent, see the path he is on, and view the future with sadness, anger, or a sense of dread. These are generally the parents who need their children to be children; these are the parents who may be uneasy, as Jody's mother was, lest their children find the "how else."

In *The Merchant of Venice*, one of Shakespeare's characters says, "It is a wise father who knows his own child." It is also a wise father who knows himself and knows what is happening around him. The wisdom of a father and a mother is tested during the time they have an adolescent in their midst. It is a time of change. Change is sometimes welcomed, sometimes feared, sometimes merely unwanted. Change is often inconvenient, usually disruptive if only a small ways, and a distraction to those who pursue routine.

As adolescents change and evolve toward maturity, their progress may disturb the parents. The adolescent may obviously and clearly show by way of open and observable behavior that he prefers the company of a girl friend to the companionship of his father. Dating can bring up rivalries between the parents and whomever their child dates. Veiled, disguised criticisms and warnings may issue from the parents.

"Are you sure she's a nice girl?"

"Be careful. Don't let him take advantage of you."

"What do you know about her family? Are they nice people?"

"Is he a safe driver?"

"Does she smoke?"

The parents may give themselves away when they say other things to the adolescent. For instance, there are two basic statements a parent may make to an ado-

---

*Intimacy is discussed in Chapter 6.

lescent when he or she leaves the house on a date: (1) "Have a good time" and (2) "Be careful." Which is the most appropriate statement? Obviously, it depends. However, if the parents consistently warn with "Be careful," their warning says more about them than it does about their adolescent. Yet, the adolescent may heed the advice and behave in overly cautious ways. Many adolescents, upon hearing the words, may venture forth on a date firmly determined to be uncareful.

As adolescents grow and develop into more physically mature persons, they grow and develop psychologically in ways that may be durable and lasting. Parents often witness the physical and psychological growth, watching with a warm enjoyment. Some parents, however, find little joy in the progress they see, for it signals the beginning of the detachment from home and parents. This is a different level of detachment than was described earlier, the infantile detachment from mother. In that stage of development—in infancy—the detachment is connected with the development of a sense of trust. During adolescence, detachment is a part of the development of a sense of identity.

Detachment, adolescent detachment, is a gradually developing change in behavior. It leads to changes in the family structure. As the adolescent person spends more and more time away from home, he typically needs his parents less and less. But they may continue to need him. Sometimes parents have such a compelling need to have a child, or children, they will try to slow down the process of detachment. In some instances, as in the case of Jody's mother, they may actively try to prevent any kind of detachment from developing. This can be as psychologically damaging as trying to speed up, to accelerate, the detachment to an overly rapid pace. In both instances—slowing or prohibiting detachment and speeding it up —the parents may be trying to maintain some control over what is happening to their family structure. And in both instances there may be clashes between parent and adolescent.

Adolescent behavior and technological change

The world revolves on its axis, slowly spinning around the sun. The sun, a star on the outer edge of a galaxy, moves through great reaches of space, a tiny part of that galaxy's spiral motion. The galaxy moves away from other galaxies with a movement of its own. Trying to describe these astrophysical movements may not be as difficult as trying to describe movements connected with the adolescent in this society.

The adolescent moves along a time line, evolving, changing, growing, developing in physical and psychological ways. As he moves, the family changes—parents evolve in their own fashion—and at the same time, society changes.* The adolescent who is right now at the age of 17 cannot possibly be the same as an adolescent, age 17, in the year 1950. Yet, some parents function as though few things have changed.

Beth

As Beth said, "It gets really crazy when we talk."

"Oh?"

"My father. My father, the king. When we talk, it gets all confused."

"*It* gets confused?"

"It. (pause) I get confused."

"How?"

"The king treats me like a little kid."

"And that's confusing."

"Yes. I want to talk with him. I don't think I try very hard, but I want to. And he sits there telling me things, acting like a teacher."

---

*The behavior of living things is not rigidified or frozen in place or cast in bronze. If living things seem immobilized, it is because we see them in that inaccurate way.

"How does a teacher act?"

"You don't know my father, he's a frustrated teacher. He acts more like a teacher than teachers do."

"How do teachers act?"

"They hang around and talk a lot. You know. Lecturing."

"So he lectures; what does he say?"

"It's all about how things used to be. How they used to be for *him* when he was a kid. He tells me how tough it was."

"Was it tough?"

"I suppose it was, but it's like I'm supposed to feel bad because he had a rough time."

"And you don't have a rough time."

"That's what he keeps telling me. He says it all the time. He had it rough, and I've got it pretty smooth."

"And?"

"I'm supposed to feel bad because I've got it so good? Doesn't that sound crazy to you?"

"What does it sound like to you?"

"Crazy. It's like I'm supposed to feel guilty because I haven't suffered."

"You've never suffered?"

"Everybody feels bad some of the time. I feel bad about the king and me."

Beth's father grew up in Florida. His family was poor, and he rarely had any time for recreation. He went through high school, but on weekends he worked in the orange groves and canning factories. After high school he enlisted in the army. Within a few months he was in combat in Korea. He was wounded twice and sent back home. After his discharge he used his veteran's benefits to learn how to pilot a plane. Eventually he earned his commercial license and went to work for an airline. By the time Beth was 17 years old her father had advanced to the job of chief flight instructor.

"He loves that uniform. I used to call him the general."

"And now you call him the king."

"I ought to call him the teacher."

"We're back to that."

"He tells me how bad television is for me. He's been saying that for years."

"But you watch TV anyway."

"Sure, why not? It's there. And then he tells me that his family was too poor to have a TV set."

"What do you think of that?"

"There's a crazy king in the house. Maybe his family was poor, but when he was a kid, there wasn't any television."

"You're right."

"And no stereo sets. What did they call them then? Victrolas?"

"I'm not sure."

"He said his family had a Victrola, and they listened to records. But he says a stereo is a lot better, and I'm lucky we have one. Well, he's lucky too."

"What else?"

"Oh, let's see. He had to work when he was young."

"And you?"

"It's against the law now. Ever hear of child labor laws? I'm a child. At least according to the teacher. And I'm supposed to feel bad because he had to work when he was a kid."

It is a long technological way from a Victrola to a stereo set. According to Lewis Mumford (1967) and Barry Commoner (1966) the technological development of recent times is more a plague than a pleasure. Stirred into the technological mix is the use of "mood food," which according to Wieder and Kaplan (1969) is used to help the adolescent not only to experience more of himself but also to contend with stressful factors in the environment.

For Beth, one of the stress-producing factors in the environment was a well-meaning but somewhat psychologically naive father. ("He doesn't know me at all. When he lectures, he's talking to whoever he *thinks* I am. I wish he'd talk to *me* once in awhile.") Partly because she felt alienated from her father and mother, partly because of the gentle pressure of some of her friends and because she was experimenting with the how else, Beth dropped acid during one summer. She was on the mood food for two months before her father noticed anything different in her behavior. Drugs, mood food, are as much a part of the technological system of society as television, transistors, and telephones.

While the central theme of the adolescent years is the development of the sense of identity, there is what David Bakan (1972) refers to as "man's intrinsic *psychophobia*—man's fear of acknowledging the truth about his own mind" (p. 88), which can operate in ways to reduce that sense of identity. It can also interfere with what the next chapter deals with—intimacy.

REVIEW QUESTIONS

1. What is the main difference between phase 1 and phase 2 of adolescence?
2. What is the spectatorial attitude?
3. Describe adolescent conflicts. What conflicts did you have?
4. Why do adolescents experiment?
5. What is the central theme of the adolescent years?
6. Can you define psychophobia?
7. What is the difference between latent and manifest?
8. Which are the years of apprenticeship?
9. Who can best describe the world as adolescents see it? Why?
10. What did Richard Quey have to say about "group insurance"?
11. What is normal homosexuality?
12. Why is parental courage in explaining sexual behavior evidently important?

6 THE ADULT YEARS

No sharp line marks the moment when adolescence ends and the adult years begin. Any definite point that divides these two stages of life is a matter of convenience. There is, however, a defined transitional state marking the end of adulthood. Some thoughts about that transition are included in the last section of this chapter.

While children and adolescents may not often consider themselves as temporary residents of the planet, adults do. They may do so intermittently during the years of early adulthood and then with increasing frequency as they grow older. The realization that life is temporary may sometimes produce a sense of exasperation and perhaps some envy of Shirali Mislimov who lived for 168 years in a distant village named Barzavic.* (Leaf, 1973).

The realization that one's own life is a temporary condition may produce a sense of the special importance of living. In turn, that may foster the development of behavior oriented toward the pursuit of the pleasures of today and only of today. More often, however, it may foster the development of a search for what Robert Jay Lifton

*Shirali Mislimov was born in 1805 and died Sept. 2, 1973.

(1973) calls symbolic immortality. *Symbolic immortality* is neither a simple nor a devious denial of death. It is instead an expression of a difficult-to-define need for an inner sense of continuity and a connectedness with what has gone on before and what will go on after one's own temporary biological existence. It is an attempt to leave a trail of personal footprints behind, an effort to make a difference in the world by one's presence in it.

Mountain climbers leave behind footprints, steel pitons, bits of climbing rope, and rock scratches as they move toward the crest. They do not, however, climb a mountain because "It's there." They climb because "I'm there" when they get to the top. If the mountain is a million years old and if only a dozen people have stood on its crest, the climber can perhaps briefly sense some feeling of his very real presence in the stream of time. His presence on the top of the mountain is temporary, but as he descends to the valley, he may be aware of a fragment of what symbolic immortality is about. If what he senses becomes a part of his personal view of reality, he may be involved in one of the kinds of symbolic immortality. While this symbolic immortality has to do with nature and his place in it, he may have had a transcendental experience so intense that time and death become irrelevant.

The other kinds of symbolic immortality are more obvious. There is, of course, biological immortality insured by the birth of one's own children. There is a theological immortality that involves the idea of life after death, ideas of heaven or of reincarnation, or some other spiritual protection against the mundane finality of death. Then there is the matter of creatively insuring a symbolic immortality. Creativity can involve such things as writing songs or books or poems that may endure beyond one's own demise. It can also involve participation in relationships with other people, relationships beyond the usual. That is what most of this chapter is about.

RELATIONSHIPS

None of us live out our lives alone, cut off, totally isolated. We cannot, even if we try, separate ourselves from our surroundings. Within our surroundings we have the opportunity to make a wide variety of connections and relationships. There are three possible relationships a person may have with another human:

1. **Relationship with a superior.** Obviously this is the first relationship we experience. The newborn infant relates to the mother who is clearly superior. The child in first grade relates to the teacher, a superior. At work the employee relates to the boss, an organizational superior, a person in a headship position. The most abstract and ethereal relationship of this sort is the personal connection some have with their God.
2. **Relationship with a peer.** Relationships with peers mean relationships with equals, colleagues, compatriots. If this form of relationship is to endure, both individuals must agree, openly or in silence, to maintain the relationship on at least one of the following levels:
   a. *Superficial.* In a superficial relationship conversation is limited to such topics as weather, sports scores, hair styles, or hobbies.
   b. *Formal.* A formal relationship includes the superficial plus conversation *and* activities that involve work or recreation.
   c. *Trusting.* In a trusting relationship both individuals are able to express their own opinions, attitudes, and beliefs openly. It is the opposite of a superficial relationship. It does not mean the two people in a relationship always agree with each other.
3. **Relationship with a subordinate.** This obviously includes the relationship the mother has with her baby, the teacher with the child, the manager with his employee.

These three forms of relationship involve one human relating to another human. Very often, though, any one of us can form relationships that do not include another person. Here are some examples:

1. **Relationships with pets.** It is possible to achieve some measure of satisfaction by developing close relationships with birds, dogs, cats, horses, tropical fish, or bees.
2. **Relationships with nature.** We can develop a sense of relatedness with a wide range of natural parts of our environment. People may form relationships with and feel attached to a lake, a mountain, a tree, African violets, or roses.
3. **Relationships with things.** "Things," in this context, include cars, bikes, model train layouts, stereo sets, and a fantastic variety of other man-made objects.

Beyond the relationships we may have with people, pets, nature, and man-made things, there are the forms of relationships we have with the imagined. Imagined relationships take place within the mind, and there are at least three forms:

1. **Daydreaming.** We can relate to our own daydreams, which can be pleasant and temporarily fulfilling. Daydreams may also be dreadful, frightening, or loaded with sadness and still be fulfilling. Daydreams satisfy in a temporary way.
2. **Fantasies.** Fantasies differ from daydreams, although both can have the same theme or content. The difference is a matter of con-

trol. Daydreams can be turned on and off like a TV set, but fantasies cannot.

3. **Hallucinations.** People may hallucinate because they have taken alcohol or other drugs. They may hallucinate because of a temporary but great loss in their physiological homeostasis caused by extreme thirst (dehydration), extraordinary hunger (starvation or malnourishment), and even under conditions of *hypoxia* (a lower-than-necessary level of oxygen in the bloodstream). Humans also hallucinate sometimes if they become mentally ill to a severe and serious degree. A hallucination may involve hearing voices when no one speaks, seeing objects and people that are not really there. Hallucinations may also involve taste and smell. We will explore the matter of hallucination

and mental illness more thoroughly in Chapter 9. For now, we will discuss what Erikson and a number of other people have to say about the matter of intimacy.

INTIMACY IN YOUNG ADULTHOOD

According to Erikson the sixth stage of development is titled *young adulthood.* It covers the years from 21 to 34. The essential task, the basic thrust, of young adulthood is the development of a sense of intimacy with a limited number of other people. While intimacy may be described and defined in a wide variety of ways, and while the word has been used in connection with everything from perfumes to automobiles, we will limit its definition here. That definition will be gradually unrolled in the following pages.

Intimacy as a factor in the relations between peers

In the beginning of this chapter, mention was made of three possible relationships a person may have with another human. The only form of relationship in which interpersonal intimacy can develop and become reasonably consistent is in the peer connection. A relationship between unequals generally has a consistent element of dependency to it. Dependency and intimacy do not easily coexist; one dilutes the other.

In relationships with peers the potential development of intimacy can be crushed if one person in that relationship plays the "boss game." Arnie played it.

"I'll tell you like I told her. I'm the boss in that house. I'm the one who works, I make the money. I pay the bills. That puts me in charge, and if I'm in charge, I'm the boss. Got any questions?"

"Do you have to be boss?"

"Hell, yes. Somebody's got to be boss. You don't get anywhere unless somebody steers. I steer."

"Does your wife ever want to steer?"

"Sure. That's the problem."

"How so?"

"Well, I'll tell you, like I told her. If two people try to steer, it's like too many cooks in the kitchen. There's going to be a crash. Only one person steers in my house, and that's me."

"All the time."

"Right. All the time. It's my duty. My old man was the same way."

"You mean he was the boss."

"You bet your banana he was. And you never crossed him. Like my kids never cross me. They know better."

"And your wife?"

"Like I said, that's the problem. If she would go along with things and do what I say, it'd be a lot simpler. It'd be easier living with her. But she keeps wanting to put in her two cents' worth, and that always leads to a fight. Well, almost always. I mean sometimes I smack her one, and she settles down right away."

"You smack the kids, too."

"Sure I do, but only when they deserve it."

Arnie was a self-employed welder. He had big arms and strong hands. What was a smack to him might have been a painful punch to his wife and four children. He treated his children and his wife in much the same way. He saw them all as dependents, subordinates. While he may have believed it was his duty to be the boss, he also believed it was their duty to be subservient, and when they were not, especially his wife, he smacked them repeatedly. Even after his wife divorced him for physical brutality, he remained rigidly stabilized at the boss level with most people. It seemed as though he would not or could not tolerate any other kind of relationship. Because of that, he never knew what intimacy was; he worked with a crude diligence to insure that other humans he came in contact with never functioned as peers with him.

In considering Arnie and his lifetime style, some acknowledgment must be given to the existence of peer relationships based, at least in part, upon an exchange of efforts to bring about physical damage. Some husbands and wives fight with great vigor, beating on each other, breaking windows, plates, and furniture. The brawling may come to the attention of neighbors who call the police. When the police arrive, husband and wife may shift from being enemies to being allies and, working in unison, may aim their assaults at the police. The violence between husband and wife may be mutually satisfying for both of them, but is it intimacy?

In contrast with Arnie and different from relationships that involve mutual physical beatings, there exists the kind of relationship in which one of the persons spends energy in trying to put the other person in a position of superiority. There are moments when this is clear, obvious, blatant, sometimes even to the person who does it. Take, for example, the behavior of this high school senior. He is still heavily involved with the adolescent tasks surrounding the development of a sense of identity. At the same time he is moving closer to the years of young adulthood. He comes from a reasonably typical family. His father works in an office. His mother works part-time for a clothing store. He has a younger sister. His name is Bill.

"Aw, you should see her. She's really beautiful. She's got really long black hair."

"You like her."

"Like her? Aw, yeah, I really do. I guess I love her. Really a lot, I—well, I feel funny saying this—but I think about her all the time, *all* the time."

"Daydreaming?"

"All the time. Yeah, I daydream away and think and think about her. I guess you could say I've got her up on a pedestal. She's wonderful."

Bill put his girl friend on a pedestal, and for a time she seemed to enjoy it. After a while, though, she tired of his adoration and refused to date him any more. He was temporarily shattered by the experience.

Putting anyone on a pedestal amounts to putting them in a superior position. It can be an indication of an attempt to avoid a peer relationship. It may also indicate a feeling of inferiority. For Bill, it was both. His main life experiences with females were with his mother and his younger sister. He had considerably less practice in relating to peer females. But he learned, and as he learned, his sense of inferiority lessened, and he became increasingly industrious and self-fulfilling in his pursuit of satisfying relationships with peers, including peer females.

Relationships with a peer may be varied, evolving, multifaceted, and they may permit wide freedoms not available in the other forms of relationships. Personal freedom, however, has its complications. In discussing the psychological aspects of freedom, B. F. Skinner (1971) stated:

Freedom is a possession. A person escapes from or destroys the power of a controller in order to feel free, and once he feels free and can do what he wants to, the literature of freedom prescribes no further action, except that of eternal vigilance lest control be resumed. [p. 41]

Rollo May (1969) wrote:

Freedom cannot be the domain of a special part of the organism, but must be a quality of the total self—the thinking-feeling-choosing-acting organism. [p. 199]

While Erich Fromm (1941) maintained:

This discussion will always be centered around the main theme of the book: that man, the more he gains freedom in the sense of emerging from the original oneness with man and nature and the more he becomes an "individual" has no choice but to unite himself with the world in the spontaneity of love and productive work or else to seek a kind of security by such ties with the world as destroy his freedom and the integrity of his individual self. [pp. 37-38]

The quotation is from Fromm's *Escape from Freedom*, which was originally published over thirty years ago. The title alone carries a message, for we humans sometimes show astonding expertise in escaping from or preventing the development of freedom. In relationships with other people we may escape from or prevent the development of peer relationships. We may do so in ways similar to those of Arnie and Bill, but more often we have subtler techniques. The techniques, subtle or blatant, civilized or savage, are designed to insure the development of some stability in (1) taking care of other people by fostering their dependency or (2) getting people to take care of us, thereby building up our own dependency. In both instances freedom is compromised, avoided, or eluded altogether.

The avoidance of freedom is perhaps as much a part of the lives of humans as self-defeating behavior. It is possible the two behaviors are identical.

Intimacy as a factor in agreement-disagreement

In an intimate relationship with a peer the individual has the right to agree or to disagree. The agreement-disagreement factors may be based on similarities and differences in attitudes, opinions, and beliefs. To put it in more useful words: In a truly intimate peer relationship the people involved will sometimes fight and sometimes agree. They will express not only anger but also affection toward each other. The leading American proponent of this idea is George R. Bach. With Peter Wyden, he wrote *The Intimate Enemy* (1968); with Ronald M. Deutsch, he turned out a book titled *Pairing* (1970). In *Pairing* Bach and Deutsch describe the beginnings of a relationship between two people:

In the beginning, it seems only politeness. No one wants to appear indifferent to a partner's wishes, after all, or self-centered about his own. It is only the courteous thing to put another's comfort or pleasure first. So no alarm bells go off when accommodation begins to meet the intimate anxiety of hiding real feelings from a partner. And once accommodation begins it is hard to stop. [p. 89]

Accommodation to the desires of the partner is the polite thing to do. It is civilized to open doors for ladies, pay for their meals in a restaurant, help them on with a coat. It is also civilized to nod in agreement or to at least be silent when a partner makes a statement that contradicts what we believe in. It is civilized and dishonest.

What lies behind the good manners, the courtesies, the accommodations? No one can be sure, for one of the purposes of manner and protocol is to disguise or to deny real feelings. In this society men are supposed to be gallant or at least courteous to women, but what exists behind the gallantry? Germaine Greer (1971) may be more honest than embittered, more open than attacking, when she writes:

Women have very little idea of how much men hate them. Any boy who has grown up in an English industrial town can describe how the boys used to go to the local dance halls and stand around all night until the pressure of the simplest kind of sexual urge prompted them to *score a chick.* The easier this was the more they loathed the girls and identified them with the guilt that their squalid sexual release left them. [p. 245]

Greer's words may be dismissed with the comment "But that's in England," or "It doesn't happen here." But it does. In some parts of the country it is called hustling. In other sectors it is called rustling, an old western American term once used to describe the stealing of cattle. Sometimes it is called "beaking" or "making the scene" or "bait and switch," a term also frequently used to describe a clever and not always ethical marketing and sales technique.

No matter what the region or the geography, the basic action is an attempt to establish a relationship with someone, perhaps with anyone who may be able to satisfy one's social or sexual needs. Masturbation can be performed alone. All other sexual activities require the participation, the presence, of another. Participation of another or others is required in the pursuit of social activities. A required participation instantly has within it the potential for dependency. In addition, dependency feelings often have given birth to feelings of anger (Berelson and Steiner, 1964; Cramer, 1959).

Feelings of dependency may more often be denied than accepted. The denial can, of course, be accomplished by way of repression. The denial can also be accomplished by the use of inaccurate labels, a feat that facilitates repressions. Dependency is sometimes inaccurately called love.* R. D. Laing (1970, p. 48) writes:

> She wants him to want her
> He wants her to want him
> To get him to want her
>   she pretends she wants him
> To get her to want him
>   he pretends he wants her.†

Individuals who live on the time line that runs from age 21 to age 34 are usually equipped with the physical apparatus of sex. This includes not only the sexual organs but also the juices, the fluids, the hormones, the lacework of neurological fibers necessary for the performance of sexual functions. Yet, for humans the most compelling and powerful need is for intimacy in a relationship, for acceptance, for personal validation, for affirmation, for confirmation of one's own existence and identity rather than sex per se (May, 1969).

Within the intricacies of a relationship between two peers there exists an opportunity for intimacy if the matter of mutual dependency can be successfully contained, controlled, and directed. That means intimacy and anger must be recognized and acknowledged, for they are packaged together. It is, of course, easier to think of intimacy and affection. That is a more popular package, a more socially acceptable and conventional combination.

---

*Love is not always dependency, however.
†From Laing, R. D.: Knots. Copyright © 1970 by Pantheon Books/A Division of Random House, Inc.

Jim and Sara

Jim and Sara were both 30 years old. They had been married for ten years. They had no children. Jim worked as a real estate salesman, but he was not very successful in his job. Sara was a registered nurse who worked in a small geriatric hospital. They lived in an apartment two blocks from the hospital where Sara worked.

Jim and Sara watched television every night, except on New Year's Eve when they went out to a restaurant to eat and during the two-week vacation they took every August. They always spent their vacation visiting Sara's parents, who lived in Kansas City. Jim calculated they watched television 350 evenings a year.

Three days after their tenth wedding anniversary they settled down to watch television. Sara tuned in a rerun of "Bonanza" as Jim lit his pipe. He noticed his hand shook as he held the match. He puffed on his pipe, waved the match flame out, and put the half-charred remains in an ashtray. His other hand began to shake, and then his arms and shoulders were vibrating spasmodically. He quickly put the pipe in the ashtray as Sara watched him. She asked him what was wrong, and when he tried to answer, the words seemed stuck in his throat. He gagged, suddenly doubled over in his chair, and vomited on the floor. Then he fainted.

Sara instantly took Jim's pulse and checked his breathing. Both were rapid. She ran to the phone, called the geriatric hospital, and asked the night-duty nurse to locate a physician who would come to the house right away. Then she sped back to Jim who was on the floor, still unconscious. She took his pulse again, checked his breathing, and found that both were less rapid than before. She cleaned his face with a towel, covered him with a blanket, and sat next to him on the floor watching the show on television.

The second set of commercials came on the tube as the doorbell rang. Sara let the physician in. He asked her some questions, examined Jim, and questioned Sara again. He nodded his head, thought for a moment, and told Sara to call an ambulance.

Jim came out of his unconscious state as he was being put into the ambulance. He smiled wanly at Sara, who rode in the back of the ambulance with him. When they arrived at the hospital, Jim was given a more extensive examination and was put to bed in spite of his protests that he was feeling all right now.

The next day more x-rays were taken, a more complete blood serology analysis was made, and he was examined by a neurologist. On the following day he was discharged. All the tests had shown negative results. There was nothing physically wrong that anyone could find. Jim was told to consult a psychiatrist. He did, but only after Sara urged him to do so.

The psychiatrist asked Jim a long series of questions during the first session. The second time they met, the questions continued, and Jim was asked to see a psychologist for psychological tests. After that he was to come back to the psychiatrist. The psychologist saw Jim, gave the tests, and wrote a report, which he gave to the psychiatrist.

When Jim saw the psychiatrist again, he was asked more questions, but this time they were directly connected with his marriage. As he answered, Jim began to see a faintly outlined and dim picture of the actual interaction with his wife. He began asking some questions of his own. He wondered why he had always been so cooperative in his dealings with Sara. He asked about the vacations—why had they not gone somewhere else? He did not like Kansas City in August, had little in common with Sara's father, yet he had gone there for ten two-week vacations.

"It's like a bird migration," he said. "We go there every August and come back home. It's like we don't even think about it. We just go. Like birds. It's bird brained."

"Does your wife know how you feel about the trips to Kansas City?"

"No."

"Have you ever suggested going to some other place?"

"Well, no."

"Why not?"

"It didn't seem important."

"What was important?"

"That Sara has a good time."

"Why is that important?"

"It keeps her peaceful."

"Peaceful?"

"Yes."

"If she gets her way, she doesn't argue."

"Do you ever get your way?"

"Sometimes."

"When?"

"I get to pick out some of the shows on television."

"Sounds like you enjoy watching television."

"Yes, some of the time."

"Not all of the time though."

"No, not all of the time."

Gradually Jim began to realize how unrealistically agreeable he was. As the weeks of psychotherapy passed, he came to see himself as a passive individual, cooperative to an extreme, losing himself in trying to do things—anything—in order that his wife remain peaceful. He was, he said, afraid of her anger. The psychiatrist asked: What about your anger?

"I'm never angry."

"Never?"

"Well, I get sort of irritated while driving in heavy traffic."

"Only then?"

"Yes, only then. Most of the rest of the time, I just feel bored."

"Bored?"

"Yes."

"What other words can describe how it is?"

"Well, bored is one, sometimes a little listless, maybe tired, not interested."

Inch by passive inch, Jim discovered he was depressed most of the time. Then even more slowly he began to realize the depression might not be simply that. There could be something else in there—impatience perhaps? Maybe it was just a lot of irritation. "Why not," the psychiatrist asked him, "call it anger?"

"Anger?"

"Think about it."

"Anger?" Then with a rush, Jim realized he was not afraid of Sara's anger. He was afraid of his own.

After almost two years of psychotherapy Jim told Sara he did not want to go to Kansas City on their next vacation. Sara was delighted. She did not want to go either.

Other changes followed. They sometimes ignored the television set and talked with each other. They began going to antique stores, browsing through dusty shelves and musty rooms filled with old furniture. And, more often than ever before, they laughed. Sara was happier, but vague concerns began to drift across her mind. She knew Jim was different. He was a lot more fun to be with and somehow more determined. He had gotten a raise and then a promotion with another raise in pay; he was increasingly successful on the job, as well as at home and with her. But what about herself? Could she keep up with his growth?

With some measure of anxiety and because of Jim's urging, she signed up in a psychodrama group. She agreed to go to four meetings just to see what it was like. At the first meeting she could barely talk. At the second session she felt only slightly more at ease. During the third meeting she briefly acted out the part of someone's older sister. The fourth meeting was almost enjoyable, and she told the director she wanted to stay in the group. She was getting something out of it, but she did not know what—yet.

Sara and Jim vacationed in New England that year. They went in the fall and marveled at the autumn colors, and when they talked, they sometimes referred to their past as the "Dark Ages."

Intimacy as a factor in psychological growth

The developing of a sense of identity occupies much of the typical adolescent's time and efforts. That development does not stop when the adolescent enters the stage of young adulthood. There is no magic point, no chalk mark on the time line, to indicate the moment when the person proclaims "This is *me*!" There is no such moment, for whomever and whatever a person may be continues to unfold, unroll, open up, reveal itself to the person throughout life.

Beginning in late adolescence and continuing throughout life, the individual who can be called a reasonable adventurer will interweave the development of self-identity and the development of intimacy. The interweaving is done with at least one other person who is on the same track. It is the ultimate of friendships. The blending of efforts involving identity development and the development of intimacy is not a laborious, daily grind. It is instead an ongoing, evolving, and growing self-aware-

ness, a growing self-appreciation mixed with an appreciation and awareness of the other person. It cannot always and perhaps should not always be a calm friendship, an untroubled alliance, a glass-smooth interaction.

This *system,* a system that involves identity and intimacy, is fundamentally a learning process. It has nothing to do with education, for education implies teaching, and as mentioned in the previous chapter, the core philosophy of teaching is "let those who know teach those who do not know" (Maier, 1971).

Person A cannot teach person B who person B is. Such an activity could easily become not only coercive and manipulative but also headed in the direction of a boss-dependent relationship, a teacher-student style of interaction. Within a peer interaction, person B tells person A who person B is, or more appropriately, who person B thinks he is, how he thinks he is, what

Michelle Stone/Editorial Photocolor Archives

he thinks he is, and the emphasis is on *is,* not on was or will be.

Goodall (1972) has described a facet of this in his report of a study conducted by the National Institute of Mental Health. To fit his report into the language of these pages, it can be said that (1) person A cannot teach person B who person B is but (2) person A can tell person B what person B does. To tell someone what they do is substantially different from telling them who they are.

Another aspect of this system of interaction is the avoidance of most questions and the development of a style for making statements. If this sounds simple, perhaps you could set aside half a day for this activity. You may discover how many questions you ask, such simple questions as "How are you?" "Did you see that TV special last night?" "Where are you going this weekend?" "Are you comfortable?" "Do you like that?"

Some of the questions we ask each other are legitimate, knowledge-seeking devices. Frequently, though, the questions we ask are shields or deflectors or devices designed to get the other person to say how he is or who he is, while we remain safely standing behind our protective device (Greenwald, 1968). Questions may imply an interest in the other person, but in this society, questions are often used to find out what it is we are to agree to. There are, for example, a number of questions people ask of each other that generally have predetermined answers, answers that form part of a social ritual when they are linked to the question. (Q) "How are you?" (A) "Fine." (Q) "Did you have a good time at the party last night?" (A) "A wonderful time." (Q) "Do you enjoy your work?" (A) "Yes." They go on endlessly, a ribbon of questions and prepared, socially correct answers leading nowhere except to what was described in the beginning of this chapter: a superficial relationship.

Making statements involves risks that do not exist when only questions are asked. Making statements means saying something about oneself, and they can be as simple as: "I feel fine." "I really liked that TV special last night." "I'm not going anywhere this weekend." "I feel comfortable right now. I'm at ease." "I don't like that very much." Another facet of this system of meshing identity development with development of intimacy is the abandonment of many obligations.

The obligations we sense are a part of our social heritage of courtesy, protocol, good manners. The obligations we sense are also a part of the heritage of socialization. We are obliged to cooperate as children in family living and in school. The cooperation may sometimes be necessary, but it often subtracts from our freedom of adolescent *and* adult experimentation. Cooperation can mean conformity. Although conformity may be vitally necessary while driving at great speed on highways (conforming to traffic laws) or while duck hunting (conforming to gun-safety regulations), it may often be unnecessary and even inhibitory in face-to-face relations with other people.

The social, interactional obligations we sense are learned. We can learn them as children at home and at school, and if we retain the obligations of childhood, we remain children. We may feel obligated to take care of someone. For example, if a person says "I'm not going anywhere this weekend," some among us may feel obligated to offer an invitation to lunch or dinner. When the invitation is offered, the person may feel obligated to accept, but the result can be the fostering of dependency or simply the living out of a "proper way to be" in which neither person finds enjoyment.

There are times when we sense an obligation to give reasons for what we do. When we explain our actions, our behaviors, to another person, we will sometimes be accurate, on target, living examples of precision and clarity. At other times we may be inaccurate, evasive, and what we say may be shrouded in a cloud of ambiguity—all these are possible without realizing it at the moment.

When we give reasons for what we do, we may range from the highly precise to the incredibly obscure. We may also range from the totally honest to the totally dishonest. In most instances, though, when we try to explain ourselves to another person, we try to make sense; we try to be believable. But are we genuinely obligated to explain? Not as often as we may sense that obligation in this system of identity and intimacy.

The system of behavior partially outlined in the preceding paragraphs takes into account some aspects in the continual development of a sense of identity, together with the development of a sense of intimacy with a limited number of other people. The system of behavior is achievable if the individuals involved have developed at least some measure of trust, autonomy, initiative, and industry as well as the firm beginnings of a sense of identity (Erikson, 1968). If these qualities of behavior have not been allowed to blossom, they may still be available to the individual as genuine parts of life if he or she is willing to accept the responsibility for their growth. That, of course, means induced change, and not everyone welcomes change in their lifetime styles, even if that change means movement from the realm of psychological pain to a life of relative but real psychological comfort.

Intimacy as a factor developed on a weak base

There are numbers of people who become involved in encounter groups, "T" groups, sensitivity training sessions, weekend marathons, and some forms of what is inaccurately called group therapy and who develop a language of intimacy on a weak base.

After an individual in the group has revealed some aspect of his being to group members, others may say to him such things as: "I feel very warmly toward you," or "You have touched me deeply, and I feel lots of empathy for you now," or "I admire your courage for saying what you did. I feel very close to you." While many of these statements may be spoken by people who actually experience, within themselves, the feelings expressed in the words, there are others who will say the same things in a ritualistic way, uttering the words as actors in a play might. They are the individuals who follow the track of courtesy and good manners, attending to the protocol of the group and society rather than attending to themselves.

By attending to themselves, people learn about themselves. If some of the people in a group choose to avoid themselves, to deny whatever it is they are thinking or feeling in a conscious way, and to opt for the courteous, they lose; perhaps it is self-defeating. They lose through good manners or because they feel some obligation to be nice, to be supportive, to connect superficially with another person on a verbal and carefully intellectual level rather than on a level of intimacy. In these instances intimacy is an act, a phenomenon of pretending, an often unwitting insult to themselves and to the person to whom they speak. Intimacy becomes a sham. In contrast, the individuals who speak from the heart or, as it is often stated, from the gut are apt to be considerably more authentic, especially in the manner in which they experience themselves.

To capsule and stress the issue: in groups, where it seems more obvious, and in one-to-one relationships, authentic intimacy can be achieved only after the individual has developed a reasonably solid beginning of a sense of identity. If the sense of identity is primitive and undeveloped, the person who speaks the language of intimacy is operating from a weak base.

If one of the central factors of intimacy is a sharing of oneself with another, how can a person share if he does not know himself?

Intimacy as transitory

Developing at least a firm beginning of a sense of identity is not a smooth uninterrupted flow of growth. It moves, as the development of human culture moves, in spurts. No one is capable of consciously placing all his energy in the consistent pursuit of identity development. In a psychological sense we can move forward for a brief period, pause to rest, move forward again, become distracted by preoccupations with the pedestrian issues of daily living, move forward once more, and then simply stop as though we had run into a barricade. The barricade, however real or invisible or unrecognized it may be, is usually a self-imposed barricade that in a careful analysis may prove to be a form of self-defeating behavior learned at an earlier age.

What has been said in the preceding paragraph about the development of a sense of identity may also apply to the development of intimacy. As with the thrust toward identity development, the development of intimacy is a movement that is and that may need to be interrupted. It cannot be sustained on a continual basis anymore than a person can sustain twenty-four hours of sleep a day for a lifetime. Yet, there is an ethic, a belief, among some (especially some of the participants in encounter groups) who maintain that working for intimacy is just that —work—and the work of intimacy development must, for whatever reason, be full time. That is impossible.

To seek the treasured intimacy on a full-time basis may damage the treasure. Any two individuals in an intimacy-directed interaction may often need to separate themselves from unadulterated sharing to the sort of being alone often sought by the individual adolescent. Each individual in an intimacy-directed relationship may require refueling from the world outside the boundaries of the relationship. They may require a variety of interactions with others who are not so consistently significant but nevertheless useful, perhaps entertaining and sometimes briefly as important as the highly significant other in the intimate relationship.

Intimacy as variety

Within the boundaries of an intimate relationship the primary and fundamental interaction takes place between individuals who respond to each other as peers. Periodically, however, that peer level may be swiftly compromised. Both individuals can and will shift into dependent-superior and inferior-dependent connections with each other. They can function as children to each other or form a temporary parent-child style of interaction to return again to the peer level.

The meshing of an ongoing identity development with an ongoing, developing intimacy is a system (Grinker, 1956). A *system* is a unified and integrated set of behaviors that exists over a period of time. A system has a past and probably a future, but the emphasis is on what exists in the immediate now whenever the system is viewed, examined, studied, or evaluated by the participant or perhaps by an outside observer.

MIDDLE AND OLD AGE

Middle age begins at the middle of a person's possible span of life. In the United States, Canada, and a few other countries, people can expect to live to be about 70 years old. Middle age starts at the midpoint, age 35, and ends at age 65; the seventh stage of Erikson's scheme lasts for thirty years. In a general sense those who can deal successfully with the more relevant factors of middle age have already experienced two prior successful achievements in living. They have formed (1) a reasonably adequate sense of their own identity and (2) a generally adequate, satisfying level of intimacy with one or a few other people.

Rosalie and Rosemary

Rosalie and Rosemary were known as the R and R girls by the men at the office. Neither one ever dated any of the men in the office, however; they found their rest and recreation with each other. They were middle-aged homosexuals who had lived together for fifteen years.

Rosalie and Rosemary were probably the best secretaries in the corporation; each worked for a vice-president. Rosalie worked for the man in charge of marketing and advertising, and Rosemary was secretary to the engineering vice-president. They drove to work together, ate lunch separately, and drove home together. They lived in a large house in the suburbs, and while they had separate bedrooms, they usually slept together.

At first, when their relationship was new, they took their vacations together, going to Europe every other year and to Canada or Mexico in between. They were, to all outsiders, good friends, and that was all. Yet their relationship had begun to change five years ago. Rosalie went to Europe for three weeks, and Rosemary spent two weeks in Oregon, fishing, camping, and visiting with relatives. In September Rosalie had her appendix taken out, and in November Rosemary had a partial hysterectomy. At Christmas they shared presents by the decorated tree, but in the spring they began to sleep apart, each in her own bedroom. A year later Rosemary began having an affair with another woman, while Rosalie grieved—angry, jealous, but mostly depressed about what was happening to her life.

Six months later Rosalie bought another car and drove to work alone. Rosemary shrugged her shoulders and continued her relationship with the other woman. The two secretaries began to eat dinner in their home at different times. The following Christmas Rosemary went ice fishing in Idaho, while Rosalie visited with friends and ate Christmas dinner in an elegant restaurant, alone. By Easter there were good morning greetings and good nights, but that

was about all. No one at the office knew there was any strain in the relationship between the R and R girls. When summer came, Rosalie went to Banff while Rosemary stayed home. When Rosalie came back from Canada, she walked into their suburban house and immediately confronted Rosemary. She could not stand it any longer, she said. She wanted to do something about the tangled-up feelings she was having. She wanted to get back to the way things used to be. Rosemary agreed.

The next morning the two women drove to work in the same car. They did not talk much on the way to their office, but that evening on the way home they talked about what might help to repair their relationship. They continued to discuss the matter over dinner, and by late evening they agreed to find someone who would give them some counseling.

The next day Rosalie called a psychologist. She made an appointment for herself and for Rosemary. Two weeks later the two of them went together to see the psychologist. Together they described the history of their relationship. They went to the psychologist for four visits that first month. At the beginning of the second month the psychologist told them that as far as she could determine, what they probably needed was usually called marital counseling. She arranged for them to see a marital specialist. They went to the specialist at the end of the month.

If an adult has achieved a sense of identity and formed intimate relationships, he can expand his life and find further satisfaction by helping the younger generation to become genuinely grown up. This means, in many instances, simply allowing young people to assume the responsibilities and the rights that are theirs. In other instances, it can mean pushing members of the younger generation to do what they are supposed to do. In both instances the middle-aged individual fosters and promotes the development of the younger generation in an activity broadly labeled generativity.

A middle-aged person need not be a parent to achieve a sense of generativity. Those who are parents are in positions in which generativity can be expressed more obviously, yet there are others—teachers, counselors, human service workers, nurses, coaches, some disc jockeys, some family physicians, and some who follow a religious life, such as ministers, priests, and rabbis—who can develop a sense of generativity.

The achievement of a sense of generativity can be diluted by concerns middle-aged people often have. Generativity can be compromised by some real and some imagined health problems. There is, of course, a decline in many physical factors: hearing and eyesight are not quite what they used to be nor are such things as stamina, speed of reaction, muscular strength, and a physical resiliency that permits quick recovery after strenuous activities.

Concurrently the middle-aged individual may become periodically anxious or angry or sometimes fearful of the behavior of adolescent offspring. Mental health practitioners often note antagonisms between middle-aged parents and adolescent members of the family, antagonisms that seem based on a combination of factors. Some parents resent the fact their children are young while they no longer are. Some parents see their children as ungrateful, too eager to move away and find their own styles of life, leaving the parents behind to mourn a loss. Other parents may feel they have somehow been robbed of freedoms they see their offspring enjoy, but perhaps more centrally, middle-aged individuals will often realize they are closer to the end of life than the beginning. That thought can foster the development of what is considered the opposite of generativity—the development of self-absorption, a turning away from a participating life, turning inward.

The body is typically old at age 65, the year when, according to Erikson, old age begins. The body may be old, and new parts are difficult to find. Yet, if the individual has managed to achieve a sense of generativity in middle age, he may be in a ready position to develop a sense of completeness and integrity. If complete-

Diana Henry/Editorial Photocolor Archives

ness and integrity are achieved, the old person has developed a successful way of fending off the opposite—despair, perhaps disgust with life, and possibly a fear of death. If the old person deeply fears death and continually expresses that fear, his children may develop a fear of life (Erikson, 1950).

In contrast to the fear of death is the feeling expressed in these words by Ilya Ehrenburg (1968) who, in examining his own history and his personal preparations for the end of his life, said:

For the past fifteen years or so, I have been learning how to be an old man. This is not nearly as easy as I thought when I was young. I used to think that desires die down along with the possibilities of satisfying them; but then I began to understand that the body ages before the spirit, and that one has to learn to live like an old man. One learns even in dying; to die in such a way that death is a fitting end to one's life is not an easy art. [p. 47]

Ehrenburg was 12 years old when the Wright brothers first got air travel off the ground at Kittyhawk. He was an adolescent when Woodrow Wilson was still on the faculty at Princeton University and 27 years old when the first World War ended. He was 37 years old when penicillin was discovered, 54 when an atomic bomb was dropped on Hiroshima, and 66 when the first man-made earth satellite was launched. He died at the age of 76, a year before Martin Luther King was killed. Before he died, he said of himself:

My trade requires a knowledge of human beings, and whereas I have some insight into the mental and emotional reactions of my contemporaries, I have to keep on studying every day in order to decipher the feelings of the young.

I am old in years, but now I know with certainty that I know little. One must go on learning as long as there is breath in one's body, and a student's bench becomes even an old man far better than the preacher's pulpit or the academicians' chair. That is my conviction. [pp. 55-56]

DEATH

The leaves were falling from the great oak at the meadow's edge. They were falling from all the trees.

One branch of the oak reached high above the others and stretched far out over the meadow. Two leaves clung to its very tip.

"It isn't the way it used to be," said one leaf to the other.

"No," the other leaf answered. "So many of us have fallen off tonight we're almost the only ones on our branch."

"You never know who's going to go next," said the first leaf. "Even when it was warm and the sun shone, a storm or a cloudburst would come sometimes, and many leaves were torn off, though they were still young. You never know who's to go next."

"The sun seldom shines now," sighed the second leaf, "and when it does it gives no warmth. We must have warmth again."

"Can it be true," said the first leaf, "can it really be true, that others come to take our places when we're gone and after them still others, and more and more?"

"It is really true," whispered the second leaf. "We can't even begin to imagine it, it's beyond our powers."

"It makes me very sad," added the first leaf.

They were silent a while. Then the first leaf said quietly to herself, "Why must we fall? . . ."

The second leaf asked, "What happens to us when we have fallen?"

"We sink down. . . ."

"What is under us?"

The first leaf answered, "I don't know, some say one thing, some another, but nobody knows."

The second leaf asked, "Do we feel anything, do we know anything about ourselves when we're down there?"

The first leaf answered, "Who knows? Not one of all those down there has ever come back to tell us about it."

They were silent again. Then the first leaf said tenderly to the other, "Don't worry so much about it, you're trembling."

"That's nothing," the second leaf answered, "I tremble at the least thing now. I don't feel so sure of my hold as I used to."

"Let's not talk any more about such things," said the first leaf.

The other replied, "No, we'll let be. But—what else shall we talk about?" She was silent, but went on after a little while, "Which of us will go first?"

"There's still plenty of time to worry about that," the other leaf assured her. "Let's remember how beautiful it was, how wonderful, when the sun came out and shone so warmly that we thought we'd burst with life. Do you remember? And the morning dew, and the mild and splendid nights. . . ."

"Now the nights are dreadful," the second leaf complained, "and there is no end to them."

"We shouldn't complain," said the first leaf gently. "We've outlived many, many others."

"Have I changed much?" asked the second leaf shyly but determinedly.

"Not in the least," the first leaf assured her. "You only think so because I've got to be so yellow and ugly. But it's different in your case."

"You're fooling me," the second leaf said.

"No, really," the first leaf exclaimed eagerly, "believe me, you're as lovely as the day you were born. Here and there may be a little yellow spot but it's hardly noticeable and only makes you handsomer, believe me."

"Thanks," whispered the second leaf, quite touched. "I don't believe you, not altogether, but I thank you because you're so kind, you've always been so kind to me. I'm just beginning to understand how kind you are."

"Hush," said the other leaf, and kept silent herself for she was too troubled to talk any more.

Then they were both silent. Hours passed.

A moist wind blew, cold and hostile, through the tree-tops.

"Ah, now," said the second leaf, "I. . . ." Then her voice broke off. She was torn from her place and spun down.

Winter had come.*

Living things eventually become dead things. All living humans die sooner or later, and there is not much that can be done about it—at least not yet. Rosenfeld (1973) has described some of the present research designed to uncover what happens in the process of aging so something can be done to correct what is now the inevitable decay of the body.

According to Morison (1971) the human body adds new cells from the moment of conception onward for a period of about twenty years. After that, however, the number of cells that make up the individual begin to decrease. A part of that decrease includes the death of 100,000 brain cells per day after the age of 35 (Rosenfeld, 1973). It seems only a small comfort to know we have a total of ten billion brain cells to draw from.

*From Salten, Felix: Bambi. Copyright © 1928 by Felix Salten. Copyright renewed 1956 by Simon & Schuster, Inc. Reprinted by permission of Simon & Schuster, Inc., pp. 60-63.

The decrease in the number of cells that make up a human body depends upon physiological controls not yet fully understood. Because they are not understood, not much can be done with them or about them, and so the decay that leads to death is unavoidable. But what is death? Morison (1971) views it as a gradual sequence. He believes the actual moment of death cannot accurately be known, for after "life has gone," various organs of the human body, which have not decayed too much, can be used in transplant surgery. In contrast, Kass (1971) believes death to be not a sequence but an event, a specific but not necessarily an abrupt circumstance. As he says:

What dies is the organism as a whole. It is this death, the death of the individual human being, that is important for physicians and for the community, not the "death" of organs or cells, which are mere parts. [p. 699]

Death at a distance is familiar and often fascinating. Tobin (1972) comments that by the time an individual is 14 years of age, he or she will have seen 18,000 deaths. With perhaps almost no exceptions these deaths will have been the result of legal and illegal homicides occurring on television. Death close at hand is not as familiar an experience. With the exception of what can happen in wars or car accidents, people die out of sight, but not necessarily out of mind, in geriatric homes or hospitals. Because of that, we have lost something our forefathers had—the awareness of death close at hand. Death has become an abstraction.

The word *death* is an abstraction. The word merely labels an event. The word does not even describe. Yet, the word is often treated as though it had some power of its own, as though the *word* were the *event*. Because of that, in part, we have managed to invent substitutes such as "passed away" or "passed on" or "not with us anymore" or "life has gone." Whatever the term or the phrase, there is a difference between living things and dead things, a difference between something that lives and the something that no longer lives. As Kass (1971) has put it, "Death is the transition from the state of being alive to the state of being dead" (p. 699).

It is a transition most of us wish to avoid as long as possible or for as long as we comfortably can. The avoidance may be related to what Diggory and Rothman (1961) found in a research study: death represents an assault on the individual's self-esteem. It is viewed as the ultimate of insults, and insults are to be avoided. But death is unavoidable. Death is our companion, our consistent and ever present companion, according to what Carlos Castaneda (1972) wrote in *Journey to Ixtlan.*

Castaneda in quoting don Juan, his teacher-mystic-witch, states that your own, or anyone's, death can be seen if you turn around and look quickly over your left shoulder. (Dictionaries tell us the left side of anything is known as the sinister side.) Death will be there, says don Juan, a wise adviser, watching, waiting. It is the consistent awareness of the inevitability of death that puts the routine difficulties of daily living in perspective.

Castaneda's don Juan made an almost living thing out of death, as clearly as Eugene O'Neill did in his stage play, later a movie, called *Death Takes a Holiday.* In the play, Death does take a holiday, appearing as a young man. He frightens most people who come to know who he is, but he also manages to meet and to love a young woman who goes away with him when his holiday is over. Does she die? It does not matter. What does matter is that death, or Death, is seen as a reality by O'Neill, by don Juan, and by Castaneda—a reality instead of an abstraction. Again we face the matter of defining reality. According to a report by Constance Holden (1973), a California research chemist named Alexander Schulgin

has defined reality as everything the mind can perceive, and that includes the reality of death.

The psychological reality of death has not been widely studied, although there is some evidence death is of greater interest than sexual behavior. For instance, *Psychology Today* surveyed its readers on sexual behavior and received 20,000 replies to a research questionnaire; that same magazine surveyed the subject of death and received more than 30,000 replies (Schneidman, 1971). Among the findings of the survey: less than one third of the respondents grew up in families in which death was openly talked about; over half believed psychological factors could influence and even cause death; one third of the respondents had some change in attitudes about death after using drugs. Avorn (1973) has described the use of drugs, including LSD, to alleviate the fears of dying in seriously ill and dying patients. As they are dying, they may, with the help of some counseling and some drugs, achieve not only a sense of peace but also a feeling of joy related to their increased understanding of what life is all about. Herman Feifel (1963) maintains over 80% of terminally ill patients want to know about their impending death. He says, "They do not want their problems ignored or reassurances they perceive as falsehoods. They feel supported rather than terror-stricken when they can express their sensibilities about death" (pp. 10-11).

The first awareness, the initial realization that one's own death is not far off rarely brings joy. The sequence of reaction to the news has been described by Elisabeth Kübler-Ross (1969) as following these five steps:

1. **Denial and isolation.** The individual denies the approach of death, says it is not so, isolates himself from the information (such as x-ray films, lab reports, and his physician) that states he is past the point of no return,

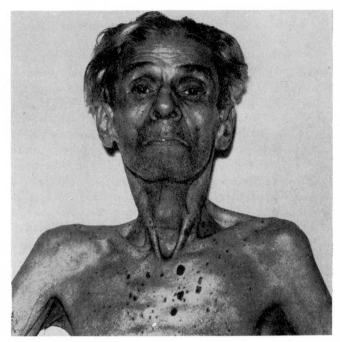

Cachexia. Photograph of a patient with widespread cancer taken a few hours before his death. (From Prior, J.A., and Silberstein, J.S.: Physical diagnosis, ed. 4, St. Louis, 1973, The C. V. Mosby Co.)

and often refuses even to talk about the seriousness of his physical condition.

2. **Anger.** The individual says "Why me?" with rage or envy that others will live longer than he. Doctors become terrible people, and healthy friends are enemies.

3. **Bargaining.** The individual says, in one way or another, "Maybe death will be postponed if I'm pleasant"—time off for good behavior. In this stage, some people may make secret pacts with their God, praying that if they are given more life time, they will dedicate their lives to Him.

4. **Depression.** The individual says "Why me?" but this time with a sense of sadness and dejection knowing life will be lost—his life, her life—and no one can stop the process. Lost also will be the whole earth-based environment loaded with familiar and known things and people.

5. **Acceptance.** The individual is not sad, but he is not happy either. There is an absence of feelings and, often, an absence of conversation. The individual may wish for the si-

lent companionship of other people, who may be nurses and doctors, or friends if they are available.

Then there is the funeral. Funerals are older than man's written history. They existed before the Caesars of Rome, before the pharaohs of Egypt, before the first tribal chieftains of China roamed the plains of that ancient land. The ritual of the funeral is in some places a time for music and dancing. In other places funerals are meant to be times of mourning and grief. Whether they are joyful or sad, funerals are designed for the living. And the living contemplate death. In the *Psychology Today* survey the more-than-30,000 people who responded contemplated their own deaths. Two thirds believed they would die in old age, and as for the kind of death they preferred, see Table 6.

L. E. Sissman (1972) may have thought

Table 6. Percent preference ratings for type of death*

Sudden but not violent	38%
Quiet, dignified	30%
No "appropriate" kind of death	16%
Death following a great achievement	6%
Suicide	2%
Death in line of duty	1%
Tragic, violent death	1%
Being murdered	0%
All other kinds or types of death	6%
Total	100%

*Adapted from Schneidman, E. S.: You and death, Psychology Today, vol. 5, no. 1, June, 1971.

about his preference, but the contemplation of death—his death—suddenly became real for him. He swiftly became an expert on dying, and his comments have a ring of authenticity.

> Throughout our lives, far more efficiently than responsibility or taxes, we evade the idea of death. This is no mean feat, in a world of massacre and genocide, of widely reported individual deaths in Belfast, in Vietnam, and in our own backyard, we keep our blinders firmly on. Even the deaths of our friends and relatives do not persuade us fully of our own mortality; it's always somebody else that death happens to. In adolescence we are reckless with our lives, as if there were more than one life to a customer; in middle age we are cautious and husbanding of them, but as an affirmation, not an admission; in old age we fight tooth and nail—or toothless and horny-nailed—to keep our licenses to live, as if they could never be revoked by the Registry of Spiritual Vehicles. We are all of us always, in the words of the noble old cliche, living a lie. [p. 18]*

Sissman could not evade the idea of his own death when a physician informed him he had Hodgkin's disease, a form of cancer. There would, of course, be radiation therapy provided by the best of modern technology, but there were no guarantees.

> My first reaction, an almost entirely unconscious one, was to clamp a tight lid of security down on

*From Sissman, L. E.: Innocent bystander: a little night music: the curvature of the earth. Copyright © 1971, by The Atlantic Monthly Co., Boston, Mass. Reprinted with permission.

overt expressions of . . . feelings. It seemed that the only way to deal with this crisis . . . different in degree but perhaps not, after all, in kind from others I had had to deal with . . . was to negate it, to pretend to myself and everybody else that, though it *had* happened to me, it couldn't happen to me. [p. 18]*

Death is a part of the lives of all of us, but for some, it occupies the mind perhaps more than is appropriate. For example, Michelangelo, one of the great sculptors and painters of our history, spent forty years in a restless fear of death. He was almost 89 years old when he died on February 18, 1564 (Hartt, 1964). Charles Darwin died in 1882, but for the last fifty years of his life he maintained a record, a diary, of his extensive health problems that may or may not have been caused by medicines he took for his chronic and often severe eczema (Winslow, 1971). Yet in his diary he described feelings of depression, headaches, agitation, what may have been anxiety, and insomnia.

In contrast to a life lived in the dark shadow of the idea of death, William Carlos Williams seemed to fight off the eventuality of death with an unusual tenacity. He wrote novels, plays, magazine articles, and poetry. (He was also a physician.) He died in 1963, but as his life faded away from him, he continued to write, pecking out the words and the sentences on a typewriter using his left hand while his other hand hung uselessly at his side, the result of a stroke (Weaver, 1971).

We live in the shadow cast by our past; our infancies and childhoods remain alive within our minds. We travel along the time line toward an obscure and distant horizon that marks the end of that personal time line. If we choose, we can concentrate on where we have been, constantly glancing at the rearview mirror, or we can

*From Sissman, L. E.: Innocent bystander: a little night music: the curvature of the earth. Copyright © 1971, by The Atlantic Monthly Co., Boston, Mass. Reprinted with permission.

peer ahead, wondering, perhaps fearfully, as Michelangelo did. Or, we can look around at where we are right now. To look around at the present time, to see ourselves and our surroundings, or at least to try to see, involves moving from the unexamined to the examined life.

The Boyds

The Boyds were a multiproblem family. They came to the attention of the staff of a mental health center after a series of changes within the family structure. For this particular family, the changes were great enough to precipitate a crisis.

The mother came to the center first. She had been referred by the family physician. After one visit with a psychologist, she was told to come back the next day with the rest of her family. The family consisted of Al Boyd, age 37, journeyman electrician, average height, muscular but slightly overweight, both parents living and in good health; Mary Boyd, age 37, housewife, average height, obese, father living and in good health, mother died of cancer one year ago; Laura Boyd, age 17, high school senior with average grades, two months pregnant; Bill Boyd, age 15, ninth grade student with failing grades, on school probation, probably attempted suicide two weeks ago.

When they came to the center, they met with the psychologist and a student who was in training for work in the mental health field. They met together for a three-hour session on Wednesday and for a two-hour session on Thursday. The sessions were aimed at determining what was going on and what had gone on in the family, which was now in crisis. The sessions, in effect, were devoted to an identification of problems.

At the beginning each member of the family was asked to participate in a discussion of themselves and to talk and to describe what they did, what they liked or disliked. The following are some condensed results of that initial discussion.

Al Boyd smoked two packs of cigarettes a day and spent most of Sunday drinking a case of beer. He had done this for the past ten years and jokingly referred to himself as a Sunday souse, a weekend drunkard. When he did not drink, he went fishing. He liked to go fishing with Frank, an old acquaintance, every once in a while. Whether he was drinking or fishing, however, Sunday was his day for himself. He rarely talked with his wife or with his children at any time, and he never said anything to them on his Sundays.

Mary Boyd was about 80 pounds overweight. She spent most of her time cleaning house, cooking meals, sewing, or watching quiz shows and soap operas on afternoon television during the week when everyone else was gone from the home. She used to go to church every Sunday with her mother and, when they were young, with her two children. She also liked to sew clothes for her daughter and for herself, but when her mother became ill with cancer, the sewing stopped, and so did attendance at church.

Laura Boyd had been a top student in grade school, but in junior high her grades went down for a couple of years and then climbed back to average in high school. When she was in tenth grade, her mother stopped making dresses for her and somehow, to Laura, did not seem as interested as she had been in anything that was going on in the family. Laura had never had much contact with her father, and she detested his beer drinking. In eleventh grade she started dating a boy who was attentive and fun to be with. In the summer before her senior year she began to sleep with the boy regularly. She asked some friends about birth control pills, but she did not follow through. When she became pregnant, she was surprised. She did not think it would ever happen to her.

Bill Boyd recalled that the best time in his life was during grade school. He said he liked school then and liked going to church with his older sister, his mother, and his grandmother. When his grandmother became ill, he went with his mother once to visit her, but he never saw her again after that. He was in eighth grade when she died. During the Christmas holidays in eighth grade he went to a party where everyone was either drinking whiskey or smoking marijuana. He did both. He liked the whiskey better, and because he was not old enough to buy it, he managed to steal a bottle from a large liquor store every once in a while. Twice a month on the average he poured the whiskey into an empty milk carton and sat under a tree in a small park, drinking whiskey and eating potato chips most of Saturday. He was usually sick on Sunday, but no one noticed. He was often too tired or still too sick on Monday to go to school, and gradually it seemed easier to go for long walks alone or sit in the park than to go to school. One Saturday he sat under the tree in the park drinking whiskey, but instead of potato chips, he chewed up half a lid of marijuana. He then decided at last to try LSD. He had been carrying the LSD pill around with him for three weeks, and it was covered with lint from the bottom seam of his jacket pocket. He put the pill in his mouth and washed it down with whiskey. He sat there under the tree, but nothing happened. Ten minutes later he drank the last of the whiskey and threw the empty milk carton under a bush. He slowly stood up and began to walk home. He had walked less than two blocks when the combination of chemicals he had taken hit him. He felt a great surge of fear and tried to run, but he could only stagger. He fell down on the sidewalk, crawled for a few yards, then stood up again. He somehow managed to get home and get to his bedroom, where he vomited on his bed. His sister came into his bedroom and saw what was happening. She called the mother, and together they held Bill down as he raved and cried.

After each member of the family had talked and discussed matters with the student and the psychologist, they were asked to answer this question: "What's it like for you, being a member of this family?" Al, Mary, Laura, and Bill thought for a while.

Al replied first. "Well, it's OK with me. I got a good enough job, and we're not in debt. Sure wish my wife could fix up the kids though. Well, hell, all the kids nowadays are having a bad time one way or another, so I guess my kids aren't any different. What's it like for me? I guess it's OK."

Mary began her answer slowly, hesitantly. "I don't know what went wrong. Things used to be pretty good. I mean like when we went to church. We don't go to church any more. We don't do anything any more. I guess it's bound to happen, though. Children grow up, and they got to go their own ways. That's natural. It seems like it's all messed up now, and

that isn't natural, is it? I feel all messed up, and I don't know what went wrong."

When her mother finished speaking, Laura said, "I'll tell you what it's like to be a member of this family. It's dumb. I mean here's my mother just sitting around getting fat and my father sitting around getting drunk, and they hardly ever even look at each other. It's a dumb marriage if you ask me. I don't want a marriage like that. I don't know what I want, but I know I don't want that. I don't want to be pregnant either, but I am, and all anyone does about that when I tell 'em is to get sad. Well, I want you to know that I'm sick of all that sadness. I'm sick of morning sickness too. Yeah. Sadness isn't going to fix anything up. I tried to get out of that family sadness, and I found this guy and—well—he's not a sad guy, but he won't go with me unless we have sex, but that's better than sitting around in a sad house. It's all pretty dumb if you ask me."

Then Bill spoke. "I guess it's OK. I mean it's OK with me, but I wish I was back in grade school. I had a friend then, but he moved away. I don't know anybody now. I got a place to sleep, and my mother cooks pretty good sometimes. I wonder sometimes what it's like to go fishing. I wonder if my grandmother can see us all now. Do you believe in God? She might be up in heaven watching us. Sometimes I pray to her. I wish she could answer back. Ever since she got sick and died, it's been different. It's OK, though. It's just not as good as it used to be."

The discussion began to focus more on the grandmother. It became clear she had been an unrecognized stabilizer, an individual with great psychological power, a person Mary depended upon. When she died, Mary lost a mother. She also lost her only source of emotional nourishment. (In somewhat technical terms, Mary had failed to relinquish her family of origin. She had constantly maintained a daughter-mother relationship with her mother and had not found a peer relationship as satisfying to her.) Al hinted at some feelings of resentment over the close relationship between Mary and her mother, and Laura became angry at her father at that moment.

"When Grandma died, you didn't do anything except drink more beer. Why didn't you do anything? Mom was real depressed, and she cried. Remember? You didn't do anything but put on a suit. It was Frank's suit, wasn't it? Well, you borrowed a suit somewhere, and you wore it to the funeral, and when we all got back home, you took the suit off and put on your bib overalls and just drank a lot of beer. I tried to tell Mom everything would be all right, but you didn't do anything."

In defense Al said that his wife didn't need anything from him. "She's a grown-up now, and folks get old and get sick and they die. That's how it is." He didn't want anyone to feel bad when he died. That was how life was. As for praying, that didn't make any sense at all.

The history of the family and the feelings they had, and did not have, for each other began to unfold and become discernible. In highly condensed form, the sequence of events in the family can be reduced to these phases:

Phase 1: Al and Mary were married. They seemed to be compatible and to have similar interests and related goals in life. They both wanted to have a home of their own and to raise a family. Al saw himself as the person responsible for financial matters. Mary saw herself as a wifely, motherly kind of person who still enjoyed a good relationship with her own mother.

Phase 2: They had two children. Al continued to see himself as responsible only for financial matters. He paid the bills. Mary loved her children and, with her own mother as a companion, tried to raise both of them as well as possible. Al and Mary gradually talked less and less with each other. Al's income seemed sufficient, but he felt excluded from much of what was happening in his family. He began to drink on Sundays when everyone else went to church. Within a few years he was a social isolate.

Phase 3: Grandmother died, and Mary went into a prolonged grief reaction. She became seriously depressed and did not make any effort to cultivate a new relationship to replace

the loss of her mother. She gradually turned inward and increasingly ignored her children who were becoming more independent of her anyway. She saw her life as a bleak and lonely path. No one really needed or wanted her except as a housekeeper.

Phase 4: The children of the family escaped from a drab and emotionally empty household. Laura found a boyfriend, but the boyfriend demanded sexual satisfaction for his company. Laura complied. Bill, in the meantime, slowly drifted away from the household, living as a social isolate, copying some but not all of his father's behavior. He silently mourned his lost grandmother, but found no one to replace her or the satisfactions that had been his while she lived. He was, it seemed, willing to die to reestablish the connection with his grandmother.

The core event of this family's crisis is based upon the grandmother's death. The matter of her death was not handled in an adequate fashion. For the most part, it was either ignored or viewed as the end of what is good in life.

Working with the psychologist and the student, the family gradually began to define the problems they faced. Laura's pregnancy was seen as a symptom, not as an isolated problem. Bill's suicidal behavior was seen as an effort to join the grandmother again, no matter what the cost. The suicidal behavior was, again, not an isolated problem, but a result of the interaction of a multiplicity of variables. Al's tunnel-vision view of fatherhood was based upon what he himself had experienced as he grew up in a home in which his own father had behaved as only the financial provider. Mary, meanwhile, was faced with some unfinished business. She had not, even after her mother's death, relinquished her role as a child to her own mother.

Matters eventually turned out well for the members of the Boyd family. Working sometimes together and sometimes separately, each individual constructed a more satisfying style of living, although Al changed the least.

REVIEW QUESTIONS

1. What seems to be a basic purpose of protocol and good manners?
2. Why can person A not teach person B who person B is?
3. Who was Shirali Mislimov?
4. Under what condition can authentic intimacy be developed? What helps that development?
5. What is it that makes death a difficult topic to discuss?
6. How many years does Erikson's seventh stage last?
7. Who is Carlos Castaneda?
8. What drug was used to alleviate fears of dying?
9. Can you list the five steps Elisabeth Kübler-Ross outlined? Which seems to be the most important one?
10. How did Morison and Kass disagree with regard to a definition of death?
11. What is symbolic immortality?
12. How did Skinner, May, and Fromm differ in what they had to say about freedom?

7. INTERACTIONS, RELATIONSHIPS, AND CONFLICT

The orienting concept of interaction was mentioned in the beginning of Chapter 1 and at several other points along the way to this page. In Chapter 6 a brief section was devoted to a listing of relationships. In this chapter we will deal with interactions, with relationships, and with a common outcome of both—conflict.

Relationships and interactions are not separate and distinct features of the human condition. Relationships are those interactions in which the individual often has some choice, some measure of personal authority or control. The control is not only a matter of choosing whether to relate but also how to relate. Conflict enters the scene when there is a difference between what an individual needs or wants and what he or she gets.

Interactions exist in a continuous stream for any individual. The most general of interactions has been previously mentioned. This is the interaction in which heredity and environment both play a part to "cause" or to "produce" human behavior. Interactions are sometimes so fleeting, so temporary, or so obscure they may be overlooked. They may also be so persistently present they are, like pure air, unseen. The interactions of a multiplicity of variables may be so complex they defy sorting. Because of these matters, it is impossible to identify which experience, via interaction, leads to a specific behavior. The specific and detailed causes of behavior are considerably more difficult to identify than the effects, the behavior itself. Human behavior itself is a cause of other behaviors in a circular linkage of interactions that seems to have no defined beginning, except the invented zero point of birth, and no defined end, if we consider the impact—however mild—of some of the kinds of symbolic immortality. Because they are so often unknown, so frequently unrecognized, or so intricate and complex, many interactions are beyond the control of the individual.

In infancy there is no real control of interactions. We are born into a world with no ability to control or to manage that world or ourselves. We do not choose the parents we have, and because of that, we cannot choose the genes and chromosomes we have. We have no vote in where we live, the economic status of our parents, the food we eat, or even the color of the clothes we wear in infancy. Later, however, because of increased abilities and greater mobility, we gradually move out of that early helpless condition to a position of more control over our own lives. That control, however, cannot be total. Most of us live in places designed by someone else, go to school or to work in preestablished locations where the choice of activities is anything but infinite, and eat a narrow selection of foods, considering the enormous variety of foodstuffs available to humans, in an urban world that is becoming more standardized and loaded with an increasing sameness as the years pass. We generally have had nothing to say about the design of the freeways we travel on, the quality of the steel and plastic in the vehicles we travel in, or the weather we travel through. We cannot paint the sunset in our favorite colors or grow paisley-patterned grass or modify the hue of the sky. There are perhaps a million other variables in our environment and within ourselves over which we have no control. We do, however, have a considerable control over the relationships we have with other people. But even in that endeavor the control is sometimes limited. The control is not so much over those others as it is over ourselves—control of our reactions to the behavior of others and not of the other person's behavior.

Not until we reach the adult years do we have the freedom of movement and choice that brings us the opportunities to select from a great assortment of possible relationships. At the same time, no matter what relationships we are free to make, the hum and rumble and silences of the total environment surround us, affecting us as, often, we affect it by way of interaction.

BEHAVIOR SETTINGS

If you have read *Robinson Crusoe,* perhaps you can recall the time he went mad. He had been on the island alone for many years. The lack of companionship, so he says in the book, affected him so much that finally he put his head down and cried. Then he ran wildly through the jungle and along the windy beaches, screaming and shooting his musket. He did not become a quiet man again until he was exhausted.

Crusoe's story is fictional, a classic tale written by Daniel Defoe who lived more than two centuries ago. What Defoe wrote, however, has some basis in fact. Prisoners in solitary confinement often experience a decline and deterioration in their mental functioning. Voyagers, traveling alone across the ocean or on a desert, are vulnerable to and often report a sense of being disconnected and drifting, their minds wandering and disorganized. Volunteers who are research subjects in sensory deprivation (in which light, sound, heat, cold, some of the force of gravity, and the company of other people are removed from their environment) will often feel strange feelings and sometimes hallucinate in the same way a person with a mental illness might. Research scientists working in the fields of space psychology and space medicine are concerned about the effects a long trip may have on an astronaut. Such a journey might take two, three, or even four years. If the capsule contained only one astronaut, would he or she be able to maintain a reasonably consistent contact with reality? No one knows yet. What is known, however, is that people seem to need other people, at least some of the time, to function adequately.

We each experience our environment in separate ways, ways sometimes difficult to describe, for our reactions to the environment can be as complex as that environment. The environment itself may be difficult to describe because it is made up of parts and sectors that may overlap one another. Yet, some of the environment can be untangled as Krause (1970) has done. He listed seven categories of the *social environment,* seven social behavior settings, each with a given cluster of activities. These activities are listed here:

1. Playing, as in nonserious, nonpro-

fessional activities, which are often carried out simply for pleasure*

2. Self-disclosing, in which an individual can appropriately reveal his attitudes, opinions, and beliefs to one or more other people
3. Serving, a social behavior in which one individual receives some form of compensation†
4. Sponsored teaching, which refers to behavior in a social setting, such as a school, in which one person works in ways designed to change or improve the behavior of another
5. Fighting, which means settling conflicts without compromise
6. Trading, which means settling conflicts with compromise, with an exchange of some sort
7. Cooperating, joint working, a social behavior that involves movement toward a mutually recognized goal with some promise of compensation

As the individual moves from the zero point onward, as he enters into more and more of the behavior settings, his life becomes more and more complex. As he moves into a more complex existence, his behavior becomes more difficult to evaluate or to gauge in any overall sense, for he may flow from one setting to the next and sometimes merge several activities into one constellation of behavior.

The flow of activities may, for example, move from social behavior setting 4 to 3 to 2 to 6 within an hour. In real life this may be seen in the day of an instructor in a large university-operated school of nursing. She may begin her hour with a brief lecture or demonstration to nursing students (4), then move to a patient's room to give nursing care to that patient (3), then pause in her work to have a cup of coffee with a friend and talk about her approaching marriage (2), and finish the hour talking on the telephone with her supervisor, trying to arrange for a day off, and to get that day off, she may agree to work on a weekend (6).

The merging of activities can involve 1, 7, and 6. An example: two men seriously discussing a business venture (7) at lunch as one pays for the food while the other buys the wine (6) during a holiday at a ski resort (1).

It is possible to combine, to merge, all seven activities into a half-hour sequence of living; there are over 5,000 possible combinations of all seven. The variety does not stop there, for any interaction within the behavior settings can vary in (1) the frequency of contacts between people, (2) the length of time of each contact, and (3) the direction or order of the interaction (Kaluger and Unkovic, 1969).

There are many possible directions or orders of interactions. In an old and now classic research study, Lewin, Lippitt, and White (1939) described the reactions humans have under three conditions of group life—democratic, autocratic, and laissez-faire. Industrial psychological consultants speak of a slightly different set of conditions of group life—coercive, competitive, and consultative. In the coercive style, someone gives orders and others follow them. In the competitive style the behavior of group members is governed by competition. Competition may be between group members, as it often is in student groups during examination time. Competition may exist between one group and another; for example, Ford competes with Chrysler, and Democrats compete with Republicans. The consultative style is more complex. It is quasi-democratic, and power, or the deciding factors in the ordering of interactions, is shared among the members of a group. Additionally and perhaps obviously, the interaction style that takes place within a group may shift

---

*Pleasure can be subjective; what is pleasurable for one individual may be painful for another.
†Compensation, in this context, refers to pay in the form of money or goods or services.

from predominantly coercive to competitive to consultative, depending upon the "needs of the organization," upon the psychological needs of the individuals in the group, and upon the job that needs to be accomplished.

The direction or order of the interactions we have with each other within our behavior settings can be characterized by the technology of our times, the changes that have taken place, that are now taking place, and that will take place or that are assumed will take place. We are, according to Boccioni, the primitives of a new culture (McLuhan, 1970). Charles Reich (1970) calls it Consciousness III, and William Glasser (1972) has named it Phase IV—The Civilized Identity Society. Alfred Adler (1972) believes we are headed for disaster unless we use the tools of science and technology in the examination and conduct of our lives, while Lewis Mumford (1967) feels disaster has fallen on our times because of our use of the science and the technology we have developed.

Blackburn (1971) and Roszak (Wade, 1972) believe we must combine the techniques of scientific methodology with the ideas and knowledge of those who know little of science or who are against it if we are to untangle the conflicts and contradictions of our times and of our interac-

tions with each other. Through it all, listening to the voices coming from different positions of belief, Borsch (1971), Toffler (1970), and Boulding (1964) maintain the central theme of our times is change.

The change, Boulding states, "may properly be called the second great transition of mankind" (p. 1). The first great change was the development of civilization, discussed by Kenneth Clark (1969) and briefly mentioned in Chapter 2. Much of what has been written about this second great transition is based upon the idea we are finished with what has been called the Industrial Revolution; we are in a post-industrial revolution (Servan-Schreiber, 1968). The emphasis is no longer on the career question of "What shall I do?" but on the broader and more personal lifestyle question of "How shall I be?" (Raskin, 1971).

The first question is a limiting one in this society, for the limits of doing are established by the tools and techniques available to us. The tools and techniques are essentially technological. The second question is almost limitless, as the mind of man is almost limitless in its searching, probing quest to form a framework upon which to build a sense of identity, of individuality. We are not, however, individuals operating at a distance from one another. We band together in groups, and while the idea of the individual remains, the emphasis in this discussion will be upon groups of humans, groups in which people interact with each other.

A group of people with common interests and objectives form an *organization.* Marine brigades are organizations; so are Girl Scout troops, corporations, and families. Almost all organizations, including families, will have, and must have if they are to endure, headship positions. The *headship position* is a position of some power, influence, and control over those who occupy the lower layers in an organization. The headship position has the re-

sponsibility, the "right," to give orders and directions. Within the family, parents have power and influence over their children; parents are also responsible for their children to whom they give orders and directions.

Headship positions are not the same as positions of leadership. Headships are granted by the larger society, in the case of families, and by closed societies, in the case of corporations. In a family setting, leadership positions are granted to parents by the children.

Leadership is earned, not given. If they wish to be leaders, parents typically must earn that position in one manner or another. The same arrangement exists in a corporation. The supervisor is given a position of headship when he is appointed to the job of supervisor; he is not in a position of leadership until his employees accept him as their leader. That acceptance is not inevitable (Myers, 1970).

Headship is concerned with organizational duties and requirements. Within a family, organizational duties and requirements consist of such matters as getting enough food, finding somewhere to live, or washing the dishes. These are the more formalized matters of family life, and they are called the *tasks.*

Leadership involves the intricacies of relationships between people; leadership is concerned with the personal and emotional aspects of living. Personal and emotional factors are sometimes called *process,* and any organization, the family included, must handle the necessary tasks and somehow deal with the process.

Tasks are what humans do. *Process* refers to the way in which people feel about what they do, how they feel about themselves, and how they feel about each other. A hundred lifetimes ago process was probably irrelevant in many ways. If a man did not like his companions, did not participate in hunting and foraging (both are tasks), he might simply have starved to death.

One lifetime ago parents, presidents, and supervisors believed tasks were far more important than process. Now, however, and particularly because of the findings and speculations of behavioral scientists, a great deal of attention is given to the way people feel about what they do and how they feel about each other and themselves. On a broad basis it is called public opinion; within a limited sphere, as in a corporation or a family, it is called morale. Nations, corporations, and many families seem increasingly aware that process is critical to the life of the organization, whatever its size or function.

Any organization, including the family, must somehow recognize and take care of the *essentials.* Within a family the essentials, the vital tasks, are tasks that involve getting the food and clothing and finding and maintaining a place in which to live. These tasks provide for the physical survival of family members. It is possible to list dozens of tasks essential to the survival of the family organization. It is also possible to make a long list of tasks not essential to survival. Each task, however essential or nonessential it may be, is linked with process; each task is linked to feelings.

Task is often easier to identify than process. In families there may be times when process is ignored, pushed to one side, or submerged because of special conditions, because of crises or emergencies. If their house is burning down around them, who in the family will stop to ponder the feelings they have about the task of escaping? Who would pause to reflect upon the feelings they have about other people and about themselves as they run from the flames and smoke? In direct contrast, there are times when process becomes so critical or overriding or overwhelming that task is forgotten, ignored. For instance, a man may become so enraged by the activities of other drivers in high-speed, heavy traffic he may abandon the task of driving to ram his car into the nearest vehicle, guardrail, or light post.

The essential tasks of any family have not changed in man's recorded history. The essential tasks have always been factors of survival, but how the essential tasks are accomplished has changed. The need for food, clothing, and some kind of shelter has remained constant. How those things are obtained has not remained constant. To stress and add to the point: the way in which tasks are now accomplished is different from the way they were accomplished one lifetime ago. The difference is a result of the changes brought about by science and technology.

Because of science and technology, lifetime styles have changed. There have been great changes since Egypt was formed into a nation. Most of the changes, however, have taken place during the twentieth century. For the most part, the changes have been in what people do, the activities they engage in, as they try to accomplish the essential and nonessential tasks of daily living. For example, not far back in man's history, most families grew and hunted their own food. Now, most families buy their food in a supermarket. Within a more recent time frame, contacting a neighbor for help or companionship meant walking or riding on a horse or in a carriage to wherever the neighbor was. Now, it is usually done by telephone.

THE EMERGENCE OF PROCESS

We live in a society that for lifetimes and centuries has placed a heavy emphasis on task, on the idea there is a "job that must be done," on work, on productivity. We have great momentum in that direction; as Rose (1972) has pointed out, the average worker today produces six times more than the average worker of eighty years ago. The trend is still upward, although it may be leveling off (Smith, 1972).

While Charles Reich (1970) forecasts a movement away from the emphasis on task, away from individual and corporate productivity in his *The Greening of Ameri-*

ca, that movement may be a slow evolution rather than a swift and irresistible revolution. Task—the work that must be done, should be done, ought to be done—remains central to the activities of most of us. As surely as we each participate in our own technology, we each participate in the almost gravitational pull of task. We have been well schooled in the importance of task; it is a vital part of our lifetime styles. In the pursuit of task, process may be overlooked or ignored; we can use the work of Frederick Taylor to illuminate that idea.

About three quarters of a century ago, slightly more than one lifetime back, Frederick Taylor came upon the scene, the first "efficiency expert." He showed that each task could be divided into subtasks. Each subtask could be performed in a way that added up to a saving of time on the job to be done. He was followed by others, such as Frank Gilbreth, and a field of study called scientific management grew. With it grew such techniques as time and motion studies, micromotion studies, industrial engineering rate standards, piecework pay plans, and job simplifications. These techniques for increasing the efficiency of task accomplishment have been used to speed up the production of work, which ranges from putting windshields on new cars in a production line to cleaning up a hotel room, from loading a machine that fills bottles with aspirin tablets to loading a ship with crated cars (Stagner, 1956). However, Zdravomyslov, Rozhin, and Iadov (1970) and Meyers (1970) point out that the techniques of efficiency lead only to short-term, intermittent gains or improvements in task achievement because process is usually overlooked or ignored.

The long and historic attention to task at the expense of process began to change around the late 1920s. The work of Elton Mayo, followed quickly by the research reports of Roethlisberger and Dickson (1939), brought into focus the importance of process in task accomplishment. There was a shift from acknowledging only the task to acknowledging both task and process. Psychological needs became legitimate, and behavioral systems that took into account both task and process began to be developed across the land; to name only a few—the Managerial Grid, the Scanlon Plan, Organization Development, Growth Opportunity Plan, Management By Objective, and X versus Y (Todd, 1971).

Douglas McGregor (1960) developed X versus Y, or more accurately, theory X versus theory Y, which he spelled out in his book *The Human Side of Enterprise.* Theory X contains declarative statements to which many in headship positions (parents, supervisors, managers) seem to adhere.

1. *The average human being has an inherent dislike of work and will avoid it if he can.*
2. *Because of this human characteristic of dislike of work, most people must be coerced, controlled, directed, threatened with punishment to get them to put forth adequate effort toward the achievement of organizational objectives.*
3. *The average human being prefers to be directed, wishes to avoid responsibility, has relatively little ambition, wants security above all.* [pp. 33-34]*

On the other hand, theory Y, as McGregor points out, takes into account the interplay of psychological needs with the necessities of task achievement.

1. *The expenditure of physical and mental effort in work is as natural as play or rest.*
2. *External control and the threat of punishment are not the only means for bringing about effort toward organizational objectives. Man will exercise self-direction and self-control in the service of objectives to which he is committed.*
3. *Commitment to objectives is a function of the rewards associated with their achievement. The most significant of such rewards, e.g., the satisfaction of ego and self-actualization needs, can be direct products of effort directed toward organizational objectives.*

---

*From The human side of enterprise by Douglas McGregor. Copyright 1960, by McGraw-Hill Book Co. Used with permission of McGraw-Hill Book Co.

4. *The average human being learns, under proper conditions, not only to accept but to seek responsibility.*

5. *The capacity to exercise a relatively high degree of imagination, ingenuity, and creativity in the solution of organizational problems is widely, not narrowly, distributed in the population.*

6. *Under the conditions of modern industrial life, the intellectual potentialities of the average human being are only partially utilized.* [pp. 47-48]*

Even though McGregor's ideas of theory X and theory Y are widely known and quoted in small and large organizations across the land, and even though a Y environment is less loaded with conflict potential, something seems slightly out of focus, out of alignment. How can the needs of the individual be aligned or correlated with the needs of the organization, whether it is familial or corporate? As Todd (1971) points out:

There is, after all, a theme continually sounded: attending to human needs solves corporate problems . . . attending to corporate needs solves human problems . . . what you can be, you must be: under this roof. [p. 92]

Which is to say that what you can and must be is permissible so long as it fits in and conforms. Generally in this society and in the surrounding environmental setting, there are more pressures for attending to tasks than there are for attending to process (Leavitt, 1964; Argyris, 1962). It seems there is a more consistent or more widespread belief or expectancy that thinking is better than feeling, that doing something is somehow better than being someone. We must, it appears, be rational or at least to others seem to be rational. But Michel Crozier (1969) believes humans "will have tremendous psychological problems in facing the pressure of a too-rational pattern of action according to

which they will have to measure up clearly and without possibility of escaping their actual size" (p. 158).

What is our actual size? What is it that we really are? Certainly we are capable of thinking. We have a relatively large brain, which seems to insure that. But the size and the structure of a brain, which weighs over 3 pounds, also insure a capacity for feelings and emotions. It is the feelings and the emotions that eventually filter through even the finest of intellectual screens to become expressed. For example, General Motors is a corporation known for its awareness of the vagaries and consistencies of human behavior. That organization has elaborate training programs for managers and supervisors, programs that often put a great emphasis upon the process, the feelings and emotions of its employees. General Motors has experienced an increase in the number of complaints its employees have made. In 1960, 106,000 complaints—grievances—were made; and by 1969 the yearly number of complaints had grown to 256,000 (Glaberman, 1972). The complaints are an obvious way of showing some measure of disaffection, of anger, perhaps, at a corporate structure and the supervisors who represent it.

It seems useful to consider that organizations cannot take care of all the needs of the individuals who are a part of that organization. This, of course, leads to an ancient conflict—the conflict between what an individual needs and wants versus what he can get. No organization and no one, single individual can meet all the needs a person may have. That can lead to frustration and then to anger and, eventually, to some form of expression of that anger. In the example of General Motors anger was expressed by way of complaints. In other settings the expression may be less obvious, as Goffman (1961) has described in his example of prisoners at church.

---

*From The human side of enterprise by Douglas McGregor. Copyright 1960, by McGraw-Hill Book Co. Used with permission of McGraw-Hill Book Co.

When the sky pilot* got up in the pulpit to give us our weekly pep talk each Sunday he would always make some feeble joke which we always laughed at as loud and as long as possible, although he must have known that we were sending him up.† He still used to make some mildly funny remark and every time he did the whole church would be filled with raucous (sic) laughter, even though only half the audience had heard what had been said. [p. 316]

Process emerges, sooner or later, and it must somehow be dealt with. The process with which we are involved at the present moment relates to the matter of power.

Power, in a psychological sense, is not the same as power in an organizational sense. A manager, a warden, a politician will have at the minimum the kind of organizational power that has been referred to as headship. Organizational power is vested more in the position or the job than it is in the individual. When a person is moved into a job as a manager, he is moved into a position of power, and he retains that power as long as he is a manager. If he is fired or retires, he loses the power that job gives him, the power to make and to transmit decisions that affect the behavior of other people within the organization (Poland, 1961).

In a psychological sense *power* has been defined as the ability to get what one wants or needs (Kuhn, 1963). *Powerlessness* refers to the belief or expectancy held by the individual that his own behavior does not determine whether he gets what he wants and needs (Seeman, 1959). Power and powerlessness are not so much based upon the rights and privileges of a job or a position an individual may have; psychologically, power refers to a more personal and more portable attribute than job-based organizational power.

According to Julian Rotter (1966) there are large numbers of people who expect to

be powerless and who see, or believe they see, their lives controlled by fate or luck or by some divine force over which they have no authority. Rotter has also identified the idea that there are large numbers of people who expect to be powerful and who see their lives as being under their own control. The expectancy of power and powerlessness has been mentioned before in connection with the study of the reaction to tornado threats conducted by Sims and Baumann (1972). (See Chapter 3.)

Powerlessness as an expectancy has been contrasted with powerlessness as an experience. Donald and Phyllis Tiffany (1973) have identified four sources of control: (1) Control *from* internal psychological and physiological conditions (FI), (2) control *over* those internal conditions (OI), (3) control *from* the environment (FE), and (4) control *over* the environment (OE). Individuals who are self-determined or self-directed and who are at least apparently in charge of their own lives are OI-OE people. Those who experience a high degree of control and who are non-self-determined are FI-FE.

Those individuals who expect to control and who often do control lean in the direction of OI-OE. Those who expect to be controlled and who, because of their expectancies, often are controlled become heavily involved with FI-FE. It may seem that people who lean toward OI-OE have a higher degree of self-esteem than FI-FE individuals. It can be assumed that OI-OE people have higher levels of reputation than FI-FE types. Individuals who can manage to control themselves and their environment certainly have more power than those who do not have and do not expect to have that control. Those who do not possess the power to control or who believe they do not have the power are typically demoralized, according to Jerome Frank (1973).

It seems that an individual who has no power over himself or his environment

---

*Prison chaplain.
†In the curiously changing language of American slang, "sending him up" means the same as "putting him down."

may be in a precarious position with regard to his own "mental health," or with regard to his attempts to adjust or adapt to the world around him and to himself. This may also be the case for the individual who has no power but who has a desire for power, having what Joseph and Joanne Veroff (1972) call a high power motivation.

A *high power motivation,* a desire for power, sometimes in interaction with other motives, appears to be linked with and to produce conflict if it is the only thing the individual is genuinely interested in. If, however, a high power motivation is a part of the individual's strivings (which may also include strivings for above-average achievement and for an appropriate level of belongingness or membership in a group), the individual may lead a zestful life. Yet, at the core the desire for power seems based upon a fear of weakness, of vulnerability. A fear of weakness in social interactions is as connected with self-esteem as is the sense of power.

Interaction and self-esteem have been studied with care in psychological research. What has been studied and researched can be seen in many real-life situations. The studies show that when an individual actively participates in a relationship with another person, his personal sense of self-esteem plays an important part in that relationship. If, for example, his self-esteem is high, he will not react very much, in any way, to the evaluations others make of him—and those evaluations are his reputation. On the other hand, if an individual's level of self-esteem is low, he will usually react, sometimes strongly, to the evaluations other people make of him (Jones, 1973).

There are two elements in the reacting and nonreacting mentioned above. The first involves active participation in a relationship. Stephen C. Jones (1973) maintains that if a person is not an active participant but merely an observer, his view of himself, his level of self-esteem, will remain at about the same level. That is, the person will function with consistency. If self-esteem is low, it will stay low as long as the individual occupies the position of an observer. If self-esteem is high, it will remain high.

The second element of reacting and nonreacting is the nature of the reaction. If self-esteem is high and solid, approval or disapproval—matters of reputation —seem to have little emotional effect on the individual. While he is a participant, active in an interaction, he may appear to be functioning as an interested observer when the matter of his reputation is in focus. He may be so self-sufficient that the views other people have of him do not lift him up or put him down. After all, the views others have of him may or may not coincide with the views he has of himself.

At the heart of the matter, the reputation he has is someone else's reality. But another person's reality more often is of some influence. If a person does not have a solid and high sense of self-esteem, he will be vulnerable to matters of approval and disapproval. In real life situations people who receive approval from others are likely to (1) talk more, (2) sense a high level of self-esteem, and (3) like other people better. The reverse also exists. When people are disapproved of, they are likely to (1) speak less, (2) have a lowered sense of self-esteem, and (3) tend to dislike other people. When an individual does not have a high and sturdy sense of self-esteem, he will be dependent upon others to provide him with whatever level of self-esteem is available. There is a tight connection between self-esteem and what the individual believes to be his reputation—and this connection is a highly personal and subjective one. If, to give an example, an individual can tolerate the idea he is genuinely liked, he is apt to say to himself, "She likes me because I'm a likeable person." If, however, someone finds it difficult to tolerate being liked (not a rare condition), he is prone to say, "It doesn't mean anything. She's friendly to everyone, even clods like me."

There is an apocryphal statement related to all of the above: "One of the best ways to live life is to treat everyone as though they loved you." More often, however, it seems interactions between people consist of a relationship Walter Kaufmann (1973) calls "the committee of two." Between the two people there is some conversation, perhaps even some fleeting moments of intimacy, but the essence of the interaction is passivity. Each waits for the other to do something, to say something of real meaning and substance, to decide, to exercise some form of active as opposed to passive power. The committee of two behaves as most committees behave: there is talk until something or other happens. What happens may often be a temporary interruption by the environment external to the two-person committee. They may be invited somewhere. If there are no interruptions, the small committee may (1) slide further and further into the passive state to the point where even conversation stops or (2) overturn passivity and show some measure of anger or affection or (hopefully) both. To overturn passivity and to show feelings in an open way can be interpreted as using power.

ANGER AND AFFECTION

The reasonable adventurer (Heath, 1964) is an individual who can identify, name, and allow himself to experience his own feelings of affection and anger. Both are human feelings, often necessary, a part of existence, an aspect of any person who is alive.

Roger

Roger was carried into the emergency room of the hospital on a stretcher. He was bleeding from a knife wound in the lower part of his abdomen, and his skin was almost the color of chalk. He was immediately operated on and after surgery, put in intensive care for three days. After that he was moved to another unit of the hospital where he was visited by a psychiatric nurse from a mental health center near where Roger lived.

Roger refused to talk to the psychiatric nurse. He yelled at her and tried to hit her, telling her to get out and go away, to leave him alone. The nurse told Roger to stop acting like a child with a temper tantrum. He might, she said, tear his stitches. Roger instantly threw off his bed sheet and began to rip at the bandages. The psychiatric nurse grabbed a lamp and hit Roger as hard as she could with it. She struck him on the shoulder, and he fell back on his pillow, screaming and crying. The psychiatric nurse pulled the sheet up, covering Roger, who by then had stopped screaming but who continued to cry. He said he wanted to die. He wanted to die, not caring how, and this time he had almost made it.

The psychiatric nurse called for help, and two staff nurses came down the hall and into Roger's room. The psychiatric nurse described what had happened. One of the staff nurses stayed in the room, while the other went to get the medical intern who was assigned to that wing of the hospital. Within ten minutes, Roger was heavily sedated, sleeping a drugged sleep and the psychiatric nurse was completing a report of the incident, which was to be kept in Roger's file.

The next day the psychiatric nurse went to see Roger again. He was still sedated, although not as heavily as on the day before. He was sleepily awake, and when he saw her, he pointed at his bruised shoulder.

"You really got me," he said.

"I had to stop you."

"Why?"

"Because you were trying to hurt yourself."

"What difference does that make?"

"How am I going to get to know you if you're dead?"

"Who cares if I'm dead?"

"Maybe I do."

So the conversation began, Roger disbelieving and disagreeable, the psychiatric nurse direct and sometimes challenging, but consistently interested in Roger's well-being.

A month after Roger had been taken to the hospital for the knife wound, he appeared in court to testify about his part in the fight. The man who had stabbed Roger was on trial for attempted murder. On the witness stand Roger admitted he had started the fight and said that he knew the man who had stabbed him well enough to know what that man would do if he was "teased enough. You know, I knew I could get him going just by calling him names and then he'd go after me."

The assistant district attorney slumped in his chair, knowing his prosecution was going down the drain as Roger spoke. The jury listened, however, and voted a verdict that led to a jail sentence for the man who had stabbed Roger. Roger was dismayed by the verdict, and as he told his psychotherapist (the psychiatric nurse) he wondered again about suicide.

Two months after the stabbing Roger went back to work at the gas station and visited with his therapist twice a week. By talking with her, he gradually learned some things about himself. He discovered he had been heading toward death for at least four years. His brother had been killed in a helicopter crash in Vietnam, and he had watched enviously as his parents grieved. It seemed to him they had never been much interested in either of their two children, but the death of one brought forth a torrent of sorrow Roger wanted to repeat. He had worked at getting killed. Before the stabbing, he had been in a car wreck that came about because of what the police called reckless driving. Before that he had "accidentally" fallen off the roof of his parent's house, but the only result had been a sprained wrist.

His therapist helped him to realize his wish to die and the hope for his parent's grief was based in part upon his deep pool of anger. When he came to understand the sources of his anger, Roger's suicidal urges decreased a great deal. He stayed in psychotherapy for a year and a half, and at the end of that time he was a vastly different person.

There are people who diminish themselves, who subtract from their own lives by denying the feelings they have. They appear in many forms. One form has been described by Theophrastus (Garnett, 1899) who lived over 2,000 years ago. He inscribed these words:

> The unseasonable man is one who will go up to a busy person, and open his heart to him. He will serenade his mistress when she has a fever. . . . He will come to give evidence when the trial is over. When he is asked to a wedding he will inveigh against womankind. He will propose a walk to those who have just come off a long journey. [p. 268]

The unseasonable man is not some rare and exotic specimen. He exists today, and he is just as denying, as subtle, and as elusive in expressing his feelings of anger as in the time of Theophrastus. At the very least, he is aware of the tasks alone.

Another example of disguised anger, "civilized" anger, has been described by Jelliffe (1920) in a brief passage from his book about the technique of psychoanalysis. Jelliffe writes of Leo Tolstoi (often spelled Tolstoy), the renowned Russian author.

> Tolstoi has given us a vivid characterization of this impulse in a record of his own boyhood. His tutor flogged him, and he reacted in the only way in which he could "get even" by not merely the thought of suicide but the vivid imagination, well set in scene, of himself dead and his father dragging the terrified tutor before the beautiful corpse, and accusing him of having been his murderer, while the friends around bemoaned him as so brilliant yet so tragically driven to death. [p. 80]

"This impulse" mentioned in the first sentence of the quotation above refers to an old technical term: *Minderwertigkeit,* a lengthy label for an overpowering sense in children and adolescents of their own insufficiency or incompleteness.

The unseasonable man and someone floating in a sea of *Minderwertigkeit* have something in common. They both deny the existence of their own anger, and both express their anger indirectly. The unseasonable man behaves in inappropriate ways, ways that make life at least temporarily awkward, unhandy, or inefficient for other people who often may be too loaded with a sense of a self-imposed obligation, too polite, to confront the individual or to ask him to leave. The individual immersed in *Minderwertigkeit* may feel so insufficient and helpless he may channel his anger into daydreams in which vengeful acts take place. In instances such as this, the anger may not be visible or recognized for what it is, even by the person who conjures the daydream.

Daydreams evolve to nightmares in civilized societies that engage in military combat. Combat amounts to an organized expression of anger. The results are usually beyond an easy comprehension, and we can read the tabulations with a cool and intellectual eye, especially if we were not there. "Let me quote, again, the figures of French casualties for the months of August and September, 1914: 329,000 killed, died of wounds, wounded or made prisoner" (Blond, 1962, p. 234). And in *one* battle in 1943: "The German losses were put at 70,000 killed, 2,900 tanks, 195 mobile guns, 844 field guns, 1,392 planes and over 5,000 motor vehicles" (Werth, 1964, p. 626). Approximately 135,000 people, most of them civilians, were killed in Dresden, Germany, in an air raid on the night of February 13, 1945 (Irving, 1963). Conventional (nonatomic) weapons of war were used in the accomplishment of a task.

The numbers are too large, the locations too remote, and the dates too much a part of history to affect us in a personal way. Closer at hand is the individual in this description, a small-town boy from Iowa, a medical corpsman in the U. S. Navy.

In a Vietnamese village, Bob set rice fields afire with his cigarette lighter and watched calmly as his unit shot down fleeing peasants. At one point he saw an old man lying in a field. "How are you going to treat him, Doc?" joked one of his officers. By way of reply, Bob leaned over and killed the old farmer. [Lumsden, 1972, p. 42]

Anger is a problem of formidable dimensions for all humans. None of us is free of it. Some of us, though, are skilled at denying its existence within ourselves, but the avoidance of awareness, the denials, diminish the individual and reduce his chances of establishing what Jerry Greenwald (1968) has called "nourishing relationships." Greenwald maintains that "the development of awareness can enable a person to modify his behavior, regardless of his past experience or his age" (p. 6).

Awareness of one's own self is a basic factor in the growth of identity and a necessary ingredient in the development of intimacy and in one's attempts to move toward self-actualization. Awareness of one's own process, feelings, is as critical a part of the psychological equipment owned by the reasonable adventurer as is the awareness of task. Awareness of one's own feelings means, inevitably, an awareness of one's own anger. Yet, anger is a word that can be lost in a thicket of other words such as "ticked off," "irritated," "bothered," or "put out." The lexicon of anger covers a great range, but then so does the feeling, ranging from apathy to rage.

Anger can result from frustration, but frustration is not a feeling. It is a condition. To be delayed or stopped in the pursuit or achievement of some goal is to be frustrated. Each of us experiences small frustrations every day. Sometimes, when we are in the greatest hurry, it seems the traffic lights magically change to red just before we get to them. When we are supremely hungry, the cafeteria line may seem to move with the speed of a crippled snail; when we are thirsty, the water fountain does not work; when we need to be recognized as brilliant, gifted, creative, exceptional, the world is oblivious to our existence. These and a thousand other conditions of frustration often exist in the environment; the anger, the feeling, exists within the person.

In our society the conventional wisdom associated with anger and frustration may be confusing. It is generally supposed that by the time an individual has achieved

Daniel Brody/Editorial Photocolor Archives

adulthood, he or she should be able to deal with a large variety of frustrations with some ease. He or she should also be able to handle anger in a generally realistic way. These "shoulds" are societal rules or a mixture of those rules and an array of self-imposed obligations to behave properly or in a polite, often highly controlled and courteous manner. The "shoulds" may not coincide with reality.

Children are typically frustrated because of the thousands of rules and regulations they must learn and follow. When a baby is born, he is an uncivilized savage, but within a few years he must learn how to control his bowel and bladder. He must learn a working vocabulary that at first is not his own, but the world's. He must learn how to feed himself, how to put on his clothes, and how to sit still at school, all factors that can frustrate.

The rules and regulations about "how to" can include rules and regulations about how to handle anger. For many people the rule seems to be "don't." While many parents are easily able to show their children how to behave in the bathroom or at a store, not many parents seem skilled in showing their children how to deal with anger. Perhaps many of them are too busy trying to contend with their own angers to be able to teach. Their own anger may be associated with not merely expected but actually experienced control from others, from the environment (FE). Tiffany and Tiffany (1973) maintain that individuals who feel powerless in relation to their environments can be expected to feel powerless over themselves, and they may react to even minimal stress with impulsive reactions, often in the form of anger. Williams (1972) indicates specific and allowable expressions of anger may differ according to the socioeconomic level of the family, but the message from parent to child may extend from "Don't be angry at me" to "Don't be aware of your anger." That can lead to repression of the feelings of anger.

Affection, feelings of affection, can be repressed. This seems to be especially the case with regard to affection for oneself. We have, as mentioned earlier, a society in which modesty and self-derogation are often rewarded. Expressions of self-approval or self-praise may go unrewarded or punished. It is, it seems, the unusual person who likes himself, who likes what he is, how he is. In describing an unusual, atypical person, Schulberg (1972) commented on Muhammad Ali and said:

> Of the past eight heavyweight champions, six have been Negro, but this was the first black champion to proclaim his blackness, to say to the white world "I don't have to be what you want me to be," the ideal practitioner to tap out on the heads and bodies of his opponents the message: Black Is Beautiful. [p. 26]

Affection, whether for self or for another, ranges along a scale from apathy to love.

In a book designed for children in elementary schools, Walter Limbacher (1970) writes:

> Like everyone else, you have a feeling toward yourself. You may not think about the feeling very often, but it's there—deep within you—and it has effects on the way you behave. [p. 25]

Limbacher continues on to describe the idea of self-image and the importance other people have, especially for the young, in the development of that self-image. An approval of oneself, an affection for one's own being, a positive self-image seems a necessary factor in the development of a satisfying life, yet at the same time it seems difficult to achieve.

As Charlotte Buhler (1971) has pointed out, there are three areas of human endeavor that have earned criticism for their negative impacts on the development of an adequate, appropriate self-image.

> The first area of criticism comprises our modes of upbringing and our ways of living which result in overwhelming amounts of emotional disturbance in people. . . . The second issue rousing criticism has to do with the aforementioned educational system's failure to develop the individual as a person. [p. 384]

It is appropriate to point out at the moment that Limbacher's writings for children and their use in schools is the exception, not the rule. Buhler continues:

Therapists know how many patients complain about their parents never having seen or treated them as persons, never having given them the feeling of the integrity and the dignity as persons, which should be the basis of all upbringing and education. . . . The releasing and furthering of creativity is the third important issue in this area, that is the releasing of that kind and amount of creativity accessible to every human being, if properly guided. [pp. 384-385]

And so, in a grand sweep, Buhler, with justice, aims criticisms at parenting, at teaching, and at our society in general. None of these interrelated sectors of the environment seem capable of developing a sense of adequacy in the individual.

These three sectors of the environment are made up of people who can be called "they," and to return to Limbacher (1970):

If they treat you with respect and kindness, you feel that you deserve respect and kindness. You believe you're all right as a person. If people treat you with unkindness, you begin to believe that you're not good enough or important enough to deserve kindness. . . . So the people around you are like mirrors. If they show you you're a winner, you will feel like a winner. If they show you you're a loser, you feel like a loser. [pp. 25-26]

It is of some interest that Limbacher's book is titled *I'm Not Alone,* for what he has described in terms of mirroring is called *reflected appraisal,* and none of us is alone in that respect. We are all vulnerable to the feelings and attitudes others have toward us and about us. It has been referred to as reputation, a factor vital in childhood and often but not always vital in the life of the adult and a factor that may stand in the way of an adult's development of self-esteem. A healthy level of self-esteem even to the point of self-love seems necessary for the growth of love for someone else. It is evidently necessary for people to be able to care about and have affection for themselves before they can care for and have affection for others. If

an individual cares for someone else more than they care for themselves, the relationship is more a dependent interaction than an affectional one.

CONFLICTS

In our interactions with others, we move through a variety of environments. It seems that, no matter what the behavior setting, we humans almost always seek the approval of others before we have the ability to develop an approval of ourselves. We begin to seek the approval in infancy and in early childhood, but as we move into the years of adulthood, we may still look for that approval, behaving in ways designed to preserve our reputations, while self-esteem often withers and dries up. For those among us who seek approval at the expense of self-esteem, these words from Jerry Greenwald (1969) may be useful:

"Approvalitis" is not a toxic pattern in childhood but it becomes toxic if it persists as the child grows to adulthood. In such cases it may take the form of "congenital approvalitis" in which the victim of one generation, having developed so little autonomy and self-reliance of his own, in his turn as parent dominates his children in the same manner as he was dominated as a child. This cycle of chronic infection is exemplified in families where each generation is obsessed with controlling and dominating the next generation. [p. 4]

"Approvalitis" can be transmitted from one generation to the next, not by way of the physical, genetic, inherited base, but by way of internalizing.

We all internalize, especially when we are young. We internalize the language we use, and we internalize the attitudes, opinions, beliefs, gestures, table manners, and often the core of whatever religious beliefs we may have from our parents. We internalize; that is, we take in other people's attitudes, and they become our own. In that manner we learn how to be, or at least some of the ways of being, and our horizons of behavior become narrowed in the process. In childhood the more powerful individuals are usually parents, and in contacts and encounters with them we usually take on, unthinkingly, their system of values, their ways of being in much the same manner they internalized systems from their own parents in an effort to avoid anxiety and other kinds of stress. Anxiety and the other forms of stress have two primary sources: the *intrapersonal* and the *interpersonal.*

Every human is born an uncivilized savage. The infant, however, evolves slowly into a reasonably civilized child, and he has done so to avoid interpersonal strife with parents and to gain rewards for conforming to their ways of being. Yet, even the most civilized child and probably every adult must deal with the remnants of the savage that still live within each person. The savage is not some inherited aspect of human behavior. The idea that humans are inherently and unchangeably aggressive is probably false. The belief—there is little proof—that humans instinctually stake out and mark off a piece of land and then defend that territory is probably also false. As Leon Eisenberg (1972) says:

To believe that man's aggressiveness or territoriality is in the nature of the beast is to mistake some men for all men, contemporary societies for all possible societies, and, by a remarkable transformation, to justify what is as what needs must be; social repression becomes a response to, rather than a cause of, human violence. [p. 124]

Tiffany and Tiffany (1973), in a similar fashion, maintain that social unrest and human violence are caused by the adverse effects of social systems upon the individual. Among the social systems that Sanford (1966) mentions are those that Charlotte Buhler (1971) has mentioned and that have been cited previously: the home, the school, and the larger society. While each has been developed by man, none seems now to serve man as well as might be expected and as might be needed. Each seems loaded to the gunwales with subsystems and demands not only unsatisfying but also frustrating, as though each were operating in ways meant to preserve what always has been (traditionalism) at

the expense of the very real and pressing needs of the individual. Is it, perhaps, that we depend upon the way things always have been for our source of law and order?

Whatever views anyone may have of man and the present society, it seems that by the time an individual has progressed to the school age stage of behavior, his conscience is in full flower, an internalized conscience, and he must contend not only with the rewards and punishments of others but also with the rewards and punishments he provides for himself. It is a delicate balance of forces that must be maintained. The forces must be integrated. Each person is glued together by an invisible bonding agent sometimes referred to as the *ego* or the *self.* The self is not a fixed or specific part of a person; it is not the end result of anything. Instead, it is a moving, fluid, modifiable, ongoing aspect of any human's existence (Horrocks and Jackson, 1972). While it may be based upon an enormous background of countless interactions of the biological, the social, and the psychological, it responds and reacts in countless ways in any immediate or present setting.

The self may be viewed as an idea or a concept, just as "time" and "reality" are concepts; self is more easily discussed than researched, more often speculated about than measured. In spite of the ambiguities about what self may or may not be, it can be assumed that we behave in a more or less consistent way because the psychological part of us called ego or self keeps us in balance. The ego or self is often referred to as the integrating sector of personality. Whenever the ego or self is threatened by forces that may push it out of balance or interfere with its integrating function, strategies and tactics of defense come almost instantly to the rescue.

If the ego or self is unable to function in an adequate manner, the individual may not be able to govern, control, direct, or channel his own behavior well enough to meet and to deal with daily problems. He may be in a state of decompensation or collapse. Yet, we are equipped with strategies of defense that are actually strategies for defending the self against what the individual may think or imagine are attacks. Attacks against the self are rooted in intrapersonal behavior. The individual may "attack" himself; that is, he may sense the rise within of a spectrum of urges and impulses that he may feel are bad or frightening or evil, almost as though they were foreign objects lodged within his brain. The person may sense some imperative need to hide these urges and impulses from view, primarily from his own view and secondarily from the views of others. The technique for hiding or for disguising the impulses and urges will involve the strategies of defense. Some of the time, however, the urges, the impulses, can become so compelling they break into the open, and the individual may see himself acting out the impulses and see that other people see him. To try to make peace with himself and with other people, he may choose, unconsciously, to bring into play the defensive strategies he has learned to use.

Attacks against the self—whether real or imagined—may be rooted in interpersonal behavior. That is, the individual may experience others as injurious or potentially injurious in a psychological, not in a physical, sense, and he will feel a need to defend. Attacks against the self then may involve the individual's self-esteem and reputation. The preservation and maintenance of an adequate (to the person) level of self-esteem and an adequate (to the person) level of reputation motivates defensive behavior when self-esteem and reputation are attacked. The individual may be motivated to defend against an imagined or expected attack. In this society and in many others the two most common assaults against the self are frustration and conflict.

As you may recall from previous comments, frustration is a condition. It is not a feeling. Frustration is impossible to avoid, and the effort to adjust, cope, get along, survive, is usually a matter of developing skills for handling the inevitable frustrations of daily living. We are surrounded by frustration, and it is useful to separate and briefly delineate their variety.

1. *Personal frustration.* This can be a source of great psychological pain for the person. It is based upon both genuine and imagined inadequacy. With regard to the genuine, a girl may spend years in seemingly endless practice on the guitar, yet her finger dexterity and sense of pitch may be well below the average. In spite of great ambition and dedicated effort, she never rises above a below-average level of skill on the guitar.

As for the imagined, we can use the example of the boy who pictures himself as an inadequate, helpless person loaded with *Minderwertigkeit* who repeatedly daydreams about being the first astronaut to set his feet down on the sand of Mars. When he surfaces from his daydreams to survey the real world (Earth) and his real position in it, he may deeply sense a rush of self-induced frustration. The frustration may thicken as he gets in touch with his own transitory *Minderwertigkeit.*

2. *Environmental frustration.* When we most desperately need to get somewhere in a hurry, the traffic lights seem always to be red. When we go to the library to read a treasured or necessary book, we find it has been checked out by some unknown person. We sit in a cafe, hungry, harried, and hurried, watching the waitress gossip with other waitresses while she should be taking our order. We call a friend, but the line is busy. In the middle of a fascinating television show, the picture tube goes blank. Someone else gets the job we needed. We schedule a picnic, and it rains. The car won't start. A shoelace breaks. Jill says no.

There are moments and days when we need the uncompromised acceptance and affection from others, but we feel unnoticed, anonymous to the point of invisibility. This may happen to us at home, at school, or anywhere in the larger society. At other times some of us may feel a need to be alone, but surprise visitors knock on the door, surge into our privacy, and try to get a party started.

3. *Conflict frustration.* There are three major types of conflict that can lead to the development of frustration (Dollard and Miller, 1950).

The first of these is usually called an *approach-approach conflict;* that is, the individual may try to achieve or to go after (approach) two different goals. On a sim-

ple level a child with a quarter may have to decide whether to buy a vanilla or a chocolate ice cream cone. He does not have the money to buy two cones, but if he gets one, he cannot have the other. He is caught between two "approaches" or ways of satisfying himself.

On a more complex level some women find themselves caught in a conflict of choice between marrying one or the other of two distinctly different men. One man is a delightful, gracious person, and she may see a great potential for the development of an intimate relationship. That man, however, is not at all interested in

Marion Bernstein/Editorial Photocolor Archives

working so she will have to support him. The other man is near-wealthy, gracious, but often tedious, and she sees little chance for the development of intimacy. Yet, the rich man has a yacht and prefers to spend long vacations cruising the bays near Barbados. If she chooses one man, the other is lost to her.

A second type of conflict that can lead to frustration is the *approach-avoidance conflict.* In this kind of conflict circumstance, examples are easy to see. For instance, a man wants to buy a sleek, expensive sports car, but if he did, he would not have much money left over for other things, such as food. With the car he could impress his friends (approach), but he would be hungry or poorly clothed (avoidance). Then there is the woman who wants a baby but despises not only the idea but also the activity of sexual intercourse. In contrast there is the woman who thoroughly enjoys sex and cannot take the pill because of health reasons but who would loathe having a baby. A student may be willing to cheat on an exam to get a good grade, but he may be fearful of the consequences of getting caught. The person who is 100 pounds overweight is ordered by her physician to go on a diet. She knows the diet is necessary, but every time she passes a bakery or a candy store, the approach-avoidance conflict is reborn.

An additional example of this form of conflict can be seen in the man who is admired by all who know him, a superbly skilled heart surgeon who can ask for, and get, high fees for the delicate work he does. Yet, he hates his work. He would rather grow cabbages and carrots, but he thrives on the deserved admiration he receives. In addition, he has two children in college whom he must support. For another example, think of the policeman who enjoys the power and authority of his position. He enjoys the uniform he wears and the gun he carries, but he spends his days immersed in worries that he may suddenly be killed in the line of duty.

A third example of conflict frustration is called *avoidance-avoidance.* In this circumstance the individual will sense a need to avoid two circumstances, two threats, two fears, two of any toxic situations. To grasp this conflict, think for the moment of the man backed to the edge of a 200-foot precipice. He can jump off the cliff or stand and fight the stalking tiger running right at him. Consider this example of an avoidance-avoidance conflict: a 16-year-old girl is pregnant. She cannot afford either a legal or an illegal abortion. Her parents can, but she is fearful of saying anything to them. She is also fearful of doing nothing as her pregnancy progresses. She knows that eventually the pregnancy will become obvious.

The three sources of frustration—personal, environmental, and conflict—briefly skim the surface of some aspects of living almost all of us experience. We also experience our own reactions to frustration. It is the way in which we handle the results of frustration that determines whether we are "adjusted" or "adequate" or "intact."

Infants respond to frustration in understandably crude ways, (Bridges, 1932). Within a very short time after birth, they may express distress in the form of anger and fear. They show a physical restlessness that increases to a level of crying, often an expression of anger or fear. Because infants almost inevitably experience frustration and their own responses to that frustration, it seems easy to assume they also experience the beginnings of a sense of mistrust in themselves. Mistrust can sometimes be defined as an expectation of frustration. To expect frustration is to be ready for it when it comes. To expect it, however, can cause the person to shout at shadows or to hide from frustration when no such frustration exists.

Frustration, whether real or imagined, can produce a number of feelings. Most frequently, these feelings are (1) anger, (2) fear, and (3) anxiety. While the infant may be able to express anger and fear in open ways, the civilizing process of socialization with its component of mistrust leads to behavior often less open, less honest, than that expressed by the infant (Rubin, 1969).

Anger has been lightly touched upon in previous pages. Anger and fear are linked together, so also are fear and anxiety. With regard to anger and fear, we can and do learn how to be afraid of our own anger. We learn, sometimes with a great inaccuracy, that anger is usually unwanted, unwelcomed, penalized, or laughed at. Sometimes our anger is ignored, and that is nearly equivalent to being ignored as a person. Many among us are taught that anger is bad or illegitimate, or that we must govern and control ourselves or else accept the governing of others (Spicer, 1971) if we are to survive within the miniature society of the family and the larger society of the family of mankind. We usually learn not only to accept the rules and regulations of society but also to welcome them. In so doing, we gradually escape from what Simone de Beauvior (1948) calls "the anguish of freedom," to be aware of and to express the anger that resides within.

Fear, when it is a result of frustration, can be fear of the anger that results from the experience of frustration. Fear may also be connected with the agents of frustration. A child may easily learn to fear and to hate a frustrating mother, a frustrating teacher, a frustrating friend. An adult may become afraid of venturing into a job and thereby frustrate himself. Fear may be connected with approach-avoidance and avoidance-avoidance conflicts. We can learn how to fear conflicts of any sort, in part because the resolution of conflict depends upon making choices that end the conflict. We can be afraid we may make the wrong choice.

Anxiety and fear are identical with one exception: in fear, the fear-producing agents or factors are known. They can be identified. This advantage does not exist with regard to anxiety. In anxiety the causative factor is unknown. As Morgan and King (1966) have pointed out, the person who is anxious may be totally unaware of the frustration or conflict that makes him uncomfortable. In addition, he may not be aware of the specific peculiarities of his own behavior that result from the anxiety. He is, however, keenly aware of the discomfort and the psychological pain.

Anger, fear, and anxiety can interfere with "approvalitis" in both children and adults. Self-esteem is injured by these feelings, and the person who experiences them may feel that because they are bad feelings (uncomfortable), he must be a bad person (guilty of something). In essence, the person may believe his level of reputation is down. He is frequently a demoralized individual.

This trinity of often intermixed feelings can form the basis of attacks upon the self, attacks that must somehow be fended off. We humans have ways of fending, of defending against the attacks, real or imagined as they may be. These ways are often called coping mechanisms, defense mechanisms, or adjustment techniques. They constitute our strategies and tactics of ego defense, and in the first part of this book they were called defending behaviors.

REVIEW QUESTIONS

1. Why is process often difficult to observe and to define?
2. In what way can relationships and interactions be differentiated?
3. Can you distinguish between leadership and headship?
4. How is McGregor's theory Y related more to leadership than to headship?
5. Can you define FI, OI, FE, and OE?
6. Why is it so difficult to define self?
7. What is our actual size? What does that question mean?
8. Why is frustration *not* a feeling?
9. How do people respond when they are given approval?
10. What are the three types of conflict listed and described in this chapter?
11. What is one advantage of fear? What is a related disadvantage of anxiety?
12. What is meant by a "committee of two"?

8
DEFENDING BEHAVIORS

Roger Heyns (1958), in commenting upon defending behaviors, said psychologists have not always agreed on the names and definitions for each mechanism or technique of adjustment. There is, however, a common agreement that these defending behaviors are learned responses designed to satisfy psychological needs.

Defending behaviors satisfy the individual because they reduce a feeling of tension. They also satisfy because their use can result in a subjective sense of (1) having maintained reputation and self-esteem at a familiar and unchanged level, (2) having enhanced reputation and self-esteem, and (3) having provided the framework within which self-actualization may take place. It should be noted that the defending behaviors which provide a framework for the development of self-actualization are few. They appear at the end of this chapter.

Defending behaviors seem to be almost a requirement for survival in our society, for we are constantly faced with real or potential frustration and conflict. In addition, there is the matter of change versus stability; we are often not where we want to be, doing things we would rather not

do, looking back to a yesterday that seemed better than today or looking forward to a tomorrow that may—hopefully for some—be better or—hopefully for others—worse than the frustrating and conflict-loaded today. In direct contrast, we can be exactly where we want to be, doing precisely what we wish to do, but knowing that in an hour or a day the pleasures of the moment will fade and we will once again meet with frustration and conflict.

Frustration and conflict seem so much a part of our environment and so much a part of ourselves—our psychological selves —as to be inescapable. We do, however, escape. We withdraw, and we compromise in our efforts to somehow defend against these incessant psychological companions. And they are incessant, for without them we would live in some different environment we could call utopia or nirvana or heaven.

AGGRESSIVE DEFENDING
There are often long moments in the histories of groups and individuals when the most apparently available means of defense is attack. Defensive attack may be

a consciously planned effort. The consciously planned defensive attack takes three forms.

1. **Momentary or intermittent attack.** A simplified example of this form of defense can be seen in the football blitz. The defending linemen rush the opposing quarterback, often with a nearly murderous intent. The defending team will not usually rush the quarterback on every play; they may do so only intermittently, alternating the rush with other defensive plays.

2. **Repeated attack.** Slightly more than a hundred years ago, U. S. citizens and soldiers had crowded American Plains Indians off much of their land. According to Dee Brown's description (1970) the Indians' attempts at living a familiar and peaceful life had been frustrated. To counter the frustrations, they attacked forts, wagon trains, and white settlements along the Powder River and the Bozeman Trail in Wyoming and Montana. The repeated attacks were temporarily successful; they amounted to a series of defensive and bloody confrontations called Red Cloud's War.

3. **Protracted attack.** The protracted attack consists of a system of interrelated tactics used over an extended period of time (1) to preserve and defend whatever it is one has —beliefs, property, perhaps certain freedoms or rights, styles of living—and (2) to take from others what are viewed as the essentials. According to Alinsky (1971) and to some degree according to Mao Tse-Tung (1952) the protracted attack is not designed to annihilate the foe, the agents of frustration, so much as it is to prevent the enemy from destroying the defender. The protracted attack is a long-term defense. The purpose is not to win but to keep from losing.

While these three forms of defensive attack are conscious and purposeful, usually planned and at least roughly calculated, the psychological defending behavior we can label as aggression seems merely purposeful, although that purpose is not generally a conscious one.

Aggression labels an attack upon the object, the circumstance, or the individual—including the self—causing the frustration. Aggression can involve name-calling, slander, gossiping, and physical attack. Aggression can also involve varieties of sabotage, such as letting the air out of the tires on the car belonging to the teacher who gives only low grades and who behaves in an imperious way in the classroom. The central feature of aggression, when it is viewed as an aspect of defending behavior, is that it does not really solve the problem of frustration. The source of frustration remains, however, and the individual may sense again the gradual rise of tensions that, in time, will be expressed by the kinds of aggression he typically uses.

The varieties of aggression are almost endless. What a person may do by way of aggression may be often consistent. Here are three examples:

1.

The little boy has a mother who is orderly, neat, demanding, and filled with rules the little boy must obey. If he does not comply and conform, the penalties are high. Once and often twice a week the little boy sits on the edge of a bed, alone, holding a pillow tightly against his face. He screams into the pillow. He screams for five or six minutes or however long it takes for the tension to drain out of him.

2.

The young woman falls off a ladder and injures her spine. She is paralyzed from the waist down. She watches other people walk and run as she sits in her wheelchair. Every three or four weeks she rages against her paralyzed legs, crying and stabbing her thighs with a pencil or a ball-point pen. When her parents see her stabbing her legs with a small kitchen knife, they begin to think about taking her to a mental health clinic.

3.

The middle-aged man is the chairman of the biology department at a large university. His work consists of some teaching, which he loves, and many administrative tasks, which he hates. He must attend lengthy and tedious meetings, plan courses, talk with problem students, act as a father and comforter to young faculty members, and write reviews of new textbooks. He feels that much of what he does is frustrating, seemingly endless and unrewarding. Before he leaves his office on Friday afternoon, he quietly closes and locks the door, sits down at his desk, and rips a book apart, page by page, with his bare hands. He puts the the torn pages into his briefcase and takes them home where he puts them in the garbage.

The little boy cannot do much about his mother's ways. The crippled young lady cannot be uncrippled, and the middle-aged department head believes he is trapped in activities that frustrate him and from which he believes he cannot escape. Each drains away the tensions brought about by frustrations. None of them, however, does anything about the frustrations themselves. Each has found a temporary way out, a transitory release, a learned technique for psychologically adjusting, even though that adjustment is only for a brief period of time.

A human behavior related to but not identical to aggression can be found in the aggressive defense called *displacement.* Displacement is the main topic of this fictional sales pitch.

"Hello, there. Got a minute? I want to tell

Marion Bernstein/Editorial Photocolor Archives

you about a new corporation. I'm selling the stock for the Little Yellow Dog Corporation. Maybe you'll buy some.

"The Little Yellow Dog Corporation is a profit-making venture designed for the busy businessman. The basic product is a little yellow dog, a live dog. We expect to sell the dogs for ten dollars each, and the buyer gets a free choke chain and an iron stake.

"The customer puts the choke chain around the dog's neck and bolts the other end of the chain to the top of the iron stake. Then he takes the dog out in his back yard. He hammers the stake into the lawn, and the little yellow dog stays right there, chained to that stake.

"Now, when the man comes home from a hard day's work, he gets out of the car as usual, but he does not go inside his house right away. Instead, he goes out in the backyard, and he walks right up to that little yellow dog and kicks him. He kicks him five or ten times, real hard. Got the picture? *Then* he goes inside the house, all relieved because he got rid of those bad feelings he picked up at work. He goes inside, but now he does not have to yell at the wife like he used to.

"Want to buy some of that stock? We're gonna sell a lotta dogs."

The Little Yellow Dog Corporation is imaginary and cruel, but it helps to describe what is called displacement.

Displacement is extraordinarily common in this society. It is supposedly a move toward a safer expression of feelings. In the example of the little yellow dog, angry feelings were displaced from the wife or the job to the animal chained to a stake in the backyard. Other examples: it is safer to throw rocks at a cat than to fight with a peer. It is safer for a woman to punish her children than to get in an argument with the policemen who has just given her a traffic ticket.

Displacement of feelings is common. Displacement of a burdening conscience is also common. There are large numbers of people who have overcivilized, burdensome consciences, and they are loaded with regulations about what is proper or right or correct. They may often try to

displace a portion of their heavy consciences as they say "You shouldn't do that," or "Do you think that's all right to do?" when the person they are talking to is, or appears to them to be, involved in some minor infraction of etiquette.

There are times when the process of displacement takes years to unroll. For instance, a girl may grow up in a home where the father is autocratic and hostile, but not to a degree that crushes initiative out of the child. She is unable to fight back, but her anger is stored away for later use. The child grows up, gets married, and gradually develops intense feelings of anger for her father-in-law. She argues with him and criticizes him, acting out against the father-in-law the feelings she was unable to act out against her own father.

Displacement may show itself in environments vastly different from the original setting, the setting in which the displaced feelings were first collected. An example of this takes us back a chapter to Bob, the medical corpsman in Vietnam who killed the old farmer (Lumsden, 1972). Bob was seen by Herman P. Langner, a Navy psychiatrist. One of the findings about Bob's behavior that came to the surface was his displacement.

In Bob's case there were personal influences molding his violent actions. As a farmer's son he had worked obediently in the fields, pushing down resentment that he couldn't go out for sports or hang out with friends. Dr. Langner speculates that killing the old farmer was, for Bob, an act of rebellion that he never expressed as a boy. [p. 42]

There are differences between defensive aggression and displacement. In defensive aggression the individual may be aware of the agents of frustration; in displacement, he is not. In defensive aggression the frustrating agents may be the targets of the expressed feelings—often, but not always —while in displacement the frustrating objects, circumstances, or people are never the targets of the displaced feelings.

Something or someone else is. In addition, defensive aggression is involved with the sensing and usually the expression of some variation of anger. In displacement, the emotion is often anger, but under some circumstances it may be affection.

Displaced affection can be seen in the behavior of an individual who, for example, is highly cautious and circumspect in relationships with most other humans. He may be generally well mannered but aloof and distant while interacting with people he has known for some time, whether these people are in a superior, peer, or subordinate position. Yet, the individual may show warmth and affection to one or two people at a time, people who are newcomers to his life. Once they are no longer newcomers, he may evolve to his more typical style of aloof interaction with them. Such an individual may be more bewildering than unpleasant.

To continue the example: if the person is cautious and aloof with humans and expresses some form of caring and affection for a pet, the direction of the expression is downward, to a target that is less than human. In such instances the feelings exist and are expressed by way of an aggressive defending behavior called substitution.

Substitution may be as safety seeking as displacement. Gilbert Rogin (1965) has provided us with an example of a man who sought interpersonal safety by way of substitution. These words are from his short story, "Hello! Goodbye! I Love You!"

When my wife left me, I bought a bird for company. I chose a bird over other creatures because I didn't want something around to which in time I would become devoted; it has been my experience that most pets fall mysteriously ill, become melancholy and droop or pine or, inexplicably, run, crawl or fly away. Besides, my anticipated life span is half over, and I will undoubtedly survive any small animal except for tortoises, parrots or carp, which are almost everlasting, but toward the end more monument than flesh. There are enough claims made upon me without having to endure these unnecessary impositions of love and death. [p. 117]

The character in Rogin's story clearly tells us he is seeking interpersonal and perhaps intrapersonal safety by choosing to relate to a pet. Substitution of a lateral sort exists when a person stops smoking and then gains weight rapidly. (In smoking and eating, there is much oral activity.) Substitution exists for the woman who, having raised all her children, goes to work as a grade school teacher. As a teacher, she might provide her students with the opportunity for identification.

Identification is the behavior involved in taking on the admired attributes of another person; identification also involves the feeling, the sense, of having some of the more admired characteristics of another person or group of others. Depending upon what we believe in, what our personal and individual values may be, and the specific facets of our strivings for self-esteem, reputation, and self-actualization, we may identify with skilled lawyers, well-known criminals, millionaires, poets, learned scholars, or tree surgeons. Identification can provide an individual with a greater sense—however fragile—of self-esteem, and the individual may believe his own reputation is enhanced. When the admired basketball team wins the big game, the statement is often "We won!" even if the maker of the statement was merely a spectator.

Identification is a factor of behavior that can be seen at the end of the childhood stage and during the school age years (Maier, 1965). As the third stage of behavior comes gradually to a close, the girl represses her sexual feelings for her father and moves into an alliance with mother. The boy represses what he has felt about mother and begins to have a closer and less competitive relationship with his father.

Generally the girl identifies with her mother, and the boy with his father. If the child does not identify, at least to some extent, with the parent of the same sex, he may have some difficulties during adolescence and in adulthood. For instance, if a girl identifies closely with her father, she may be so masculine when she is an adult that most men will be repelled or frightened by her. She may, however, build a relationship with a man who, in his youth, identified with his mother. The result is a paring off of a masculine woman and a feminine man. This sort of pairing, which involves sexual role reversal, is not rare.

In this matter of identification there is an element of unreality that, in this society, seems to be based upon a need to make the world more sensible, more predictable, more orderly. Girls *do* identify with mothers, and boys *do* identify with fathers, but cross-identification also takes place, to a great and compelling degree. The result is a blend in the person, a merging of some characteristics of father and of mother.

At the core of defensive identification is what is sometimes referred to as identification with the aggressor (Hoffman, 1968). Identification with the aggressor can be seen in the behavior of a child who is treated harshly by a parent but who, fearful of even more harshness if he rebels, avoids conflict with the parent and seeks approval by taking on the characteristics and the viewpoints of that parent. There is, it seems, an element of internalization in this sequence. The child may internalize the views the parent has about him and treat himself harshly (self-persecution) in a number of ways. However, he may have identified with the aggressor parent to such a degree that he treats most other people as harshly or as punitively as he himself has been treated. By the process of identification, he learns how to be; the behavior becomes a part of his reality.

Another aspect of identification relates to the development of conscience, and it is called *developmental* or *anaclitic identification* (Hoffman, 1968). It is based upon the child's fearfulness over the loss or potential loss of a parent's love. To defend against the fearfulness and to assure himself of parental affection the child will work with diligence to become like the parent, imitating the parent and becoming in time a near carbon copy. An example of extreme identification may be seen in *folie à deux;* the term is French for "the folly of two." An example can be seen in the relationship between two people, one of whom is psychotic and who is the aggressor in the relationship. The other individual is not psychotic at first, but through identification he becomes so.

Another commonly used aggressive defensive maneuver is called projection. *Projection* typically involves a transfer of blame, a disowning of a characteristic or behavior. The usual mode is to put one's own unwanted feelings onto another person. Sometimes an angry person, who may be almost totally unaware of the anger residing within him, may believe someone else feels angry. (This is a central feature of paranoia.) Disowning projection can also be witnessed in connection with feelings other than anger. Here are two examples:

1.
He works in an office. The secretary is a lovely brunette, and he likes to watch her get up out of her chair and walk down the hall. The bookkeeper is another brunette with a body encased in clothing that is either short or tight or both. At noon he eats lunch in a small cafe, and the blonde waitress has on a filmy-foamy blouse. When his afternoon is finished, he drives home, watching for female pedestrians. When he gets home, his wife greets him at the door. She is friendly, but he looks carefully at her and asks, "Hey, how come you're so nice? You been playin' around with somebody?"

2.
She is a student in a large university. She takes a course in modern dance and finds herself fascinated by another student who is also female. She watches the other student during exercise sessions and while they learn

dance movements. She intently watches the other student in the locker room and in the dormitory lounge, and then she discovers the other student looking back, watching *her*. She whispers to a friend, "Watch out for that one. I'll bet she's a lesbian."

The man in the first situation was loaded with daydreams, and perhaps fantasies, at the office, in the small cafe, and as he drove home from work. It is possible to assume the daydreams were sexual and that he felt guilty about them. He disowned the daydreams by projecting them onto his wife. He could then worry about her activities rather than his own troubling and unsatisfied daydreams.

The student in the second situation probably had what amounts to a widely felt concern. She was probably concerned about her own homosexual feelings, but she disowned them and projected them onto the other student. She could then be worried or feel hostile toward that other student, perhaps feeling some relief because she no longer owned her own feelings on the subject.

Perhaps one of the most overlooked aggressive defenses is called sympathism. Eric Berne (1964) calls this the "ain't it awful?" game. In *sympathism* the individual works with diligence, an unconscious diligence, to gain the sympathy of others. Sympathy is a form of recognition, and sympathetic recognition can help to boost an individual's sense of self-esteem, sometimes improve his reputation, but rarely foster the development of self-actualization.

Sympathism may develop out of chronically self-defeating behavior, for in making use of sympathism the individual typically tries to maintain a sense of self-worth after having failed. It is an unconscious attempt at trying to salvage something good out of something bad. Anyone involved with the use of sympathism will seek suffering, make mistakes, allow themselves to be taken advantage of, or fail in some other

way so they can describe their blighted life to someone else who will then give them sympathy. There are times, however, when the individual gains not sympathy but rejection (Lerner, 1971), and if rejection follows failure, the person may be deeply frustrated in his attempts to adjust, to cope.

Another example of aggressive defensiveness can be seen in *trivialization.* It is essentially an effort to make great things trivial and unimportant or harmless. It is a way of equalizing or minimizing. For instance, a man involved in a conversation about Albert Einstein, one of the great minds of this century, may dismiss Einstein's unusual intellectual gifts with the comment, "Oh, well, he put his pants on one leg at a time just like I do." Or a woman may say of her husband who is world renowned for his expert and artistic photography, "He's just like anybody else. He's an ordinary guy. That's all." On a larger scale, trivialization may take the form of dismissing the vast multitudes of poor and starving peasants of India with a shrug of the shoulder, a wave of the hand, or a comment such as, "It's always been that way."

Trivialization may take place over many years, perhaps especially when the thing made trivial is monstrous. Take, for instance, one of the major events of the twentieth century, World War II. No one knows how many people were killed in that conflict, but estimates of military and civilian deaths run as high as thirty million. Countless and other unknown millions were injured, wounded, starved, imprisoned, and otherwise afflicted, yet the classic war story of that bloody epoch is a wild and hilarious book titled *Catch-22* (Algren, 1973). On a parallel track the situation comedy known as "Hogan's Heroes" trivializes life in a prisoner of war camp. In thirty years, trivialization has, it seems, reduced a great and world wide tragedy to popular comedy.

Stefan Kanfer (1973) has traced the sequence of trivialization of a European nobleman and his deeds. Five hundred years ago the nobleman, a count, ordered and authorized the killing of twenty percent of the population of his small realm's half a million people. His favorite method of dispatching people was to impale them. From time to time he would dine in the presence of his victims' dead bodies. He himself was killed in 1476, but he became a grisly legend and the basis for a novel published in 1897. In 1930 the count showed up in the movies portrayed by Bela Lugosi. Within recent years a child's breakfast food was devised and given a faintly disguised name that goes back to the actual, evil person who lived 500 years ago. The name of the breakfast food is Count Chocula.

A somewhat related defensive tactic, perhaps more subtle than trivialization, is *discounting.* While trivialization is meant to minimize and make harmless the greatly evil or greatly beneficial, discounting involves exclusion. Anything outside the individual, in the environment, can be excluded. When environmental matters are excluded, the excluder—the person who discounts—believes or at least acts as though he believes he is of more importance or of more significance than whatever or whomever has been excluded.

According to Aaron and Jacqui Schiff (1971) there are four possible ways to discount:

1. *Discount the problem.* Example: a boy is failing in most of his third grade classes at school. Neither of his parents asks any questions or calls the school or urges him to do some homework. Instead, they may all watch television together.

2. *Discount the significance of the problem.* Example: a boy is failing in most of his third grade classes. One parent or the other says, "He's always gotten poor grades," and goes on to think of other things.

3. *Discount the solvability of the problem.* Example: a boy is failing in most of his classes at school. A parent says, "There's nothing we can do."

4. *Discount the person.* Example: a boy is failing in most of his classes at school. A parent says, "He's so much trouble. I've tried my best but, after all, it's his problem."

To be on the receiving end of either trivialization or discounting can be like being on the receiving end of rape.

DEFENSIVE FLIGHT

We are all escape artists. We all have a capability to avoid, to flee, to run away from, or to simply ignore what we do not like. One of the factors of living we do not seem to like very well is uncertainty.

If we are uncertain, we can and often do invent answers to explain behavior and to relieve the tensions of ignorance. We can explain away the varieties of the human condition by using whatever happens to be handy at the moment. Some of the phrases are familiar. We can say to children that "education is the best investment in the world," but if they use that education in a disagreement with us, we can say, "experience is the best teacher." If someone moves away and we miss them, we may claim that "absence makes the heart grow fonder," but if we do not regret their leaving, we may state, "out of sight, out of mind." The old saying "birds of a feather flock together" is sometimes useful, but so is "opposites attract." The invented reason, the manufactured answer, can bring temporary relief from the aches we get from living in a world in which few things are absolutely certain. We can be uncertain about our own behavior, unclear in our own minds why we have done what we have done, but we can defend against the uncertainty by way of what is called rationalization. The following description of *rationalization* was given on a previous page but was not identified as such: "There are times when we sense an obligation to give reasons for what we do. When we explain our actions, our behaviors, to another person, we will sometimes be accurate, on target, living examples of precision and clarity. At other times we may be inaccurate, evasive, and what we say may be shrouded in a cloud of ambiguity—and all these are possible without realizing it at the moment.

"When we give reasons for what we do, we may range from the highly precise to the incredibly obscure. We may also range from the totally honest to the totally dishonest. In most instances, though, when we try to explain ourselves to another person, we try to make sense; we try to be believable."

We work at being believable, credible, sincere when we try to explain to others and to ourselves. The essential ingredient of rationalization is the attempt to make sense or to appear to make sense out of what we do in an effort to earn social and intrapersonal approval, especially if what we have done has been irrational or neurotic in a transitory way. Rationalization is an attempt to make ourselves look better to ourselves and to other people. If the individual feels it is inappropriate to "look better," he may rationalize a behavior in the other direction; that is, he may try to make it look worse than it really was. An individual may have done something creative and self-fulfilling, but when he describes what he has done to someone else, he may report it as an episode of irrational or neurotic behavior. Perhaps he may say his success was a matter of luck, although the "luck" was based on great effort and considerable sweat.

A somewhat related escape technique used in defensive flight is called intellectualizing. *Intellectualizing* involves an escape from frustration or conflict—or expected frustration and conflict—by making use of inappropriately complicated thoughts, which are often expressed in words. For example, a man can say to a woman, "I love you," or he can say something almost equivalent, such as, "You're very important to me," or he can say, "I perceive you in a positive manner," or "Whenever you exist in my conscious awareness, I feel the presence of a positive transference combined with highly libidinal ideation." The last two statements are intellectualized versions of the first two.

It is not so much the big words that make the last two responses intellectualized. It is their indirectness, their evasion of the supposed intimacy that exists. For an added example: "How do you feel about Jane?" "I think she's nice." The answer does not answer. In this common type of interchange the question is about feelings, but the answer is about thinking. How humans think and how they feel are two different sectors of behavior. Cognitive, thinking behavior is not typically the same as affectual, emotional behavior.

If you would care to explore some further reaches of intellectualizing behavior, invent a question and ask a series of individuals that question. Sooner or later someone will respond with an intellectualized answer. To illustrate the point, here is a question: "What would be the first thing you'd say to a peaceful creature from outer space?" Here are a few possible responses:

Person A: "Hello."

Person B: "Goodbye."

Person C: "Let's talk."

Person D: "What do we humans look like to you? I mean, what kind of beings do we seem to be?"

Person E: "Well, the first goal is to find some way to communicate. It is my opinion a computer code, a binary code maybe, would work. The code could be transmitted on a broad spectrum with a geometric increase in signal strength in order to . . ."

The last response (Person E), besides not answering the question, indicates a flight, a withdrawal, an intellectualized but perhaps only temporary escape from the question.

If you were to conduct a rough exploration of intellectualization by asking a question and recording the answers, perhaps you might feel some sense of superiority over the people who responded. This may be especially the case when an individual gave an obviously intellectualized response. A mild sense of superiority is, of course, understandable, and it might illustrate another form of defensive flight. It might indicate reaction formation.

According to Veroff and Veroff (1972) an individual may strive for a sense of superiority, may spend energy in trying to capture a sense of influence or control over others because of an often unconscious fear of his own weakness or powerlessness. This effort is an example of reaction formation. *Reaction formation* is an adjustment or an attempted adjustment to fears, desires, hopes, and attitudes the individual views as dangerous or unwanted in some way or other. He may feel or think the expression of the fears or desires might lead to great frustration or conflict. Instead of expressing the actual fears or desires, the individual will express the opposite. A person, for example, may unconsciously feel his fears and desires are evil, but consciously he may think they are good and behave toward others in a saintly way. A woman may feel ugly, yet she may behave in ways that suggest she thinks of herself as beautiful. A man may feel he is basically a stupid person, but that feeling is not easily tolerated, and to avoid the feeling, he works with considerable effort to show other people how educated and erudite he is. This may include an unknown number of textbook authors.

There are times when reaction formation evolves slowly, over the years. A boy may be an absolute antisocial terror in his childhood years and on into high school. As time progresses, he may gradually change to become the opposite sort of individual, at least superficially. The urge to be antisocial and wildly adventurous is still there, but as a man he may become a prudent lawyer who eventually becomes a judge. In contrast with the evolution of a life-style based on reaction formation, we can witness the seemingly instant conversion of an alcoholic derelict into a fanatically religious prohibitionist. The examples can be found almost daily, examples in which the individual functions in ways opposite to what lives in his unconscious.

What lives in the unconscious can be and often is what is intolerable to the individual. What is intolerable can vary from one person to the next. Mothers who feel homicidal toward their children may act in incredibly overprotective ways toward them. The thoughtful and meditative guru of a commune may really prefer to live the life of a wild libertine, moving from one sexual orgy to the next in a thoughtless and uninhibited way. The extraordinarily cooperative, good little girl might really want to run away from home.

Reaction formation will sometimes be confused with negativistic behavior. Negativistic activities are, however, conscious, purposeful, often loaded with anger, and designed to preserve and enhance one's own sense of apartness from others. For instance, in families that impose many rules, in families filled with regulations, the child may react in negativistic ways. While internalization and identification with the aggressor are perhaps more common, both involve an unconscious acceptance; negativism is a consciously acted out behavior running in the opposite direction.

A light flavoring of reaction formation exists in the mechanism called *undoing*. We all must contend with the savage and the civilized portions of ourselves. We must somehow keep a balance between the two by integrating the wild with the calm, the hot with the cool. Sometimes we slip slightly, a bit of the savage shows itself, and we can experience a sense of disapproval. When that happens, we will often apologize in one fashion or another. Many of us learn to apologize at an early age. An apology can be made with words, with gestures, with actions of one sort or another; apologies are a form of undoing a mistake, of making amends for some disapproved thought or act. Within the sequence of undoing, there is an element of self-accusation. The individual who excuses himself or tries to undo may be accusing himself of whatever he has done; the disapproval may have come from the conscience, not from another person.

Another common, probably universal, and sometimes dramatic strategy of defensive retreat is called *regression*. Allan, the fireman-student, regressed in his panic. He ran from the classroom in the back of the firehouse, jumped aboard the fire truck, and roared out of town seeking the comfort of the familiar countryside. He moved with speed from one setting to another, from a stressful setting to one that had meant peace to him during earlier years. In trying to cope with an imagined assault on his reputation (the woman pointing at him and telling everyone what he did), he *regressed* to an earlier and, for him, a more satisfying sort of behavior.

There are other examples of regression. The parent who does not get his way with his own children may regress and give a demonstration of a temper tantrum that can sometimes be viewed as appropriate behavior during the childhood years. The self-sufficient female college student who acts—unwittingly—like a little girl on a date is probably regressing. The regressing person tries to escape from a present-time stress by moving back along the time line to an earlier level of behavior. It is common for individuals who become physically ill and who are hospitalized for that illness to regress (Peplau, 1952), sometimes to a

level that challenges the patience of nurses and physicians who have been trained and who often have years of experience with regression in patients.

Many people regress when they are afraid. Sales (1972) has provided an example of regression involving the majority of the people of Germany. Following World War I the German people were in great difficulties, partially because they had just lost a long and costly war. Their country was in great economic trouble with runaway inflation and high unemployment, and there was strife and confusion in the government. The average German citizen, it seems, was fearful of what the next set of troubles might be. That fearfulness apparently helped to develop a need for a harsh, substitute "parent" who appeared to be able to take care of all the problems. That "parent" was Adolph Hitler who was given a headship position and who was accepted as a leader by most of the citizens of that country.

While individuals and groups may regress during times of crises, they may also become involved in what is known as denial of reality. *Denial of reality* protects against what are thought to be unpleasant realities. The unpleasant realities of the consequences of global pollution, potential warfare, and overpopulation and crowding in our cities can be denied in a variety of ways. So can the unpleasant realities of everyday life. A parent with a child who is acutely mentally ill can say, "Oh, she's just going through another phase of growing up." Any person who smokes a great many cigarettes a day can joke away the disease potential by talking about getting a lung transplant. Worries about tomorrow's final exam can be temporarily swept away by drinking a lot of beer, and the troubled corporate executive may take off on a vacation as his company gradually goes bankrupt.

The essence of denial of reality is escapism. Escapism may be found in daydreams and fantasies. If reality is so assaultive to the self, so frustrating, and so seemingly insurmountable, the individual may withdraw from any problem-solving contemplation of that reality and slide into a world of his or her own making, the world of daydreams and fantasies, a separate kind of reality.

Daydreams and fantasies, briefly touched upon in Chapter 6 and in the description of adolescent behavior, can involve fantastic and temporarily pleasant journeys of the mind. When we daydream, as we conjure fantasies, we can be anything, do anything, go anywhere. But then we must, if we still can, return to the world as it is more commonly known, a world of pleasant and unpleasant circumstances. Daydreams can provide a pleasurable rest stop, a pleasing side trip or excursion away from dreary routine, unsatisfying days, empty weeks. Fantasies may bring periods of pleasantness too, but as mentioned before, fantasies are not so easily turned off. They may occupy the thoughts of the individual more than is wanted, but they remain, nevertheless, escapes.

Daydreams and fantasies, even though they may be escapes, can be considered as useful and productive if they lead to some form of creative self-expression. The poet, the sculptor, many architects and theoretical mathematicans, as well as cabinetmakers, quarterbacks, chess players, and inventors, depend upon controlled or goal-oriented daydreams and fantasies. Perhaps these people and many other kinds of artists and craftsmen escape unpleasant realities in at least a temporarily productive way.

Another facet or technique of defensive flight can be seen in behavior labeled emotional insulation. *Emotional insulation* is an attempt at adjustment in which the individual withdraws into passivity. The primary purpose of the passiveness is to protect against hurt, to safeguard the self from psychological pain. The individual may detach himself emotionally from the realities of a painful, to him, situation or circumstance and drift passively, perhaps hoping that someday something nice will happen. It rarely does, for the individual who overuses emotional insulation may be safe from the psychological pains, but he is usually unable to feel the psychological pleasures of life.

DEFENSIVE COMPROMISE

We continually must face an ancient and frustrating circumstance, a circumstance that for some promotes the growth of what can be called "psychological strength." For others, that same circumstance proves to be catastrophic. The circumstance: we do not get from ourselves or from our environment all we need or all we want. The result is frustration. Whether it is personal or environmental or conflict frustration, it is essentially unending and inevitably inescapable. We do escape, however, at least temporarily. We withdraw and attack; we attack and withdraw. The activity helps keep us awake on dull days.

If it were possible to construct a totally benevolent, absolutely satisfying, supremely untroubled environment for an infant, that infant would remain an infant until he withered and died of old age. If an adult were placed in such an environment, he or she would regress, perhaps swiftly, to an infantile level of behavior. In effect, environments that provide everything and anything do not call into action the resources a person may have; there is no challenge to overcome, no measure of success or failure. Psychological development and growth become unnecessary and, in the end, impossible.

In contrast with the totally benevolent environment is the world as we commonly know it. While that world is not totally hostile, the birth of a new human is rarely greeted with the sound of trumpets. Red carpets do not unroll. There are no welcoming committees, no dignitaries to award medals for surviving the trip through the birth canal, no presentations of the keys to the city and no parades. There is instead an environment with people in it, some of whom wonder what the infant will do when he grows up. The infant may grow to spend his peak years in a mental hospital, a prison, on a ranch, in the White House, or in a ghetto. The infant may become a surgeon or a spy, a thief or a chief of police, a locksmith or a dock worker. Whatever the outcome, the infant will have to do something, and whatever he does will be touched by technology.

Before the infant can grow *to be,* he must learn how *to do,* though the doing may seem to compromise the being, even in what many consider the most personal of activities. Rollo May (1969) has discussed the idea of "the sexual technician," a label that could not have been invented in a society that did not have a large component of technology in it. Gadpaille (1972) has reviewed and written about the technological messages contained in eighteen books designed to be instructive about sexual behavior. For the most part these "how-to" books concentrate on what to do, not how to be. Yet, it is the how-to-do aspects of life that form the basis of how to be. We must, in this society, learn how to talk, how to read and write, and how to operate machines and tools before we can begin to "be." The machines and the tools we learn to operate are often obvious: cars, trucks, typewriters, television sets, vacuum sweepers. Some are so common they are not viewed as the tools and machines they in fact are: spoons, cups, forks, doorknobs, faucets, pencils, can openers.

We must learn the how to do of making a speech before we can be a speechmaker, and we must learn how to function in sexual activities before we can be a sexual partner. To do comes before to be, as surely as an infant's crawling comes before a child's walking.

Robert Coles (1971) has expressed the idea that the doing of work can overshadow and obliterate a positive sense of being. He reported the work of Simone Weil, a French woman, "a serious and scholarly French lady," who worked as a worker not as an observer in factories and on farms. What she discovered in France is what Coles has seen in America. He writes:

> Working people with whom I have talked make quite clear the ways they feel cornered, trapped, lonely, pushed around at work, and, as Simone Weil kept on emphasizing, confused by a sense of meaninglessness. These feelings, I have noticed, often take the form of questions—and I will take the liberty of paraphrasing some of them that I have heard: What am I doing that *really matters?* What is the point to it all—not life, as some philosophers say, but the specific, tangible things I do or make? What would I do if I had a real choice—something which I doubt I ever will have? Is there some other, some better way to work? Might we not break up these large factories and offices, work closer to our homes, closer to one another as workers—and work together on something that is not a fragment of this, a minor part of that, but is whole and significant and recognizable as important in our lives? [p. 104]

Anyone who has worked in a factory knows what Coles is saying. Even with a high degree of technology and in spite of the skilled use of automation, which reduces the physical demands of work, the psychological cost of much we call work often remains high. The sense of powerlessness exists. The tedium is often incredible, whether the person works in a factory that makes suitcases, television sets, automobiles, hiking boots, plastic bottles, cookies and crackers, or frozen meals for people to thaw and eat. It is not much different for bank tellers, typists, file clerks, office machine operators, and many nurses. Nor does the sense of powerlessness or meaninglessness and the tedium seem to be absent in our schools (Illich, 1970).

The sense of helplessness, of meaninglessness, the tedium of work and schooling can be found in the home. Not long ago it was common for people to state that a man's home was his castle. More frequently now it has been described as his and his wife's prison (Greer, 1971), a location in which neurotic interactions take place (Aldridge, 1969) and one of the sources of the increase in mental illness (Buhler, 1971).

There are those who survey the scene, see what is happening around them at work, in the schools, and in the homes of this land, and conclude—as Keniston (1968) has—that our time, our era, is marked by the development of an increasing psychological distance between people; an insulation—an emotional insulation—exists between individuals in this society. He also states that great numbers of individuals sense an increase in personal and social disorganization, a rise in the degree of meaninglessness and incoherence in the lives they lead. Keniston has, it appears, named these behaviors as the responses many among us make to the present crisis of change. And yet, in the midst of tech-

From Wagner, N. N., and Haug, M. J.: Chicanos: social and psychological perspectives, St. Louis, 1971, The C. V. Mosby Co.

nologically based change, there are opportunities. Some of the opportunities involve the potential uses of defensive compromise. That opportunities exist is based upon the idea that *the principal activity of defensive compromise is the attempt to contend with the variety and the effects of frustration in ways that lead to the reasonably consistent fulfillment of psychological needs.*

The psychological needs for social interaction, the needs related to reputation, self-esteem, and self-actualization, may be met most effectively by a conscious, purposeful, and—most centrally—a skillful use of defensive strategies based upon compromise. The compromise may be with oneself. It may involve oneself and the environment, and it may involve matters relating to conflict.

Compensation is one form of defensive compromise. Compensatory behavior has great variety. Here are some examples that take into account members of the same family:

1.

He was 45 years old, a large, restless man who worked as a truck driver. He was gone from home most of the time, hauling freight across the state—often driving fifteen hours without a real rest—on into the neighboring states, 700 miles a day. When he stopped for fuel, he would sit in noisy roadside cafés slowly drinking a cup of coffee or a glass of beer, wondering what his wife was doing at that moment. Once in a while, he would meet a woman who happened to live near whatever truck stop he was in, and the woman would invite him to her place for a quick visit. None of the visits lasted more than fifteen minutes, and they usually cost him twenty dollars. After each visit, he would climb up into the cab of his truck and start the motor, telling himself twenty dollars wasn't too much for a little recreation, a little companionship.

2.

Her husband had been a truck driver for ten years, and she still wished he could spend more time at home. He made good money

hauling freight, though, and they had some nice things in the house. Still, she was bored most of the time she spent at home. A couple of years ago she started bowling, and now she got away from the house three evenings a week. She was on a team, bowling with other women, all of whom were close to her in age. She liked the other women. She could joke with them and laugh, and that, she thought, was a lot better than sitting around watching television. She was glad her daughter was old enough now to take care of herself, but she wondered why Cindy was so quiet all the time and so fat. Maybe she was just going through a phase. Kids were like that.

3.

Cindy did not like fifth grade. She thought fourth grade was more fun, and third was better than fourth. She did not like it when her mother went out at night. She did not like it because the house was empty, and whenever her mother went bowling, Cindy turned the television up loud and watched the shows and the movies, eating jam sandwiches and drinking a lot of milk. She always got to bed by 10 o'clock, loaded with food, listening to the television as it blared its sounds down the hallway and into her bedroom. She listened through the news, the weather report, then the sports, and when the man talked about games and scores, she thought about Jack and his basketball. The house was a better place when Jack was there, but he had gone away to college when she had started fourth grade, and he only came back for short visits now. By 10:30, she was asleep.

4.

Jack was almost 7 feet tall, and sometimes he felt like a freak because people were always looking up at him. The height was only good on the basketball floor. The height, though, and his quick movements had gotten him a scholarship. He did not like college all that well, but it was better than a job, and it would help him to make it to the pros. He knew he would not be one of the tallest on the team there, but his playing would be better. He would see to that. He practiced and worked out every day, running and dribbling and shooting baskets. He knew he was getting better every year, getting stronger. Once he made it to the pros, he thought, he would never have to worry about being a truck driver the rest of his life.

In each example there is an element of real or potential failure to be guarded against. Each individual is faced with frustrations linked to failure, and each individual compensates. The compensatory behaviors have variety. The truck driver compensated for his failure to maintain a consistent and perhaps rewarding relationship with his wife. He compensated by quick visits with strange women who charged twenty dollars. His wife, meanwhile, compensated for her own lack of marital companionship by bowling. Their fifth-grade daughter overate to compensate for loneliness. The son, the basketball player, compensated with a future in mind. It seems from the information at hand that the daughter's compensatory behavior is essentially unconscious. It is doubtful she sits down and says to herself, "Well, I'm home alone again, and I'll eat jam sandwiches to get *something* good out of life." The father may not be much more aware of what motivates his behavior. The mother seems to be handling her home-based frustration in a conscious manner, taking care of herself in the immediate circumstance. The son's compensations take into account the future in a planned way. He has, it appears, turned a mild disadvantage, his height, into an advantage to avoid working in a job he thinks he would dislike. Compensation involves making up for a lack of success or satisfaction in one area of living by developing an increased level of satisfaction in another area.

Sublimation is a defensive strategy often confused with compensation. Sublimation is simply the channeling of energies from socially unacceptable activities (individualized savagery?) into activities that are typically more acceptable. For example,

there are some people who would like to be in a rough and bloody fight with another person at least once a week. If they fought that often, however, they might not survive long, or if they survived, they would be in constant difficulty with the law or their families or with society in general. Yet, the need for physical battle remains, and they must somehow satisfy the need. As a way out, some may become sparring partners in a boxer's training camp or physical education instructors known for their toughness and durability. Others may play professional hockey or pro football. Still others may become gymnasts or karate instructors or fencing masters.

Sublimation is not limited to the area of channeling a need for brutal physical activity into a recreation or sport with rules and regulations. Sublimation exists in the man who dreams his way through the adolescent years, thinking of nude women. In adulthood he becomes a skilled and well-known artist who produces oil paintings of nude women. Sublimation is a move "upwards," a more civilized or more productive manner of responding to frustration and conflict than any of the other defensive behaviors.

Sublimation, functioning with what Tiffany and Tiffany (1973) describe as OI and OE, appears to be central to creativity. Creativity, one of the potentials for development mentioned at the beginning of the book, seems to come in three forms. According to the *Carnegie Corporation of New York Quarterly* (1961) the creative person may create for the following reasons:

1. Because what exists within the person, the individual's inner, intrapersonal state can be and is directly expressed in musical compositions, paintings, writings, and sculptures.
2. Because the environment needs or demands a new and useful thing. The thing may be a new gear system, a unique and previously unseen way of teaching arithmetic in second grade,

or a method for communicating effectively with whales.

3. Because what exists within the individual as a potential can be expressed to merge with an environmental need or demand to produce something unique or otherwise special. The merging may result in a new form of architecture, a new style or format of film making, or a different, more efficient, and simpler way of harvesting food from the oceans.

The difficulties of capturing the essentials of creativity have apparently been experienced by Rosner and Abt (1970). They distinguish between the creative experience, the creative process, and the creative product. John Nicholls (1972), however, believes the research in creativity can be viewed from only two vantage points. The first has to do with the creative product, the thing produced. To be the genuine article, the product should be something that can be given a rating on a "creativity scale." There are difficulties here, though, for how can creative productions be rated on a scale when they differ so much? It may be possible, however, to gauge the creativity rating of such disparate items as the invention of the light bulb, the deciphering of the dance of bees, and the composing of a masterful symphony. Nevertheless, if an individual actually produces a creative thing, it seems proof he is a creative individual.

The second vantage point that Nicholls mentions in the research on creativity has to do with the characteristics of the creator. (Donald MacKinnon [1965] has perhaps been the best known researcher in this endeavor.) The results of the research seem, at best, to be of limited value in viewing all humans in general as being potentially creative. In a speculative sense, it may be that most people have as much difficulty in producing an original and useful thing as they have in accepting a high level of psychological freedom in which it is subjectively comfortable to perform at the peak levels of behavioral adequacy.

In closing this chapter, it seems appropriate to consider that creativity, at present, may be best defined by the production of a unique, original, useful thing. It also seems appropriate to consider creativity as one large slice of the more productive and beneficial outcomes of using the compromising behaviors compensation and sublimation. But we should not lose sight of the idea that compensation and sublimation sometimes may be used in counterproductive and perhaps even in destructive ways, if not to society, then to the individual who becomes involved with them in an awkward and unhandy manner.

REVIEW QUESTIONS

1. Count Chocula helps to define a defensive behavior. Which one?
2. Can you give examples of discounting behavior from your own experience?
3. What is the essential ingredient of rationalization?
4. What are some benefits of defensive compromise?
5. Why is projection used?
6. Can you differentiate between substitution and displacement?
7. What is a *folie à deux*?
8. "Ain't it awful?" is an aspect of what defending behavior?
9. How can regression and emotional insulation seem sometimes to be almost the same?
10. Can you differentiate between how to do and how to be?
11. Creativity can be linked most clearly with which defending behavior?
12. What is the Little Yellow Dog Corporation?

9
COLLAPSE

The life of each individual human consists of a sometimes fragile set of interconnecting links between the biological, the social, and the psychological factors of his existence. Biologically, physically, humans are so intricate, so delicately balanced, and compared with many other organisms, so frail, it is something of a wonder there is such a thing as good health. Socially, within the interpersonal network of relationships, the complexities of interactions are so abundant it seems almost odd any human can build a durable relationship with another person. As for the psychological factors, they seem so elusive, so often immeasurable or simply unknown, it is almost mysterious the way people manage to stay glued together. What is not strange or odd is that many among us become unglued, disconnected, emotionally disordered.

This chapter is about that which is not strange—emotional disorders. Although emotional disorders are to be expected, especially in a society and a culture as many faceted as the one in which we live, emotional disorders are not very well understood.

Because of our technology and our science we are in a slightly better position than the Greeks and the Romans of 2,000

years ago. We have an arsenal of chemicals designed to alleviate some factors present in emotional disorders, and we have, spread across the land, a great many community mental health centers, psychiatric hospitals, and student counseling offices. The Greeks and Romans, however, had the same kinds of establishments. They did not have the sophisticated drugs used in present day psychopharmacology (drugs are discussed in Chapter 10), but they did have places where patients could go for rest and reprieve from the clamor of daily living. They had what McNeil (1970) refers to as temples, where emotionally disordered people could receive quiet counseling including dream interpretation. The mental health workers of that era were called temple priests. That era came to a close when the Roman Empire fell apart.

The Middle Ages or the Dark Ages followed, and during that time, people with emotional disorders were viewed as evil, sinful, dangerously different, to be avoided at all costs if possible, and to be penalized for their sins. In some ways, we now find ourselves halfway between the humanitarian practices of the Greeks and the Romans and the incredibly inhumane activities of those who were in power during the Dark Ages. While there are many among us who view emotional disorders with compassion or a desire to understand, others see the seed of Satan in anyone who is "disturbed." No one seems neutral or deeply disinterested in emotional disorders. Everyone, or almost everyone, has a viewpoint about them, and that viewpoint is often unwittingly based upon what Menninger (1966) has called the *king's peace.*

The king's peace has come down to us from more than a dozen lifetimes in our past. It is made up of a small set of rules that may be applied almost anywhere by almost anyone. The rules are as follows:

1. There are certain people, ideas, beliefs, organizations, and social customs that must be treated with respect. (Others may not be.)
2. Certain persons may not be mistreated, injured, or killed. (Others may be.)
3. Certain persons must not be sexual partners, and some methods of sexual gratification must be avoided. (But there are exceptions.)
4. Certain objects belong to a person or an organization, and they may be used only with permission. They may be taken away only with permission. (But again, there are exceptions.)
5. Certain activities, especially in the realm of services, must not be required of employees, servants, or other subordinates. (More exceptions.)

While these rules can be interpreted and applied with some ease by one individual, they are so unclear, two people may find it difficult to agree on what they mean. They are, however, a part of the code of behavior, a part of our culture. If these rules of the king's peace are seriously broken, perhaps repeatedly broken, the rule breaker may be placed in a prison or a psychiatric hospital. Sometimes there is little difference between these two kinds of institutions as they are viewed by the

occupants and as they are often viewed by many members of the larger society.

Acts of violence and crime are often acts of defensive aggression. They are meant to help in personal adjustment. Although active violence and the committing of crimes may temporarily free the person from feelings that result from frustration, they may in the end be self-defeating. Acts of defensive aggression may often be energetic attempts to escape from madness, and there is little room for doubt that much of what we call "mental illness" is a defensive withdrawal from the individual's own wish, often unconscious, to act in violent ways to break the rules of the king's peace (Menninger, 1966).

PSYCHOTIC AND NEUROTIC DISORDERS

A psychotic disorder is a severe form of "mental illness" in which these conditions frequently exist:

1. The individual has great difficulty in functioning adequately in a variety of social behavior settings; interpersonal behavior is often disorganized.
2. Contact with and the awareness of reality *as it is commonly known* is impaired. The psychotic individual has a highly personal sense of reality.
3. The person may believe in things that are obviously not so (delusions) and may see or hear things that are not there (hallucinations).
4. Cognitive behavior may be fragmented and disorganized.
5. The individual may behave in ways that are dangerous to himself or to other people. The dangerous behavior may range from great aggressiveness through extraordinary carelessness.

Psychotic disorders are a tangle of these five and a great many more secondary features. In a very general sense the varieties of psychotic disorder may be condensed to these few:

affective psychoses emotional disorders in which the individual exhibits or displays inappropriate extremes of emotional response, such as mania or depression

paranoid psychoses disorders in which the individual reacts with suspicion and hostility to those around him

schizophrenic psychoses disorders characterized by a general withdrawal from reality and the development of a life composed of fantasies

While these categories may appear clear cut and distinct, they are not that way in real life except, perhaps, for the paranoid psychoses.

A paranoid psychosis is uncommon. The individual generally can speak in an organized and often highly literate way describing his feats or his fates with great fluency. There are two basic forms of this kind of psychosis:

psychotic grandeur a psychosis in which the individual sees himself as supremely gifted or extremely powerful or both. (He may believe himself to be Christ or Moses or Thomas Edison or some other special person.)

psychotic persecution a psychosis in which the individual sees himself as a hunted person, always in danger, perhaps both feared and hated by others because he "knows what the real truth" is or, sometimes, because he has some special talent valuable to the enemy

These improbable delusions may be accompanied by hallucinations of great variety, and often there is an obvious attempt —usually successful—to deny the existence of feelings by the use of projection.

In contrast with the purity and rarity of a paranoid psychotic state, are the ambiguities of the state referred to as schizophrenia. *Schizophrenia* has been viewed for a very long time with what can only be called a careful and intellectualized confusion. It has been the subject of debate for decades, but to define schizophrenia more clearly and thus slow down or halt the debates, O. Spurgeon English (1963) assembled a group of specialists made up of clinical observers, a research team, and psychotherapists. The team met together for weekly two-hour conferences for a period of six years before they could produce a list of characteristics of individuals labeled as schizophrenic. Their list consisted of the following:

1. A schizophrenic individual has his own special and personal ways of communicating with himself and with other people.
2. Usually during childhood or adolescence the individual comes to the decision that it is unnecessary or undesirable or useless to pay attention to the systems of values the society around him believes to be correct or realistic, such as the king's peace.
3. He concludes he can or should withdraw from others to "go it alone."
4. Once he has become involved in his own style of life, the schizophrenic person likes it as well as a normal person likes his own way of life, and he will defend and maintain his own style of living with vigor. (It is an attempt to maintain stability and balance.)
5. The family from which he comes helps to make the schizophrenic style of living acceptable to the schizophrenic individual.
6. To be successfully treated, a schizophrenic person must be moved to a new environment that invalidates his psychotic thinking and psychotic behavior.
7. While it may not be simple, the schizophrenic must learn new ways of living, thinking, doing, and relating before he can recover from the psychosis.
8. While the schizophrenic person will hang on tenaciously to a psychotic way of life, it is possible to demonstrate to him that his methods for finding security through delusions and hallucinations are not as useful as the ways more normal people use to establish a sense of security.

These eight characteristics of the person

labeled as schizophrenic have a strong element of understanding, kindness, and tolerance well beyond what used to exist. Only two and three lifetimes ago, schizophrenic people and other psychotic individuals were put in chains, often locked up, and once in awhile, killed by a village mob because they were thought to be "possessed by the devil," owned by Satan, evil in some unknown and fearful way.

As Davies (1953) said, commenting on persecution:

> The urge to persecute, though always latent, cannot get very far in a country where freedom is loved and human rights are respected. The extent, therefore, to which persecution becomes active and is not rebuked by public opinion is also the extent to which freedom is no longer loved and respect for human rights is languishing. [p.68]

It seems, however, that there is a persecution of schizophrenic people. Probably the most subtle persecution, if in fact that is what it is, is to label individuals with that diagnostic term. The label gives a false sureness about schizophrenia.*It oversimplifies. Schizophrenics may be viewed as people with a "mental illness" or a "mental disease," but as Thomas Szasz (1969) has maintained:

> "Mental illnesses" are thus regarded as basically no different than all other diseases (that is, of the body). The only difference, in this view, between mental and bodily diseases is that the former, affecting the brain, manifest themselves by means of mental symptoms; whereas the latter, affecting other organ systems (for example, the skin, liver, etc.), manifest themselves by means of symptoms referable to those parts of the body. [p. 4]

Although the word itself has been in widespread use for over half a century (Opler, 1957), there is a marked inaccuracy, a severe lack of precision, in its use. As Laing and Esterson (1964) have pointed out:

---

*Peter Koenig (1973) writes that labels in general are more useful to the label makers than to those who are labeled.

No generally agreed objective clinical criteria for the diagnosis "schizophrenia" have been discovered. No consistency in pre-psychotic personality, course, duration, outcome has been discovered. [p. 3]

In spite of the comments quoted above the terms "mental illness" and "schizophrenia" continue to be used widely. The terms have, it seems, a life of their own, affecting the lives of a great many individuals involved with mental health either as workers or patients. To illustrate the power and the misuse of these terms, Rosenhan (1973) conducted a study titled "On being sane in insane places." In his study, Rosenhan assembled a small group of "normals," five men and three women. The youngest was a graduate student in psychology in his twenties. The other seven individuals were older, and among them were three psychologists, a housewife, a painter, a psychiatrist, and a pediatrician. Their assignment: become mental patients.

Each person in the study called a hospital, arranged an appointment, and went in to tell of vague auditory hallucinations. They also gave false names and fake work records, but everything else they described about themselves was true. They told of satisfactions and frustrations and described significant events and the meaningful people in their lives. Each was hospitalized for an average of nineteen days. All but one were diagnosed as schizophrenic.

Although the pseudopatients were sane, adequately functioning people, they were systematically labeled, and the label received more attention than the realities of the pseudopatients' behavior while in the hospitals. As Maslow (1968) has pointed out:

> To place a person in a system takes less energy than to know him in his own right, since in the former instance, all that has to be perceived is that one abstracted characteristic which indicates his belongingness in a class, e.g., babies, waiters, Swedes, schizophrenics, females, generals, nurses, etc. [pp. 126-127]

To place a person in a system, to categorize him or her, can bring a feeling of correctness, of certainty, a rewarding release from tensions we may feel when we are not sure. We can react to that categorization rather than to any of the realities existing alongside it. Rosenhan has described this form of reacting to categories with regard to the pseudopatients in his study. When a pseudopatient was diagnosed (categorized) as psychotic, his behavior in the hospital was viewed as the behavior of a psychotic individual. The background of experiences with family and friends was seen as a background that contributed to and was indicative of a history of psychosis. Yet, there was no psychosis. None of the pseudopatients had a history of "mental illness"; they were all "normals."

While psychotic people, and people who are labeled as psychotic, are no longer persecuted as obviously as they once were, there remains within this society what seems to be a well-developed capacity for the persecution of the self. Persecution of the self has several facets, and it is a combination of these facets that can contribute to a genuine psychotic state of existence.

Persecution of the self is not a part of the genetic, inherited factors that may contribute to the existence of some psychotic behaviors in some individuals. Nor is it directly connected with the way many individuals are biologically damaged by the incredible variety of toxic molecules in some foods and in some drugs, including alcohol. As you may recall from Charlotte Buhler's criticisms (1971) of the smaller and larger social scenes in which we live (Chapter 7), Buhler aimed her brief and pointed volleys at (1) the family, (2) the educational system, and (3) the society in general.

Psychotic behavior may be generated within the individual by his family. As English (1963) pointed out, it is the family that helps to make the psychotic style of living acceptable to the psychotic individual. Children usually internalize the language of their parents at an early age. They also internalize the attitudes, opinions, and beliefs of the parents. If one or both parents are not very well integrated, children will internalize not-very-well-integrated sets of attitudes, opinions, and beliefs.

The child may also take in and learn the parental reactions to frustration, including conflict frustration, with the subsequent development of anger, fear, and anxiety. During the same years of growth and later on into adolescence, there will probably be an internalization of psychphobia, the fear of knowing oneself.

As Abraham Maslow (1968) has pointed out:

> From our point of view, Freud's greatest discovery is that the great cause of psychological illness is the fear of knowledge of oneself—of one's emotions, impulses, memories, capacities, potentialities, of one's destiny. [p. 60]

Within the schools, from the preschool setting and kindergarten and through the elementary grades, children fortunate enough to come from families that are reasonably integrated may often be subjected to predatory teachers and a close association with other children, some of whom will be psychotic. In the larger society, especially the fragmented, pluralistic, sometimes chaotic society in which we all live, children may easily experience a sense of personal disorganization as they try to make sense out of what is happening around them and in them.

Persecution of the self—one of the by-products of chronic psychophobia—seems to be composed of several factors that, although intermixed, can be separated and examined. Each factor may contribute to the development of psychotic behavior.

1. **The constellation of anger.** The sword of anger has two cutting edges. We use one edge to cut other people. Other people use

the second edge to cut us. To view this double-edged sword with caution and carefulness is perhaps understandable but only sometimes necessary.

We usually put up our defenses when someone is angry at us. The defenses we may use automatically are agonistic; that is, they may involve fight or flight. We may defend ourselves aggressively or we may take flight psychologically, escaping from the person's anger by psychologically withdrawing, becoming passive, hoping that if we offer little resistance, the other person's anger will quickly subside. The main strategy involved in fight or flight is an effort designed to stop the other person's anger or at least to lower it.

We usually need to stop the other individual's anger, not because that anger is so dangerous but because *their* anger may ignite *ours*. Very often when a person expresses anger at us, we can sense within ourselves a swift rise of fear and anxiety. Very often that fear and anxiety will be connected with our anger, not theirs. We may struggle unconsciously with a pool of anger within ourselves, fearful lest that anger break out in a rushing torrent to destroy the other individual. At such moments we treat ourselves as lethal devices instead of humans, which is an aspect of persecution of the self.

2. **The constellation of affection.** The plume of affection has two feathery edges.* One edge is used for stroking others; the second edge is used by others to stroke us. As with the sword of anger, the plume of affection will be viewed with an understandable but not always necessary caution.

We often feel the shadow of caution pass across the mind when someone is affectionate toward us. This seems to be especially the case if the affectionate individual is neither a stranger nor an intimate associate or ally. It may be that we feel a need to respond with an automatic self-derogation, a persecution of self. Examples of this automatic self-persecution, which often effectively destroys incoming affection, were given in

---

*Psychoanalysts may enjoy the phallic metaphors used here.

Chapter 3. The athletic young man responded to a slight piece of affection, a compliment, by saying, "Aw, my legs are too thin." The lovely woman responded to an affectionate comment about her beauty by saying, "Oh, but my eyes are so bloodshot."

By the time we are grown up, many among us have developed a plethora of skills for avoiding, denying, destroying, or ignoring affection coming from others. The strategies for defending against the affections of others operate so automatically and so unconsciously, we cannot find the reasons for the loneliness we feel. One of the more intricate ways of avoiding affection is to be overly affectionate, overly warm and giving to others. If we can manage to maintain an almost constant bombardment of kindness, we may protect ourselves from the kindnesses and affections of others. In genuine affection it is often easier to give than to receive. When anger is on the scene, it is easier to receive than to give (Branden, 1969). The combination leads to persecution of the self.

Persecution of the self and psychophobia are linked. Both define slightly different aspects of not knowing about oneself, of not becoming acquainted with what is happening within, of stunting the growth of identity, which in turn severely limits the opportunities to become involved in a developing intimacy with another person. To return to Maslow (1968), "We tend to be afraid of any knowledge that could cause us to despise ourselves or to make us feel inferior, weak, worthless, evil, shameful" (p. 60).

At the same time we often tend to avoid knowing about our own competence, strength, adequacy, and worth. We may become involved in a number of activities designed to improve our own level of self-esteem, but it seems there is a ceiling on self-esteem. We feel we can legitimately have some, a little, but there is sometimes a feeling of being fraudulent about having what seems like too much. If we cannot allow ourselves to be adequate, we may be forced into accepting ourselves as inadequate. *The least adequate level of behavior is psychotic behavior.*

So far in this chapter the emphasis has been on the psychological and sociological factors that contribute to the development of psychotic behavior. It is time now to return to what was known between 400 B.C. and A.D. 200, to the information about emotional disorders that was put together by the Greeks and the Romans. They were aware, according to McNeil (1970), of the following: (1) After childbirth some mothers may experience what is called a postpartum depression, which may be the result of feelings poorly controlled and not acknowledged by the mother that (a) she may not really want the baby or that (b) she is intensely angry or in some other way disturbed because of what childbirth has done to her body. (2) Hysteria does not mean crazy wildness. It means avoidance, the avoidance of knowing what one's feelings and emotions are; the avoidance of oneself is the opposite of what has been referred to previously as a sense of identity. The psychological aspects of hysteria are best described as the ultimate of psychophobia.* (3) Emotional disorders may have a sudden onset with no previously identifiable difficulty. If so, they are called acute. (4) Some emotional disorders are characterized by wild and unpredictable emotional states, while others are identifiable by their level of apathy, diffidence, and indifference. (5) In addition to psychophobia, there are other phobias. Phobias can be described as intense and penetrating fears in which the specific agents are known. The person knows what it is he so greatly fears. The Greeks, more than the Romans, named these fears, giving

them labels that now seem slightly exotic. For a sampling, regard this brief list:

acrophobia fear of high places
claustrophobia fear of enclosed places
mysophobia fear of uncleanliness
nyctophobia fear of darkness
zoophobia fear of animals

Perhaps the Greeks and the Romans knew that phobias were an attempt to adjust, to cope with difficult—for the individual—circumstances by avoiding those circumstances or preventing their occurrence. The background reason (the source) for the phobia has been repressed, but it is there somewhere in the individual's psychological history, even though it may not be easily or quickly identified. As a result, phobias may seem irrational, unexplainable, and—to those who do not have the phobia—extraordinarily outlandish.

If the Greeks (primarily) did not say it and if the Romans (secondarily) did not mention it, then Shakespeare must have. In *Hamlet* he identified the depths of ambivalence, a paralyzing indecision, and an immobilizing conflict found in some psychotic states when he wrote, "To be or not to be: that is the question." The same sentiments are expressed in *Macbeth* with these words of mixed evaluation, "Fair is foul, and foul is fair." In *The Merchant of Venice* he named the central and personal core of what the Greeks called hysteria when he wrote, "What! Must I hold a candle to my shames?" A sliver of the sense of depression can be found in these words from *As You Like It*, "Oh! How bitter a thing it is to look into happiness through another man's eyes." In *King Lear* he wrote, "I am too old to learn," a statement that will be brought up again in the next section of this chapter.

For the moment it may be appropriate to point out that there has been and continues to be a great deal of research into the causes and the treatment of psychosis. At the very least, the research indicates

---

*The Greeks and Romans must have been at least slightly on the side of male chauvinists, for they viewed hysteria as an essentially feminine affliction. Hysteria, as a psychological term, originated in the Greek language, which gave us the genuinely and exclusively feminine term: hysterectomy.

psychotic behavior develops in the ways that nonpsychotic behavior develops; that is, the individual is involved in intricate and often unknown interactions with his own environment. Within the individual and within that environment is a multiplicity of variables that interact in ways that produce psychotic behavior. Through it all, as the individual grows and develops, the factor called modifiability comes into focus. Because of the human characteristic, this orienting concept, individuals learn to respond to their world and to themselves in psychotic ways. Modifiability also contributes to the individual's movement out of a psychotic state. People do "get over" being psychotic, although how that happens can be as poorly understood as the sequence of becoming psychotic.

To "get over" a psychosis is sometimes called being in a state of remission, which implies that sanity is a temporary state. That may not be an accurate implication. With regard to remission, however, here is a fragment of a diagnostic report written by a psychologist who saw a young psychotic individual at the request of a psychiatrist.

It is inconceivable to me that this lad has the capacities to function in any but the most rudimentary and primitive ways in almost all environments. In his test responses and in conversation, he exhibits a marked looseness of thinking, disorganization in his approach to and solution of even simple problem situations, and what is apt to be aperiodic episodes of hallucinatory behavior. (It is my impression that the hallucinations are visual.)

The diagnostic tests suggest he is extremely fearful from time to time. The great fear may be triggered by external (environmental) stimuli that may be, in reality, irrelevant or very small and insignificant aspects of that environment. It seems as though the fear response is an almost "all or none" sort of phenomenon. That is to say that he may experience either a total absence of fear or a total envelopment by fear in unpredictable and erratic ways.

I am of the opinion the lad needs immediate, intensive, long-term psychotherapy. I doubt that he can avoid hospitalization at sometime in the near future.

The patient is described in grim terms with a sure hand. Yet, within six months he somehow regrouped his forces, found a job, and for what may have been the first time in his life, enjoyed the world around him as a nonpsychotic person. What happened? Not even the patient could explain.

People do grind down and slide into psychotic behavior. They do recover, sometimes seemingly on their own, sometimes with the help of specialists with a long background of training and experience, and sometimes simply with the minimum assistance of a friend or two. In almost all circumstances others are involved, others available to the person with a psychosis. But more about those "others" on a later page.

Before we move on to the next section and information about other psychoses, we will briefly review another consequence of modifiability. That consequence is called neurosis. *Neurotic behavior* is psychologically awkward behavior, inefficient, unhandy, and the individual is typically uncomfortable in some vague way, perhaps sweating too much or laughing too loudly or being too quiet and shy according to some standard or other.

Neurotic behavior may have many of the elements of psychotic behavior, although in the neuroses, these conditions prevail:

1. Behavior may be disorganized some of the time in some social behavior settings.
2. Contact with and the awareness of reality as it is commonly known is not usually impaired.
3. While persons may believe in things that are obviously not so (delusions), they are not apt to have hallucinations.
4. Cognitive behavior may be slightly disorganized at times, but on the whole it is intact.
5. The individual may sometimes behave in ways that are somewhat dangerous to himself or to other people.

This list of five characteristics has some

similarity to the characteristics previously listed for psychotic behavior. The difference can be found in the matter of degree. Neurotic behavior is less severely disturbed, less disorganized, less troubling to the individual and to those who know him than is psychotic behavior.

In 1905, Sigmund Freud (1969) wrote that neurotic behavior was based upon inadequacies in the psychological development of sexual behavior. Joseph Wolpe (1969), on the other hand, has more recently described neurotic behavior as learned behavior that can be unlearned. Essentially, though, and whether you follow Freud's footsteps or the path marked out by Wolpe, neurotic behavior typically involves an overuse of the defensive behaviors briefly surveyed in the previous chapter. The overuse can involve aggressive defending, defensive flight, and defensive compromise, either separately or in combination. Whatever the case, the overuse of the defenses prevents the development of an adequate sense of identity, and the individual must almost constantly struggle with what can be called the neurotic variance.

The *neurotic variance* can be seen in individuals who are confronted with a conflict between how they think they should be versus how they see themselves as being. In general, the greater the variance, the greater the degree of neurotic behavior. A neurotic variance, however, does not typically exist if the difference between "should" and "actual" behaviors is overly great and obvious. For instance, a boy who sees himself as and who actually is thin and frail may never believe he should be a varsity quarterback. An attractive and intelligent girl may not believe she should be a janitor for the rest of her life. If, however, the boy does actually believe he should be a quarterback and the girl a janitor, and if they persist in these "shoulds," their behavior may depart far enough from reality to be called psychotic.

A neurotic variance is usually more subtle than the gross examples given in the paragraph above. For example, the attractive and intelligent girl may believe she should be admired by everyone who knows her. She may behave in ways designed to get everyone to like her all the time. That is a rare achievement for anyone; failure is almost inevitable. The boy may believe he should get the highest grade on every exam he takes in each course at school. That is a rare achievement too, especially if the boy goes on to college. Again, failure is almost inevitable. The result, in these examples and in many other possible examples, is the growth of a feeling of inadequacy. Feelings of inadequacy can indicate neurotic behavior if those feelings run deeply enough and are persistent. Those feelings may motivate the individual to an even more strenuous use of the ego defenses.

In addition to the neurotic variance, neurotic behavior is characterized by the neurotic paradox.

The *neurotic paradox,* a result of the overuse of the ego defenses, can be recognized in individuals who consistently use strategies and tactics that keep them from getting what they say or feel they want. The lonely man who laughs heartily and slaps people on the back and who spins off five jokes in thirty seconds so overwhelms everyone around him that people avoid him and he thus behaves in ways that perpetuate his loneliness. On a more subtle level: the little girl who wants and who needs the friendship of her father may hold back shyly, trying to be the good little girl with such dedication she is almost invisible as a person. She is so little trouble that father rarely notices her. Hopefully she may develop some measure of aggressiveness.

The neurotic variance and the neurotic paradox are both self-defeating. They are behaviors that may bring some measure of temporary satisfaction, but over a period of time, both may produce a gradually increasing level of frustration that must be dealt with, and that, in turn develops an even greater need for the ego defenses, which are overused to start with.

In neurotic behavior, there is a component of fixation. *Fixation* refers to a stoppage, a cessation of some aspect of psychological development. In a wide and general sense individuals fixate on those behaviors that satisfy certain psychological needs. For example, there are men who welcome the hunting season. Whether they are after ducks or deer, possum or quail, they enjoy the smell of oiled leather boots, and they enjoy the heft of a rifle or shotgun. Most of all, it seems, they enjoy the company of other men.

There are men who prefer fishing, and they will fish with other men. Some prefer a poker game or a game of pool or golf or, if they are wealthy, a chukker of polo. Poker, pool, golf, and polo usually call for male companionship. Women may not hunt or play polo, but you can find them getting together over coffee in the neighborhood, forming gardening clubs, organizing bridal showers and baby showers, running parent-teacher organizations, and lobbying in Congress.

Men often enjoy the company of other men. Women find satisfaction in socializing with other women. The enjoyment and the satisfaction are not entirely based on purely adult motivations. The behavior is related to an earlier period of life called the school age stage. In some respects the behavior may be fixated at that level.

An individual may fixate at almost any level of psychological development, but fixation in itself is not necessarily neurotic. It is neurotic or is at least one aspect of neurotic behavior if the fixation perpetuates childhood or adolescent behavior that interferes with psychological growth in other sectors of behavior, mainly in those sectors that contribute to a developing sense of identity.

An example of neurotic fixation exists in the behavior of the supremely clean mother, the mother who scrubs her house almost daily, demanding that her children bathe twice a day, the mother who boils the silverware after every meal and whose hands are raw from constant washing. Another example: the man with the short-wave radio who spends every evening sending out his call letters to foreign stations, contacting other radio operators in distant lands, collecting postcards from them to tape to the walls of the room where he keeps his radio equipment. The clean mother is not a rare example. Neither is the overly dedicated ham radio operator. Both are fixated on behaviors that may have been somewhat appropriate at an earlier age. For the clean mother the fixation may be connected with the early learning of cleanliness during toilet training. For the radioman the behavior may have been an appropriate response during the years of apprenticeship, just prior to adolescence. The multiplicity of variables in anyone's life, however, makes these conclusions more speculative than accurate. They are apt to be assumptions, not necessarily facts.

At this point in your reading it may be useful to turn back to Chapter 8 and review the material on regression. Regression and fixation sometimes appear to be similar behaviors. They are not.

ORGANIC PSYCHOSIS

One of the penalties of growing old has been mentioned in Chapter 6. It is death. A less frequent penalty associated with age is the chance of a senile psychotic disorder. While humans are a combination of biological, physical, factors combined with psychological and social factors, the biological factors come to the fore with advanced age. This does not mean the psychological and social aspects fade far into the background—not, at least, in this society.

In this society the old person is usually the unwanted person, unadmired, unproductive, unemployed. Generally he is retired, living on Social Security checks, sensing the decline of physical skills, and knowing the end of life cannot be far away. There are exceptions, of course, but the typical old person interacts with an environment that sees him as less than he once was. His reputation is diminished, and self-esteem may be on the decline as surely as his biological status is. A part of decline in biological status is the slow but inexorable decay of the brain and associated physical equipment.

Acute brain disorders are based upon biochemical changes in brain functions that produce temporary disorganization of behavior. *Chronic brain disorders* are based upon normal and progressive degeneration of brain tissue. You may recall from Chapter 6 that, after the age of 35, humans lose the use of about 100,000 brain cells per day. This high casualty rate does not clearly begin to show itself until old age. Chronic brain disorders are not temporary; disorganization is a permanent feature, as well as is an inability to concentrate and a markedly reduced ability to understand and think through problems— even routine problems—in a coherent way (McNeil, 1970; Goldstein, 1969).

The two most common forms of chronic brain disorder in old age are (1) senile brain disease, which is based upon the degeneration of the brain, and (2) cerebral arteriosclerosis, which is due to thickening of the arteries in the brain (Marks, 1961).

Cerebral arteriosclerosis often produces a set of symptoms such as headaches, dizziness, depression, a variety of emotional outbursts, and convulsions. The individual's intelligence is not usually impaired, and the disease itself may be of short duration, but it ends with death.

Senile psychosis is a gradual, more long-lasting condition in which intellectual skills are impaired, but symptoms such as headaches, dizziness, depression, convulsions, and emotional outbursts are not commonly seen (Coleman, 1964). The end of course is death, but before that transition takes place, there may be and often are years of gradual decline. As McNeil (1970) has pointed out, the decline is similar to the peeling off of the layers of civilization. What has been learned most recently is lost most quickly.* The person generally cannot recall what he has had for breakfast, but he may be able to remember what his mother served for dinner on a Christmas day fifty or sixty years ago. Emotional controls begin to slip, and as the disease progresses, depression may surge forth. Temper tantrums are common, as well as other poorly controlled aggressive and hostile reactions. It is, as it has often been called, a second childhood, but it is a childhood of decline instead of growth, a childhood with few if any pleasures and no future. What has been repressed gradually returns as civilization slides away from the individual. He may become extraordinarily demanding, selfish, greedy, and inconsiderate. He may become sexually aggressive and suspicious of almost everyone. In the end there is a welcomed reprieve as the person moves through the transition from a half-life to death.

There are other organic psychoses. They are not so directly connected with age, any age, as senile psychosis. Among them are the organic psychoses resulting from infection. A common source of cerebral damage due to infection is syphilis. Organic psychosis based upon cerebral damage can be found in the damage resulting from accidents. Accidental injury to the brain (in a car wreck, for example) will bring about changes in behavior

---

*Jules Masserman (1950) has found this same sequence of loss in the behavior of cats that have been fed alcohol. For humans however, this is the stage or level of decline that evokes Shakespeare's words from *King Lear:* "I am too old to learn."

depending upon the extent and location of the damage (Goldstein, 1969).

Most accidental injuries of the brain bring about acute and transitory changes in behavior. The person may briefly be delirious, confused, and anxious and may show some memory loss. The memory loss is sometimes called *retrograde amnesia;* the greater the brain damage, the greater the extent of retrograde amnesia. Memory does not instantly return if the person is hit on the head again. That is a myth from the movies. Some accidental injuries are severe enough to produce chronic change in behavior, sometimes to the point where the individual's behavior looks like an arrested and frozen-in-place version of senile psychosis.

Organic psychoses, whether they result from the process of aging, from infections or other substances toxic to the brain (e. g., many chemical fumes, drugs, and insect sprays), or from accidental damage, are increasingly more common because of the developments of technology and some developments of science. People live longer now because we can keep them alive longer. Since 1920 the diseases of degeneration associated with age have outranked any of the other causes of death (Glazier, 1973). The percentage of older people in the total population is higher, and more old people mean more cases of senile psychosis. As Amasa Ford (1970) has said, they are casualties of our times. There are other casualties too—those involved in accidents that can be traced to our technological environment. Hundreds of thousands of individuals are injured in automobile accidents in this country every year. Many of them receive injuries to the brain, and some of them experience so much cerebral damage, psychosis results. In addition, there are others who, because of technology, ingest or inhale toxic substances that cause brain damage. But through it all the connection between brain damage and psychosis remains a partial mystery. Brain damage does not directly cause a psychosis. Laboratory examinations of brain tissue from psychotic patients show no relationship between the damage or degeneration and the ways in which the individual behaved. Brain damage in almost any form reduces the individual's capacities to adapt and to adjust. With a great enough degree of damage, the person may be unable to cope effectively with himself or his environment. His adequacy is lowered, and as mentioned before, the least adequate level of behavior is called psychosis.

DEPRESSION

Because feelings of depression are so common in our society, a section of this chapter is devoted to the matter. Redlich and Freedman (1966) maintain depressions occur in all age groups but that they often go unrecognized in infants and children. Elkind and Hamsher (1972) reviewed a considerable amount of information on depression and commented that, according to the National Institute of Mental Health (NIMH), a quarter of a million people require hospitalization every year for severe, often psychotic feelings of depression. There may be, again according to NIMH data, as many as eight million people in the United States who visit their physicians every year, asking for help to fend off feelings of depression. Perhaps many more than eight million visit with their minister, rabbi, or priest for assistance with their depressions (Frank, 1973).

The language and terminology of depression is as extensive as the condition itself. No one seems certain of the dividing lines between (1) normal but transitory depression, (2) mild to moderate but persistent depression, and (3) depression severe enough to be psychotic. While depression is usually viewed as an affective disorder, Beck (1963) believes there are cognitive distortions of the commonly held view of reality, which include impaired judgments or evaluations of that reality, including misevaluations of relationships with other people.

With regard to self-esteem, there can be a high degree of affectual disturbance combined with a typically lesser degree of cognitive distortion. The person may express depression with such statements or thoughts as "I'm no good" or "I'm a failure," concentrating upon their own flaws while overlooking their areas of competence.

In matters relating to reputation, there may often be a high degree of affectual disturbance together with a high degree of cognitive distortion. Depression may be expressed with such comments as "She doesn't really like me" or "They think I'm a failure." Palmer (1970) believes one of the factors motivating suicide is the fear of losing what the individual believes to be his good reputation.

Suicide, like death, is a topic generally avoided. Heyns (1958) maintains that suicidal fantasies are common during the adolescent years, while Choron (1972) com-

ments that some individuals, especially older adults, may consider suicide as a method of dying that has more meaning than the acceptance of physical degeneration of old age. In the *Psychology Today* survey concerning death, two percent of the more-than-30,000 who responded to the survey preferred suicide as a way of dying (Schneidman, 1971).

Ed

Ed was bearded and hairy, and he loved three things: his wife, his piano, and skiing. One day while he was skiing he broke his arm, and that meant he could not play the piano. Within a week he was yelling at his wife. In two weeks he began to beat her with his good arm.

She left him. She moved in with a former high school classmate and wrote Ed that she would not come back until his arm was out of the cast and he could play the piano again. The day he got the letter, Ed called the area mental health center and asked for an appointment with someone, with anyone. He was given a time to come the next evening.

When Ed came to the center, he was drunk. The intake worker took his name, asked him a few questions, and then asked him to come

Daniel Brody/Editorial Photocolor Archives

back the next day when he was sober. Ed walked steadily out of the center, got into his car, and drove home. He put the car in the garage, but he left the motor running. He closed the garage door and sat down on the floor. Neighbors found his body the next day.

Pattison and Elpers (1972) state that one of the primary developments in mental health work in the 1960s was the opening of suicide and crisis prevention centers in many cities in the United States. The most famous and probably the best one of these is the Suicide Prevention Center in Los Angeles. Edwin S. Shneidman, a moving force in the founding and effectiveness of that center, has written (1964) of the following four kinds of suicidal behavior:

1. **Intentioned.** The individual wants to be dead and will do things to insure that death takes place.
2. **Unintentioned.** The individual may accidentally kill himself in a suicide attempt that was not originally designed to be successful.
3. **Subintentioned.** The person may have some goal important to him, such as fame or the need to make other people feel bad, that he feels he can achieve through suicide.
4. **Counterintentioned.** The action may appear suicidal, but it is nonlethal, and although self-destruction is threatened, it is not carried out.

Included among counterintentioned actions is *self-mutilation,* an activity in which the person may attack his own body (Lester, 1972). Attacks on the body by the individual may range from head banging through hair pulling (trichotillomania) to wrist cutting to self-castration. Self-mutilation is considered to be counterintentioned with regard to suicide simply because suicide does not result from self-mutilation.

In suicide and in self-mutilation there is an element of depression. Aggressive impulses that result from frustration are poorly controlled and are expressed outwardly, at the environment, and inwardly, at the person who has the aggressive impulses.

The terminology of depression includes what are known as *reactive depressions.* Reactive depressions are also called secondary depressions, neurotic depressions, and exogenous depressions. This variety of terms refers to depressions that are serious but not psychotic, usually long lasting, chronic depressive reactions to external, environmental circumstances that ordinarily bring about a feeling of grief. Whatever their label, the feelings are usually the result of a loss.

The experience of loss is universal. Parents die; friends move away; favored pets are put to sleep; wallets, cars, and bicycles are stolen; physical beauty fades with age; flowers wither and grow dry, the wine glass is emptied. Middle-aged married couples may experience a deep sense of loss and quietly become depressed over the death, not of their children, but of their children's childhoods. When their children are grown and gone, many mourn their departure from the home, sometimes briefly but often with a sense of loss great enough to induce a reactive depression.

Individuals immersed in a reactive depression may talk of how they cannot concentrate, how they have difficulty attending to even the essential tasks of group life, how they tire easily. They may talk slowly and in their facial expressions show some sense of pain as though they were close to tears. There is generally no real disturbance of cognitive functioning other than a slowing down, a retardation of thinking as though they were trying to swim in a pool of cold glue. This is sometimes referred to as *retarded depression.*

In addition to the slowing, the retardation, of thinking there may be changes in eating habits. The amount of food eaten at meals and between meals may increase; constipation is common, and vomiting may be frequent. There is often a sharply decreased interest in sexual matters, and insomnia is prevalent. Individuals who are depressed to a neurotic degree and who in addition are agitated—often referred to as an *agitated depression*—may have difficulty in getting to sleep, and they may awake after a few hours and not be able to get back to sleep even though it may be two or three or four hours before they actually need to get up. When they are up, they may feel the sense of depression more deeply at the beginning of the day than at the end.

While lack of adequate sleep may cause discomfort and fatigue in depressed adults, the penalties and consequences with regard to children are much higher. Lytt Gardner (1972) has investigated the effects of loss of sleep, which in turn affects physical growth in young children. Gardner provides examples of sleep loss in children. Among his examples is that of a boy whose father had left the home. The mother, angered by what her husband had done, displaced her anger. She directed it toward the infant son who experienced the loss of his mother's affections. The boy became depressed, agitated, restless and slept poorly. By the time he was 1 year old, the boy's height was equivalent to that of an average 7 month-old infant. The boy was hospitalized for a time and began to recover his physical growth pattern. Later the boy was released from the hospital, his father returned to the home, and the boy grew normally.

The case of the boy who failed to grow for a time ended pleasantly. There are instances, however, and Gardner cites some of them, in which children do not recover their growth. They remain small, and their smallness has been traced to the interaction between lack of sleep resulting from depression and the failure to produce the growth hormone, somatotrophin. An infant apparently must have adequate sleep for that and other hormones to be produced. If the infant sleeps poorly,

growth is stunted. The result is labeled *deprivation dwarfism.* It is evidently a physiological result of a psychological condition that falls under the general heading of agitated depression.

The mixture of physical and physiological factors with the psychological aspects of depression is not limited to changes in eating habits, loss of sleep, or retarded growth. There is often an increase in concerns about health. The depressed person may become hypochondriacal; that is, he may start thinking he has or is about to have a disease of some kind. Cancer seems to be a favorite concern, as is heart disease, brain tumor, and veneral infections. In extreme instances of depression the individual may believe he has no stomach or no brain or that he is dead.

Extreme or severe depression is often referred to as *psychotic depression,* autonomous depression, primary depression, and endogenous depression. The language and terminology is deceptive, however, for it is sometimes difficult to separate clearly exogenous from endogenous, mild and moderate from severe, neurotic depression from psychotic depression.

Diagnostically, though, there is a thin lead that may be helpful. In endogenous or psychotic depression, there is no loss. The depression results from psychological factors that operate within the individual. That may seem a simple distinction from exogenous depression, which results from loss. Yet, loss is universal; we all experience it. That experience is highly personal, subjective and often difficult to trace. A wealthy stock broker may lose a half-million dollars in a stock market transaction and merely shrug his shoulders. The next day he may be unable to find a favorite pair of cuff links for his shirt, and thinking they are lost forever, he may swiftly slide into a depression. A woman may stand in the street watching her house burn down and live for years afterward feeling sad about the loss of a favored book of poetry destroyed in the flames. So in proposing the idea that in endogenous or psychotic depression there is no loss, the diagnostician cannot be certain even if he carefully surveys the individual's personal history, for what is lost may cause such pain in the individual that the experience of loss as well as the memory of the lost object is repressed. Nevertheless, the general thinking on endogenous depression holds that no loss is apparent. The depression comes from within. What lives within? Primarily, it seems, body chemistry and the delicate fibers of the brain interacting in ways that are extraordinarily complex. Depression can be the result of even small imbalances in the electrical and chemical activity of the brain. Depression, endogenous depression, may also result from feelings within, feelings such as anger, fear, and anxiety.

Charles

Charles was wealthy. He had inherited a mountain of money from his father, money he spent with great freedom and carelessness. He had a large home, two servants, and a matched set of British sedans equipped with stereo systems and telephones. Each car was air conditioned, supercharged, and could travel seven miles on one gallon of gasoline. Charles never worried about repairs, for he was an absentee owner of a foreign car repair garage. He was also, by inheritance, a major stockholder in a minor oil company.

When Charles was 30 years old, he married Marjorie. A year later Marjorie got a prescription for some potent tranquilizers and downed twenty of them with a glass of vodka while Charles was in Africa on safari. A servant found her body the next day. Charles flew back for the funeral.

Several years later Charles married Sally, who left him within a month. Three years after that, he married Nancy. On his wedding night he killed Nancy with a hammer and put the barrel of a small pistol into his mouth and pulled the trigger.

In the kitchen a servant heard the muffled

sound of the shot and ran upstairs to find Nancy's dead body and Charles unconscious on the floor. An ambulance took him to a hospital emergency room where a small bullet was removed from the left side of his upper jaw bone. He was put in a private hospital room guarded by police as the district attorney prepared a case for first-degree murder.

Charles pleaded insanity and he was seen by two psychiatrists and a psychologist. At the trial his plea of insanity was upheld, and he was sent to a state mental hospital where he was kept on a securely locked ward. He was allowed freedom only for work.

He was a model patient. He worked in the hospital laundry for three years and then was transferred to the hospital library, where he worked as a clerk. He was there for two years. He appealed for release on the basis of being cured, although he had received no treatment except infrequently administered tranquilizers whenever he had difficulty sleeping. His appeal was granted, and he was released from the hospital.

After his release, he worked at odd jobs and tried to locate his second wife Sally. He learned she had remarried and was living in Minneapolis. One evening he called her long distance, but she refused to talk with him. He decided to try to forget about her. He got a steady, full-time job working with a construction firm as an assistant bookkeeper. In three years he was the office manager, and he was allowed to have a company car to drive. Five years after that he was promoted to corporate vice president in charge of accounting and finance. He was 53 years old.

His promotion brought him a greatly increased income, and he decided to put some of it into psychotherapy. He tried psychoanalysis for six months, but he did not think it was worth the effort. He then tried psychodrama, but that proved too emotional for his tastes. At about that time in his life he began to experiment with drugs. One day he came to work with a terrific high, and he did not make sense when he talked to anyone. He left the office and went back home, an apartment now, well before noon. The next morning he woke up and walked out onto the balcony of his apartment. The balcony was eleven stories above the level of the green lawn. He crawled up on the balcony railing and dived toward the green.

The next morning the president of the construction firm, an educated and relatively sophisticated man, called the office of the lieutenant governor of the state. He asked for a psychological autopsy. The lieutenant governor, president of the state senate, honorary board member of half a dozen charitable institutions, and intellectually a decisive and capable individual, brought together a small committee of mental health personnel to conduct a psychological autopsy concerned with the background reasons—developmental, social, and biological—for Charles's suicide. The small group assembled data about Charles, and a portrait of the man began to emerge. What do you suppose that portrait showed?

Endogenous and exogenous depressions may be the result of unexpressed anger, anger held in check by an overuse of repression and other ego defenses. Anger held in check and not directed outward does not simply evaporate. It remains and is often directed inwardly. In such instances, depression is anger directed at oneself.

Anger directed at the self relates back to persecution of the self, and it is often clearly obvious in what are termed guilt depressions. *Guilt depressions* may grow out of guilt over a subjective sense of having broken one or more of the rules of the king's peace. A guilt depression may arise out of the psychological pain that is part of the neurotic variance. The person *feels* guilty, senses a loss of self-esteem, and perhaps imagines a loss of some degree of reputation. To combat the effects of a guilt depression, the individual may often show a quick and sharp humor. He or she may make cruel and only superficially humorous remarks about himself, other people, anything. The person may like to tease others endlessly. He may indirectly invite others to tease him. The overall behavior is designed to somehow contend with guilt feelings and feelings of depression. It can become unhandy, awkward, and

predictably follow the course of action noted in the neurotic paradox. Furthermore, an individual may become fixated in this behavior. Over an extended period of time the person may continue with the humor and the teasing long after the depression has lifted (Redlich and Freedman, 1966).

Feelings of depression often simply lift. They seemingly evaporate. The individual once again senses an adequate level of self-esteem, believes his reputation to be intact, and often manages to strive once more for self-actualization. This shift back to the usual level of functioning can be noticed most often after an episode of normal but transitory depression. It can be seen in neurotic depression. It also exists in instances of psychotic depression. Often, however, a psychotic individual may go beyond the usual and rise so far above the previous level of depression he appears to be an almost totally different person. In psychotic behavioral disorders the severely depressed person may change so drastically he rises to a condition called mania.

Manic behavior is the other side of a psychological coin. Instead of slowness, sadness, and cognitive retardation the person is almost continually elated, expansive, moving with great speed from one task to another, intellectually quick—although not necessarily precise or accurate—and physically mobile to a high degree. If the individual is psychotic, the shift to mania changes the diagnostic label from merely depressive to *manic-depressive*. In neurotic behavior the level of manic activity may be nearly as frenetic and swiftly moving, but it is not often as disorganized as in psychotic behavior. It may even be productive.

When a woman reaches the end of her biologically productive years, when menstruation becomes irregular and there is no doubt she is in middle age, she may suffer the onset of depression. If, at this time in life, the woman experiences her first psychosis, and if that psychosis is associated with the "change in life," the condition is called *involutional melancholia.* Mild but nevertheless painful versions of this condition may often go unrecognized, or else they may be shrugged away as part of the normal stream of life.

The stream of life is loaded with goals and hopes and aspirations for many people. When an individual has achieved a long-sought goal, however, he or she may feel a sudden letdown, a rush of depression. Achievement of a goal removes that goal; the person may experience the loss of motivation that sustained him in his strivings for the now lost goal, and the result is called a *success depression.* He or she, in addition to feeling depressed, may also feel fearful the achievement will be somehow taken away. There may be anxiety connected with the idea of being penalized for the success.

However widespread depression may be, it is commonly based upon (1) the experience—however subjective—of loss, or (2) anger directed toward the self, or (3) both. There is usually a reduced sense of self-esteem and a belief that reputation has been compromised. There is often the need for psychological repair, the topic of the next chapter.

PSYCHOPATH-SOCIOPATH

Three decades ago they were called constitutional psychopathic inferiors. Later they were referred to more simply as psychopaths. Still later and in the present day they have been labeled as sociopaths. "They" refers to the large group of individuals who often have a superficial charm and, seemingly, a better than average level of intelligence but who sooner or later exasperate almost everyone.

Hervey Cleckley (1964) has described their behavior in detail in his book called *The Mask of Sanity.* Their behavior is neither genuinely neurotic nor psychotic, but they are, in spite of how they may appear at first or even second glance, unreliable. In conversation they can be convincing and sincere; at the moment they *do* mean what they say, but that moment passes, and they no longer mean what they said. They can, while appearing to be convincing and sincere, fill the room with one lie after another, spinning yarns and telling sea stories endlessly. They cheat with expertise and steal with skill, and if they are caught, they may pretend a remorse they do not really feel, make promises to behave, and then repeat their minor and major crimes, often carrying with them a sense that they have been treated badly because they were caught. They are caught repeatedly, for their apparently above-average level of intelligence is never as high as it seems, and in addition, they continually show poor judgment and a failure to learn from past experiences.

Sociopaths can appear to be unbelievably gutsy, but it seems more accurate to often call their bravery a kind of semi-planned blundering that succeeds because other people are so often so trusting. Because of their appearance of sincerity, they can seem to be trustworthy, but they are not. Furthermore, they do not trust anyone; they are unable to really love or to feel any sense of affection, warmth, or loyalty. Yet, they can give the impression of caring if that will help them to get whatever they are after. They are life's chronic imposters, gifted with an ability to impress other people with their goodness as they exploit them. They may be successful for years as crooked and devious politicians, con men, prostitutes, and in their own peer group, highly successful for brief periods as criminals.

Not all criminals are sociopaths, and not all sociopaths end up in jail. More often they move from place to place, changing jobs, living a life that appears adventurous but that is more often a matter of impulsiveness with few real anxieties and no goals except to survive in a world they view as a jungle in which only the "fittest" endure. They baffle almost everyone.

McConnell (1970) believes some of the sociopaths among us may be treated by behavioral modification techniques (discussed in the next chapter), but Eysenck (1960) reports they may be physiologically different from the norm, different enough to elude the attentions of a modification specialist. In general any efforts to get them to mend their ways, to cease their supremely self-defeating style of living, have failed. Perhaps a massive research program will provide useful information about how to change their behavior. At the present time, success is seldom seen.

REVIEW QUESTIONS

1. In what ways are psychotic and neurotic disorders similar?
2. What is the difference between chronic and acute?
3. What is fixation? How is it different from regression?
4. Who is Edwin S. Shneidman?
5. Can you differentiate between retarded depression and agitated depression?
6. Who wrote *The Mask of Sanity?* What was it about?
7. What appears to be the two primary psychological causes of depression?
8. Can you define involutional melancholia?
9. What is the cause of deprivation dwarfism?
10. What are the two most common chronic brain disorders associated with old age?
11. What is retrograde amnesia?
12. What is the neurotic paradox?

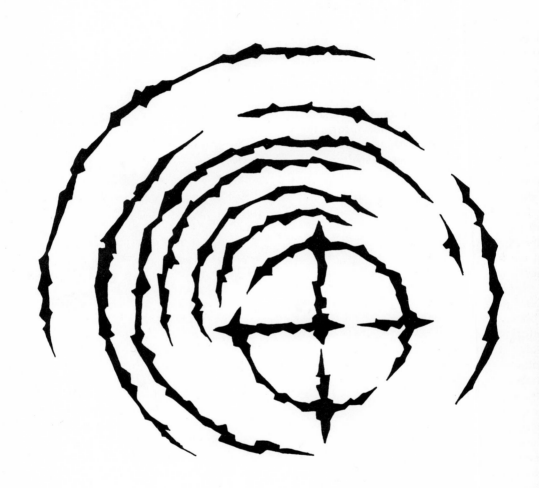

10 REPAIRING BEHAVIOR

Repairing behavior was first mentioned in this book as one of the potentials for development. Repairing behavior may be informal. It can involve many of the aspects of interaction that help in the development of identity together with the development of intimacy as outlined in Chapter 6.

Repairing behavior may be a formal endeavor and that is what this chapter is about. Formal, purposeful, and conscious efforts at repair and self-rescue may involve any one or some combination of the following: (1) psychoanalysis, (2) psychodrama, (3) behavior modification, and (4) psychopharmacology.

These four methods or techniques or approaches to repairing behavior are reasonably distinctive; they can be differentiated from each other on the basis of (1) the activities of the patient, (2) the activities of the therapist, (3) the history of development and use each one has, and generally (4) on the basis of the degree to which each focuses upon (a) the biological, (b) the social, and (c) the psychological aspects of the patient's life.

Each of these four methods of psychotherapy can be viewed as four points on the psychotherapy compass. Other forms

of therapy may be considered as combinations or blends of these four, and the blends are more common than pure applications of the four. Whatever the therapy, however, the goals are always about the same. They are (1) increased understanding and awareness of the self and of the surrounding environment, (2) the reduction or elimination of maladaptive behavior, (3) the learning of more effective defense strategies, and (4) assistance in personal growth toward a higher level of maturity that includes self-actualization (Coleman, 1969). These goals vary over a wide range because of the specific and general characteristics of the patient, because of what needs to happen in and as a result of therapy, and because of the therapist's beliefs and orientations, including his subjective sense of reality.

PSYCHOANALYSIS

Psychoanalysis is two things: it is (1) a method of treatment, a highly specialized kind of psychotherapy, and (2) a body of knowledge, semiknowledge and speculations about human behavior.

Psychoanalysis was originally developed by Sigmund Freud, who spent fifty of his adult years discussing, lecturing, writing, rewriting, and revising his views of the human mind. He wrote more than twenty lengthy and sometimes difficult to read books on the topic, poineering his way through previously uncharted realms, often meeting with resistance and rejection. From the beginning and on to the present time many learned and thoughtful people have considered Freud and freudianism to be silly or dangerous or irrelevant or simply wrong. Some thought he was pornographic, especially in his lectures and published books about sexuality in children. Today, however, almost any skilled kindergarten teacher can describe sexuality and sexual behavior among the very young with perhaps greater knowledge and a higher precision than Freud could have done in midcareer.

Freud walked a tightrope during his career. He was trained as a physician and as a scientist. He was also an intellectual adventurer who tried to build a science that had to do with the human mind. The mind is not the same as the brain. The human brain can be studied scientifically. The brain is an organ, a physical reality, a 3-pound collection of tissues and fluids that can be looked at, touched, dissected, and viewed through the lens of a microscope. In contrast, the mind of man is not a real thing. It is an abstraction, or, rather, a collection of abstractions. In the hands of Freud, abstractions about the mind often had an element that comes under the heading of biological science. He believed in *biological determinism*, the constitutionalist viewpoint that behavior is essentially rooted in genetic, inherited, factors.*
Along this line of thought he wrote of instincts that can be defined in part as inherited behaviors.

Freud wrote about instincts in humans, and in the last half of his career, he settled on what he believed to be two great clus-

terings of instincts (Hall, 1954). One cluster consists of instincts directed toward life, the "life wish" or the "life instinct," which he called *Eros*. The other great cluster of instincts was directed toward death; it became labeled "the death wish" or *Thanatos*. Freud maintained that these clusters of instincts would sooner or later be verified by direct biological investigation of human physiology, including the brain.

Freud (1927) also developed abstract ideas concerning other sectors of human behavior. In addition to Eros and Thanatos, he became known—somewhat inaccurately—as the originator of *id, ego,* and *superego*. Humans, he said, are born with an id, which remains and out of which within the first six or eight months of life the ego develops to become well established as an entity of the mind by the age of 2 or 3 years. The superego, he maintained, does not begin to be developed until the individual is 5 or 6 years old. The superego is not firmly developed until the person reaches 10 or 11 years of age.

The id is one of the sectors or divisions of the psychic apparatus or, to use an alternate term, the mental apparatus. Id is the Latin word for "it." Freud wrote in German, and some of the early translators of his books and lectures preferred to use Latin for some of the freudian terminology. If they, the translators, had been less classically minded, the id would have become the it.

The id, or the it, is there at birth, the first component of the psychic apparatus. It is composed of instinctual impulses, unconscious surgings thought to be primitive, charged with emotions usually inaccessible to the individual within whom they reside. The impulses, the surgings of primitive emotions, may range from great affection to great rage. This range of emotion develops from the interaction of the inherited with the results from a variety of perceptions of the environment (Moore and Fine, 1968). Freud believed the id could best be

---

*See Chapter 1 for an initial note on this idea.

defined by comparing it with the ego; whatever the ego was not could be a factor of id (Rycroft, 1968).

The ego, in psychoanalytic lore, has gone through some changes and revisions of definition. It is one of the principal divisions of the psychic apparatus. In the beginning, however, Freud sometimes described it as the total mental self. At other times he thought of it as the conscious mind. Later writings by Freud and by others indicated the ego to be composed of some conscious and some unconscious factors. According to Rycroft (1968) anything an individual can do is called an *ego function*. Ego functions include, but go well beyond the following behaviors:

Regulation and control of drives the ability or inability to tolerate frustration, to overcome or fail to overcome unexpected situations, and to sublimate.

Interpersonal relationships the ability or lack of ability to maintain durable and long-lasting relationships with other people

Thinking cognition

Defending behaviors ways in which the individual protects himself from real or imagined psychological assaults

Autonomous functions according to psychoanalytic theory, those functions safe from disturbance or interference by what can be the upsetting and uncomfortable surges of the id (Autonomous functions include, for example, speech, physical movement, planning, and life-purpose.)

Relationship with reality the manner in which the total person develops and maintains or fails to maintain a sense of reality and an adaptation to reality

Integrating or organizing functions those functions that bring into focus the superego

The *superego* is essentially the individual's conscience. It is viewed by psychoanalysts as the third division of the psychic apparatus. The integrating or organizing functions of the ego can be compared to a balancing act. The balancing act involves the id and the superego. The id, according to Freud and many of his followers, is in an almost constant contest with the superego. In analogy form the id says "I

want!" but the superego says "You can't have it." The ego, the rational balancer, says "Let's figure it out." And figuring out the balance often brings into action the defending behaviors mentioned previously.

Unlike the id, the ego is directly connected with the surrounding environment. It is that aspect of a person's being—that division of the psychic apparatus—that functions in ways designed to develop and maintain control over that environment. At least in part it is the "I" or the "me" that behaves in ways meant to make that environment more orderly, more predictable, less awesome. The ego is oriented toward impression management (Tedeschi et al, 1971) and the control of perception (Powers, 1973). It is that aspect of the mind, according to the psychoanalysts, more devoted to seeking a reasonably achievable level of psychological comfort rather than finding out the precise characteristics of the environment. The ego in effect is an abstraction, an idea, designed to label and account for some factors of human behavior.

The ideas and abstractions that grew out of Freud's work have been used as starting points for the works of others. In Europe, Carl Jung, Alfred Adler, Otto Rank, and Wilhelm Stekel developed their own special modifications of freudianism, and what they conceptualized became known as jungian psychoanalysis, adlerian psychoanalysis, and so on.

Freud visited the United States in 1909; his influence spread slowly at first and then more rapidly. The names of those whose lives and careers he influenced include Melanie Klein, Harry Stack Sullivan, Edith Jackson, Smith Ely Jelliffe, Jule Eisenbud, who was also influenced by the ideas of Carl Jung, and Marianne Kris. Freud also made his mark on the minds of those who are a mixture of European and American. One such person who falls within this category is Erik Erikson, whose ideas on human psychological development are superficially covered in several previous chapters. Another individual who can be considered as both European and American (he lives in Cuernavaca, Mexico) is Erich Fromm.

Fromm's work separates itself in some notable ways from Freud's ideas. For example, Fromm places substantial weight on environmental influences in the development of personality, differing in this respect from the biological determinism of Freud. Fromm also appears to be less pessimistic about humans and human behavior, although the traditional and orthodox freudian psychoanalyst would prefer to be called realistic rather than pessimistic (Brams, 1968). In addition, Fromm takes into account the effect of work, of needing to have a job, of having to buy food instead of growing and harvesting it. He also considered the impact of power structures—governments and corporations—on the individual (Fromm, 1941) dealing with some of the practicalities of daily living in ways that Freud did not. Perhaps Erich Fromm is more in touch with the modern world than Sigmund Freud was. That is understandable. Fromm began collecting his ideas together at the time Freud was an old man, and he published his most notable early works shortly after Freud's death in 1939.

Both Freud and Fromm checked their ideas out in the laboratory. Most psychoanalysts who think and write abut the human mind have a laboratory. Typically it consists of a room with a chair and a couch in it. The analyst sits in the chair; the *analysand* occupies the couch. Although some analysts put their patients in a chair, most prefer their patients on their backs, supine. Analysts, whether they be psychiatrists, psychologists, or from some other field, expect their patients to talk about themselves, their personal histories, parents, friends, enemies, hopes, wishes, fears, dreams, goals, the varieties of pains and pleasures they have experienced.

The first part of psychoanalysis is called the *analysis*. The second part is called the *synthesis*. The analysis is simply that: an analysis of the patient's past, the effect of that past, the ways in which the past experiences influence present behavior, especially if that influence is toxic or gets in the way of achieving some reasonable level of psychological comfort and achievement in life. The synthesis, on the other hand, is an effort designed to restructure and redirect behavior along lines that hopefully will lead to a greater level of psychological comfort and achievement for the patient. It is a lengthy effort for the analyst and the analysand, and most of the responsibility is with the patient. They may meet as often as four times a week for three or four years—sometimes longer—and through it all, most of the time in each session, which can last as long as an hour, is taken up by the patient, talking.

To be a "successful patient" the analysand must wage a subtle war against his own psychophobia, often digging for hidden and repressed memories of past experiences and present feelings. If that subtle war is won or at least partially won, the analysand may gradually shed some of his old, overused defending behaviors and develop what has been called an openness to new experience. That is, he may experience not only the environment but also himself with a greater degree of freedom and self-directedness.

Psychoanalytic theory, the body of knowledge, semiknowledge, and speculations, is based upon (1) what psychoanalysts believe to be the essential ingredients of human behavior and (2) what psychoanalysts have charted as their patients tour through their own minds. The application of psychoanalytic theory has been widespread. The clinical aspects of psychoanalysis, the couch and chair work, the sessions attended only by the analyst and the analysand, have severe limitations. While the theory is and has been used widely in the treatment of mental illness, the practice of psychoanalysis itself has made only a small dent in that treatment. There are reasons for this. In the first place, psychoanalysts require extensive training. To gain acceptance in an institute that trains analysts, the individual must usually prove competence in the clinical practice of psychiatry, psychology, or in a few, select instances, in psychiatric social work and mental health, psychiatric, nursing. One highly unusual exception is Erik Erikson, a teacher in a small American school in Vienna, a man with no genuinely professional training of any kind when he was accepted as a trainee in the Vienna Psychoanalytic Institute (Maier, 1965).

Related to the stringent requirements for entrance into an institute are the high standards for patients who wish to become analysands. Usually they must be at least average or, preferably, above average in intelligence. They must have a good command of the language, mainly the spoken word, for they are required to speak about themselves at great length. They must be psychologically intact, mentally organized to a degree that helps to insure a more or less sensible listening to the analyst whenever he has something to say. In other terms, psychotic analysands may not fare well on the couch. Added to all this is the idea of time and money. Patients for psychoanalysis are usually required to have enough of both to afford the experience. In sum, the clinical practice of psychoanalysis is a limited endeavor reaching a small fraction of those who need or who think they need help with living.

The psychoanalytic method of psychotherapy and almost the whole of psychoanalytic theory depend heavily upon the use of language, especially the spoken and the written word. There is some room for nonverbal language such as laughter, crying, and other gestures of the body. Psychoanalysis is, however, essentially verbal. Psychodrama, on the other hand, is not only verbal but also heavily action-oriented and nonverbal.

PSYCHODRAMA

Psychodrama began in 1911. It was started by Jacob Levy Moreno, who found that if he allowed children to act out their problems in a "let's pretend" kind of game, they could more easily identify their problems and begin to do something about them. In 1921, Moreno founded the Theater of Spontaneity, *Stegreiftheater*, in Vienna. Sigmund Freud was 65 years of age at the time, living in the same city, famous throughout the world. Erik Erikson was 19 years old, unknown, a wanderer whose potential had not yet been realized.

Beginning with his work with children, extending that work to adults in his *Stegreiftheater*, Moreno demonstrated the versatility of the psychodrama. In time the theory and practice of psychodrama was used and continues to be used in mental health clinics, prisons, mental hospitals, corporations, schools, theological seminaries, and in the training of officers in the military. This widespread use of psychodrama stands in direct contrast with the limited use of psychoanalytic practice. Another constrast involves the theoretical aspects. Psychoanalysis is loaded with theory, so much so that it is doubtful anyone has ever read all the available material. Psychodrama is not so heavily laden. In comparison, psychoanalysis is elephantine, while psychodrama is like a deer. One moves ponderously through the forest, leaving a wide and well-marked trail. The other streaks across the landscape, moving with such speed and agility it often leaves few tracks to follow. This is not to say that one is better than the other; the comparisons are meant to convey the idea of the difference between the two types of psychotherapy.

Another contrast exists in the numbers

of registered and certified practitioners within each of these two fields. According to Moore and Fine (1968) there are fewer than 1,500 members of the American Psychoanalytic Association. The precise number of fully qualified, practicing psychoanalysts in the United States is probably less than 2,000. In addition, there are some people on the fringes, some who have not graduated from an approved institute and a scattering of "psychoanalysts" who have had no training of any kind except in salesmanship of the self.*

There are fewer than one hundred individuals from varied backgrounds who have enough formal training and experience to call themselves a certified director of psychodrama, sociometry, and group psychotherapy.† Directors are certified by the Moreno Institute in Beacon, N. Y. There are, however, additional hundreds of uncertified individuals who have enough training and experience to conduct psychodrama in an adequate, often superb, and useful way. But here again, as in the area of clinical psychoanalysis, there is a sprinkling of individuals across the land who have had no training, no genuine experience, but who manage to sell themselves as knowledgeable experts in the field.

The activities that take place in a psy-

chodrama involve several different stages. The main stages are called (1) *exploration* and (2) *integration*. These stages are similar to the psychoanalytic phases of analysis and synthesis mentioned on a prior page. Exploration and integration, however, usually take place in one psychodrama session that may last for from one to five or six hours. Psychoanalytic analysis and synthesis may take several hundreds of hours, perhaps 1,000 hours and more, spread out over many years.

Exploration and integration can perhaps be best understood by taking a look at the Hollander psychodrama curve (1969). Three steps are represented on the curve, and two dimensions. The dimensions are time and "emotional quality," or degree of overt emotional expression.

An adequately directed psychodrama generally follows the sequence of events partially shown in the curve. Those events require that a group be present and be guided by the director through the steps of the psychodrama.

Step 1, the warm-up, is somewhat similar to "getting acquainted" or "establishing rapport." Initially it involves the encounter, or the *Begegnung* (Moreno, 1953), during which the director asks the individuals in the group to encounter themselves. The individuals are told in various ways to think only of self, to look inward and examine the emotional feelings they have at that moment, the physical tensions they might have, their general and overall sense of being. This activity may take as little

---

*It is possible to obtain a membership list of the American Psychoanalytic Association by writing to them at One East 57th Street, New York, N. Y. 10022.
†Carl Hollander, personal communication.

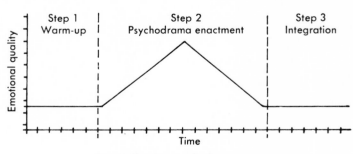

The Hollander psychodrama curve

as five minutes or last as long as an hour, depending upon the level of tension and wariness in the group and upon the style of the director.

Eventually this activity is followed by the second aspect of the *Begegnung*, the encounter of the individual in the group with other individuals of the group. The shift is from "me with me" to "me with you." This second aspect of *Begegnung* involves increased activity on the part of the director and the participants, the group. The participants may be directed to engage in one or a variety of action techniques. The action techniques range from group singing to a pairing off of group members. In pairs, one person may pretend to be a child, while the other individual may pretend to be a parent or a teacher. Sometimes the individuals in the group are asked to pretend to be whoever they most admire, and individuals may choose to be Moses or Mark Spitz, Mother Goose or Muhammad Ali. Some may pretend they are Sigmund Freud, Diana Ross, Garfunkle, or Jesus Christ. While they pretend, they talk with each other. Hopefully the tensions and the wariness of the individuals begin to subside.

The action techniques used in the second aspect of the *Begegnung* end when all the group members are asked to sit down, either in chairs or on the floor. Then it is time for the beginning of the sociometric process. This is the last part of the warm-up (Moreno, 1953).

During the sociometric process the director allows anyone to talk about anything, but as can be expected, the conversation generally involves what has just taken place: the action techniques of the *Begegnung*. Eventually, and in various ways, the director asks if anyone would like to work. It is an invitation. As with many invitations, it may be accepted or refused either directly or indirectly. If the invitation is refused, the director may return to action techniques or continue with the group discussion, or he may slowly bring the session to a close. If the invitation is accepted, several members of the group may speak out. Each may express a wish to work on a given problem or difficulty with life. The problem or difficulty may be with life as it exists now or as the now is tainted and compromised by past experiences. For example, if the invitation is accepted, group members may say things like the following:

Person A: "Well, I'm flunking out of school, and I don't care. But I'm worried that I don't care, and besides it's almost fun to watch my father climb the wall. I guess I'd like to work on what's happening between my father and me. We hate each other, sort of. And we like each other. He and I had a big fight the other day, and I'd like to to work on that."

Person B: "I'd like to work on my acne problem. I don't have acne now—you can see that, but I used to and sometimes it's like I still have it. I mean I feel pretty ugly, but I'm not ugly. Know what I mean?"

Person C: "My mother died two months ago. We had relatives come from all over, and there was a big funeral and all that, but I got all closed up and acted like a robot. I didn't cry or laugh or anything—it felt like I was almost paralyzed, and it still feels that way. Everything's dull."

Other members of the group may speak up, disclosing information about themselves, talking of problems or difficulties they would like to work on. In time the disclosures end. The director then asks the members of the group to choose, to vote on whose problem or difficulty is to become the focus of the psychodrama. The person with the most votes becomes the *sociometric star* of the psychodrama, the *protagonist*. At that point, the actual psychodrama begins.

Step 2, the psychodrama enactment, takes place on a stage. There may be an actual stage available, or the stage may merely be an open area in a large room. The protagonist is asked to get on the stage with the director. At that moment the group becomes the audience. The protagonist is asked to set the scene, to construct with tables, chairs, and imagination a genuine physical setting known to the protagonist. If, for example, person A is chosen by the group, he may set the scene at home in the room where he had the fight with his father. Person B could set a scene years ago in a high school classroom in which she experienced strong feelings of lowered self-esteem because of an acne problem. Person C could set the scene at the graveside. In any case the protagonist sets the scene with physical objects and also, under direction, describes and outlines time of day, perhaps the weather, or sounds coming from other rooms. When the scene is established to a degree comfortable to the protagonist, he is asked to play himself in that scene, to be as he was in that setting, and to pick someone from the audience to be the father, as in the instance of person A, or the dead mother, as with person C. These other actors in the psychodrama are substitutes for the real people and are known in psychodramatic terminology as *auxiliary egos.* They represent significant individuals who exist as a part of the protagonist's *social atom,* the smallest number of individuals necessary to fulfill the interpersonal role the protagonist plays.

When the protagonist begins to act out his role with individuals chosen from the audience, scene 1 of step 2 is under way. Scene 1 normally begins at a slow pace as protagonist and auxiliary ego talk about routine matters. If, to continue the example, person A is the protagonist, he will work with an auxiliary ego who plays the part of his father. They may begin with "Hi, Dad" and "Hi, Son" and progress to "Sure was a good game on television" and "Yeah, that sure was" as each gradually settles into his role. At this point or perhaps later the director or an assistant or someone chosen from the audience may

act as the protagonist's *double.* The double stands behind or to one side of the protagonist, often imitating his gestures, his body position and movements. At the same time the double may say out loud things the protagonist might be thinking but not saying. For example, if the protagonist smiles and says, "Sure was a good game on television," the double will smile and perhaps say, "I'm trying to be friendly."

At the beginning phase of the actual psychodrama the complexity of Moreno's ideas-in-action can be seen. On stage are the director, the protagonist, one auxiliary ego, and a double—four people—functioning in a physical environment that has been constructed and described by the protagonist. If the director is skilled and if the protagonist has the psychological freedom to live rather than merely act his role, the psychodrama increases in emotional intensity and often complexity. There may be additional auxiliary egos selected from the audience. Perhaps person A requires the addition of his mother to fill out his social atom, perhaps a sister or a brother. The drama unfolds. As it does, the protagonist moves from the highly cognitive scene setting and initial contact with an auxiliary ego to less cognitive and gradually more affectually intense interactions. Person A, for example, may explore the depth of his feelings for his father, and those feelings may involve only words at first and then physical fighting, using not fists but fighting pillows or punching bags. In contrast, person A may discover that his feelings are weighted on the side of affection, the anger being merely a defensive mask covering over the affection. Or person A may discover his feelings are a combination of anger and affection, feelings that can be separated one from the other to be more clearly understood, more adequately managed.

Optimally the high point of the psychodrama is an emotional peak, which may be reached in scene 1 (rarely), in scene 2, or 3, or 4, or beyond. Scene 1 is of course a subpsychodrama that takes place in a setting that has been carefully constructed by the protagonist from chairs, tables, and imagination. The other scenes may take place in the same setting or in different, imagined locations such as the backyard, a car, school, or a store. Whatever the case, the high point of the psychodrama enactment is represented by the peak of the Hollander psychodrama curve as it is shown in step 2. The high point is called the *climax of catharsis*. During the climax of catharsis an *abreaction** often takes place; that is, there is a discharge or expression of previously repressed feelings and thoughts. It is possible for the protagonist to see himself in a somewhat different light, with a slightly altered view.

Once the climax of catharsis has taken place, the nature of the psychodrama begins to change. As Hollander (1969) points out, exploration is over, and integration begins.

> Once the emotional peak has been achieved, the director should assist the protagonist in "closing down" the drama. Rather then further exploration and disclosure, the protagonist is urged to concentrate upon closing the session and building integration into the psychodrama. [p. 11]

One aspect of the building of integration, which in the psychodrama refers to an attempt at interweaving the feelings and thoughts of the protagonist to enhance understanding and control of both is called providing for what is called *surplus reality*. In many psychodramas the director can guide the protagonist into using whatever he has learned about himself in a rehearsal for the future. The protagonist may find, in this rehearsal, alternatives to old ways of behaving. If, to stay with our example, person A has discovered he genuinely dislikes his father, he may come to realize

---

*Abreaction is a term borrowed from psychoanalysis.

during an episode of director–controlled surplus reality that it may be more useful to express the disliking more directly than by the old method in which he (Person A) became engaged in self-defeating behavior (flunking classes) to antagonize the father. Surplus reality refers to the extension and expanison of the individual's typical or normative behavior; it is an effort designed to bring into view alternative and perhaps more realistic behaviors.

Directors of psychodrama may, with experience, have a variety of techniques that can be used during surplus reality. The director, for example, may place the protagonist in a chair, facing an empty chair. The protagonist may be asked to pretend that he, the protagonist, is in that empty chair. He may be directed to talk to himself, often suggesting alternative behaviors. Sometimes the protagonist will be directed to engage in a conversation with his own double or to have some winding-down talks with one or more of the auxiliary egos. In the end, at the last part of step 2, the protagonist usually is required to finish on a positive note, sometimes planning his real-life activities along more productive and more beneficial lines of behavior.

*Step 3, integration,*begins when the protagonist and the director and anyone else on the stage return to the audience. They sit back down in their chairs, or on the floor. The audience is asked for comments, for self-disclosures. At this point members of the audience often are able to describe how they felt as they witnessed the psychodrama. Often the participants will be able to describe events in their own lives that were similar to those they have just seen on the stage. The discussion may take five or ten minutes; often it may last for an hour.

The final phase of step 3 is a summary of what has happened. The summarization may be furnished by the director, by the protagonist, or by anyone in the audience, and the shift is from affective to cognitive. Hollander (1969) writes:

> As the members endeavor to integrate their feelings, experiences, and thoughts into a congruous whole, they simultaneously insure themselves against the possibility that anyone will exit from the session in "psychodramatic shock" or in a state of incompleteness, pain or panic. One way to close an emotionally energized group is to help members return to their "heads," i.e., their intellectual processes. [p. 16]

Several features are central to Moreno's work. One of these is the belief that acting a part in a controlled and guided psychodrama promotes the development of a clearer picture of oneself in action and fosters the idea there may be alternate and better—more productive, more mature—ways of behaving. Another central feature of psychodrama is that it takes place in a group, an admittedly synthetic group, but the longer a group stays together, the more it comes to resemble a natural group (Moreno, 1959) engaged in self-disclosing social behavior. Moreno's psychodrama can be considered a reaction against Freud's elitist psychoanalysis. Over the years, however, psychodramatists have adopted a great many terms of psychoanalysis.

BEHAVIOR MODIFICATION

Behavior modification is eight syllables long, which amounts to one syllable for each decade of its development. The term can be shortened to two syllables, B-mod, which may help anyone to remember that the major thrust in developing this kind of psychotherapy has taken place in America in the last two decades.

B-mod's development can be traced back to the early works of Edward L. Thorndike. As a 22-year-old graduate student in 1896, Thorndike became involved in research in learning in cats, fish, chickens, and monkeys. (Sigmund Freud was 40 years old that year.) Thorndike later went on to other areas of study,* but he is remembered as the first individual to adapt modern laboratory research techniques to the study of animal behavior.

Ivan Pavlov, the famed Russian researcher, gave credit to Thorndike for helping him in his own work in respondent conditioning or, as it is more often called, *classical conditioning* (Larson, 1972). Pavlov is the man who conditioned dogs to salivate at the sound of a bell. To illustrate what he did, we can shift from dogs and bells to humans and the sound of a small truck engine. The sound of the engine is recorded on tape in a tape recorder operated by pressing "on" and "off" switches that click. Additional equipment includes two chairs facing each other. Between the two chairs is a table upon which rests the tape recorder and a very bright light. The experimenter (E) sits in one chair; the subject (S) of the experiment sits in the other chair. E and S meet together, facing each other, for two hours a day for two weeks. S sits, looking at the bright light, which is turned off most of the time. E is substantially more active. His activity, though, is rigidly governed by a procedure he goes through every thirty seconds. He must follow this sequence:

1. Sit in chair with both hands in lap.
2. Move right hand up to tape recorder; press the "on" switch.
3. Move right hand to light switch; turn on light.
4. Move right hand back to tape recorder; press the "off" switch.
5. Move right hand to light switch; turn light off.
6. Move right hand back to lap.

This is a technologically crude arrangement. The tape recorder and the bright light could be switched on and off automatically by the addition of some apparatus such as electrically timed switches.

---

*He wrote fifty books and hundreds of research articles in various areas of psychology.

The procedure could be automated, and E could read a book or write letters during the two-hour session. But as it now exists, the procedure can be used to illustrate some factors in the experiment. In that experiment, E is busy, and S is required merely to sit in the chair looking at the light that E turns on and off. The light is called the *unconditioned stimulus* (US). Every time the US is used, a predictable and normal event takes place. The pupils of S's eyes contract to adapt to the sudden brightness. That contraction is called the *unconditioned response* (UR).

We are, as humans, almost constantly in some circumstance that involves US and UR. When the weather is hot and humid (US), we perspire (UR). In cold weather (US) we shiver (UR). At twilight, when the light grows dim (US), our pupils expand (UR), but in this small experiment there are some added features. There is the taped sound of a truck engine, which in this experiment and in the language of conditioning is called the *conditioned stimulus* (CS). The CS is presented to S by E just before the US is brought into use. CS and US are paired repeatedly during the conditioning. The conditioning, in the *experimental design* or the plan and procedure, lasts for two weeks. E and S work together two hours a day, and in the span of fourteen days a total of twenty-eight hours is set aside for conditioning of the pupillary response. During those twenty-eight hours E is required to move through his procedure every thirty seconds. E does this 3,360 times in the twenty-eight hours. By that time S's pupils will probably contract before the light is turned on. S's pupils will contract, it seems, whenever the sound of the truck engine is heard. The light is no longer necessary to bring about the UR. The CS does the job. Conditioning has taken place, and the pupillary response is no longer called UR. It is now CR, a *conditioned response*.

At this point, E may choose to explore more about CS and the CR. E no longer requires the bright light, the US. Every time E presses the "on" switch of the tape recorder and a truck engine can be heard, S's pupils contract (CR). E can remove the tape from the recorder and press the "on" switch. S's pupils may contract simply because of the clicking sound of the switch.

To take matters one more step, perhaps S's pupils will contract each time E moves a hand from his lap toward the tape recorder. In effect, in this experiment there is more to consider than the original and single CS; there is a complex of stimuli. The *stimulus complex* developed because (1) the experimental design and the conditions in which the experiment was conducted lacked precision and adequate controls and (2) humans as well as many other organisms may focus in on and pay attention to or may be affected by a great variety of factors in the environment, factors that E or any observer (O) may overlook. There is a multiplicity of variables even in this small slice of life.

The small experiment mentioned above was a sloppy one, but it may be useful to illustrate some other factors that form a part of what is called conditioning. Consider S, for example. If he were to leave the laboratory, walk down the corridor and out of the building, he would leave the artificial experimental environment and enter a more real-world environment. Suppose he walked half a block to a busy street corner. There, pedestrians are talking to one another, cars are going by, and trucks. It is an environment considerably different from the laboratory. But, let us say, a truck passes by, and he hears the engine. If at that moment his pupils contract, the CR is said to be *generalized;* that is, stimuli other than but perhaps similar to the original can cause the same response as the original. In contrast, let us say a truck passes by, and his pupils do not contract. That differential in responses indicates what is called *discrimination,* which means the ability to differentiate between stimuli or between the same stimuli in different environments.

Generalization and discrimination are often important aspects of behavior. In learning the alphabet, for instance, it is important for children to discriminate between A and B and C. Generalization comes into view, however, when a block letter A comes to mean the same as a script letter *A* or a Teutonic A. They are all the letter A, and it is necessary to respond to them in a generalized way. To continue the example, it is useful for a girl to discriminate psychologically between father and brother and boyfriend. To discriminate is to expand the number of possible responses an individual may make. To discriminate between different individuals is often to see them as the individuals they actually are. On the other hand, to generalize is to limit the possible number of responses. In specific circumstances, generalizations may be appropriate. For instance, it is appropriate for the girl to expect all males to go to the men's room if they need a rest stop. It is not appropriate for the girl to expect all males to read *Time* magazine, drink beer, and drive a three-year-old sedan simply because her father does.

Discrimination and generalization are two aspects of classical or respondent conditioning. They also exist as aspects or factors of operant conditioning. *Operant conditioning* differs from classical conditioning in that S is not passive in the operant situation. In the crude experiment in which S's pupillary responses were conditioned, S simply sat in the chair looking at the light. S was a passive recipient. In contrast, operant conditioning requires or uses the active participation of S.

Operant conditioning is also known as positive conditioning and instrumental learning (Skinner, 1953; Grossberg, 1964). The pathway that led to the use of operant conditioning as a method of repair began

in early attempts to tighten up and make more precise the language, the terminology, of psychoanalysis. Approximately a quarter of a century ago, Dollard and Miller (1950) wrote *Personality and Psychotherapy*, a book that tried to unite and blend portions of psychoanalysis with what was known about human learning. They did not, however, develop a new or different form of psychotherapy. Not long after, Eysenck (1952) reviewed the success rates of psychoanalytically based psychotherapy and found those rates to be no better, on the average, than if the subjects had received no psychotherapy at all. Spurred on by these findings, a few psychologists began to consider operant conditioning with greater interest as a real but untapped form of psychotherapy. Neurotic behavior was defined not as a cluster of symptoms but as a set of habits learned by way of conditioning. And it was deduced that by way of conditioning, neurotic habits could be *extinguished*. The focus was and still is on the modification and change of behavior through operant conditioning. What is changed is what can be observed, more or less, in the now, in the present circumstance. Little attention is paid to the individual's life history, his underlying motivations, or his unconscious. In B-mod the unconscious does not exist. As Mikulas (1972) explains:

> If a person has a fear of cats, eliminate the fear rather than look for subconscious conflicts which produce the fear. If the person is an alcoholic, stop his drinking behavior rather than look for underlying causes. [p. 6]

His comments sound sleek and simple. They are, compared to the arduous prose of psychoanalysis and psychodrama. Yet, beneath the seemingly sleek and simple rests an extensive foundation of research. At the core of that research is knowledge about the effects of (1) rewarding adequate or desirable behaviors, (2) punishing inadequate or undesirable behaviors, and (3) combining reward and punishment in the guidance and control of behavior. It is through the use of reward and punishment that behavior is reinforced and extinguished. Reward and punishment can be considered as information the patient uses as he works on the modification of his own behavior. That information the patient receives, those rewards and those punishments, are called *feedback*.

We all receive feedback. It can come in the form of a smile or a frown for something we have done. Feedback can be a promotion on the job or getting fired. It may be a passing grade in a course or a flunking grade. Our behavior may bring rewards or punishments, or it may be ignored, which often is a subtle form of punishment. Through the effects of reward and punishment, we learn. To learn and to unlearn is modification of behavior. But in our daily lives the feedback varies and can be confusing. We can, for example, behave in a certain way, and some of those we know will frown while others will smile. On the job we can work with energy and diligence and be rewarded with a promotion. Or we can, because of that energy and diligence, trigger a sense of anxiety in the supervisor, who may think the diligent worker is after his job, and we may be fired. This variability of feedback can be controlled in the design of a B-mod therapy experiment. The feedback can be made consistent and specific. For an example we can look at B-mod from the viewpoint of extinguishing behavior. For our example, we can use the habit of smoking cigarettes.

In our therapy experiment a cigarette smoker is required to smoke a pack of cigarettes in an hour. He may stand or sit or lean against the wall, but every time he puts the cigarette to his lips and inhales, he is given a small but slightly painful electric shock through some wires attached to his wrist. In an hour he smokes twenty cigarettes. Each cigarette requires twenty inhalations to consume it. Each inhalation is punished by an electric shock. In an hour the patient has received 400 shocks, and he may be slightly less inclined to smoke. But, let us say, this hour of punishment is repeated every day for a week. That amounts to 2,800 shocks for 2,800 inhalations. After that many shocks the smoker may be a confirmed nonsmoker.*

To sail off briefly in the opposite direction, consider not the extinction of smoking behavior but the reinforcement of what can be agreed upon as adequate or desirable behavior. Consider, for example, the matter of physical fitness. Our cigarette smoker no longer smokes. His lungs, however, have been ravaged by five years of smoke inhaled from over 36,000 cigarettes consumed at the rate of one pack a day. His body is not in the best condition, and his lungs of course are in bad shape. In addition, let us say he is a college student almost always in need of money. A physical fitness therapy experiment may be built upon the data so far assembled.

The student is asked, and he agrees, to run and walk a mile before breakfast every morning of the week for three months. During the first week he is allowed to run-walk a mile in twenty minutes. If he is successful, he gets twenty-five dollars as a reward for the week's effort. During the second week he must run the mile in fifteen minutes, and when he finishes that week, he gets another twenty-five dollars. This procedure can be continued to the point where the student can run the mile in six minutes. The reward of money is a reinforcer. There are, however, additional reinforcers that may come into being as a result of the running. The student may simply "feel better," have more general stamina, perhaps even easily do better in

---

*The reader is cautioned not to try this kind of therapy experiment unless there has been a careful review of the risks of using electric shock.

his course work because of the running (Ismail and Trachtman, 1973).

B-mod activities go well beyond the operant conditioning therapy experiments mentioned above. J. G. White (1959), for example, described a young girl who stopped eating when her father died. White began his modification procedure by becoming involved in playing (play therapy) with the young patient. The play therapy consisted of setting up tea parties attended by the girl, her therapist, and a doll. In the beginning the girl would merely pretend to eat. She then began to eat doll-sized portions of the tea party food. White guided the girl through successive steps of eating more in different settings (generalizing her behavior) until the girl ate independently.

James McConnell (1970), in describing the variety of ways in which B-mod may be used, mentioned some of the work of Ivar Lovaas at UCLA. Dr. Lovaas worked with an 11-year-old boy who had spent seven years in a mental hospital for children. The boy was violently self-destructive. He tried so consistently to hurt himself that he was tied down in his hospital bed for almost twenty-four hours a day. When he was brought to Lovaas, the boy was not tied down to anything, and he began to physically hurt himself. Lovaas leaned forward and touched the lad with an electric cattle prod. The boy instantly stopped his self-destructive behavior, looked around, perhaps with some sense of surprise, and then began to hurt himself again. Again Lovaas touched him with the cattle prod. The boy stopped. But he started up again, and once more Lovaas touched him, giving him another electric shock. After that the boy had had enough. He did not tear at his own flesh anymore when Dr. Lovaas was around. The first stage of B-mod therapy was successful. The whole sequence of conditioning took thirty seconds.

The electric shocks that Lovaas adminis-

tered to the boy were a painful feedback the boy received for his own seemingly psychotic behavior. Before he met Lovaas, however, the boy had received a much different kind of feedback for that same behavior. In the hospital when he would try to hurt himself, a nurse would rush up to him and hold the boy and make gentle sounds until the lad calmed down. It must not have taken long for the nurses to condition the boy by rewarding his self-destructive behavior with loving attention, a positive and rewarding feedback.

The possible effects of feedback, according to Mikulas (1972), include the following:

1. Feedback may function as a reinforcement or punishment.
2. Feedback may produce motivational changes such as in how hard the person works or the goals he sets.
3. Feedback may provide cues about appropriate future behavior.
4. Feedback may result in a new learning experience or rehearsal of previous learning. [p. 95]

Feedback is an essential ingredient of biofeedback. *Biofeedback* is a term used to describe highly specialized applications of B-mod in which the individual learns how to control previously uncontrollable parts on his own physiology. With sufficient biofeedback training, persons may control their own heart rate, blood pressure, and other physical aspects of existence including certain brain waves and stomach contractions. Biofeedback is relatively new in the United States, but it is old in Asia. In this country it can be traced to the work of Neal Miller (1969), who tied together the work of others and went on to contribute his own.

B-mod is based upon a long and extensive heritage of research. Some few may consider it scientific, but more accurately it can be viewed as an aspect of technology (Lanyon, 1971). While the examples of B-mod treatment given so far have involved only one patient and one experimenter-therapist, B-mod has been used successfully in group settings. There will be some mention of group applications of B-mod principles in the next section of this chapter. For now, it is appropriate to move on to another kind of formalized repair called psychopharmacology.

PSYCHOPHARMACOLOGY

Psychopharmacology has roots that can be traced back to the nineteenth century when Pasteur and others began to develop vaccines that helped to bring communicable diseases under control. Diphtheria, whooping cough, scarlet fever, and a variety of other illnesses were prevented by the use of vaccines. Later, penicillin was developed to combat infections and prolong life. Then came the tranquilizers. They have been widely used for only the past twenty years (Ray, 1972). The realm of tranquilizers and other *psychoactive* drugs can be viewed as a carefully developed scientific enterprise. There are, of course, laboratories and research centers that compound and investigate the effects of various drugs, but their use may be another matter. According to Lewis Thomas (1972), dean of the Yale University School of Medicine, physicians are often faced with the demand to do something—almost anything—for the patient to (1) cure (sometimes), (2) relieve (often), and (3) comfort (always). Partially because of the demands placed upon the physician, the use of various drugs cannot be viewed as being as carefully governed by scientific principles as their discovery or manufacture. Charlotte Muller (1972) maintains we have an overmedicated society, but Michael Halberstam (1972) states that patients rarely take their medications as the doctor has ordered. They take far less than has been prescribed. Ray (1972) states that the use of drugs has affected society, but the changes within our environment, the social and technological changes, have also affected the use of drugs. The primary change in the use of

drugs in recent times has been the rapid growth in the illegal use of what Ray calls the phantasticants.

Phantasticants include LSD, peyote, DOM (STP), *Amanita muscaria*, henbane, deadly nightshade, teonanacatl, DMT, and mandrake, all of which induce hallucinations and are called hallucinogens. There are, in addition, such drugs as ololiuqui and ergot, which causes Saint Anthony's fire* (Fuller, 1968), marijuana (also spelled marihuana), and hashish or hash, which is sometimes called charas (Grinspoon, 1969). While some of the phantasticants, such as LSD, are of recent development, others, such as ergot, have a very long history, but perhaps not as long a history as opium, which has been part of man's environment for almost 6,000 years. Morphine was first derived from opium in 1800, and in 1853, Alexander Wood perfected the hypodermic syringe. Morphine could then be easily administered, to be quickly absorbed by the body. By the time of the American Civil War, hollow needles and morphine were available for use by military physicians, and addiction was so common it became known as "the soldier's disease." In 1874, heroin was derived by slightly altering the morphine molecule, but by then Americans already had codeine. Not long afterwards, meperidine came into existence. None of these will be included in the general area of psychopharmacology in this book. Neither the phantasticants, the narcotics, nor such chemical compounds as nicotine, alcohol, caffeine, aspirin, various laxatives, and cold or cough remedies will be focused upon in this chapter. Instead, we shall concentrate upon psychopharmacology from the vantage point of the psychotherapeutic drugs.

---

*Saint Anthony's fire is an unusual physical condition in which arms and legs become gangrenous and drop off the torso of the living person.

Psychotherapeutic psychopharmacology stands on a foundation that consists of the following:

1. Drugs are to be administered to patients only under the direct control and ultimate responsibility of a physician. While nurses, especially psychiatric nurses, may be of assistance in a drug program and while useful information may be provided by physiologists, behavioral biologists, and some specialized psychologists, drug control rests with the physician.
2. There is no such thing as a "bad" or a "good" drug. A drug may be used improperly or carelessly, but to state that drugs are bad makes as much sense as calling a car or a camera bad. The *use* of these things may be bad, but in and of themselves, they are neither good nor bad.
3. Psychopharmacology may be a *treatment* effort involving patients. It may also be a *research* effort in which individuals, some of whom may be patients, consciously volunteer as test or research subjects in programs designed to investigate the effects of drugs on behavior. In the event that treatment and research are combined, the physician and his associates must follow carefully outlined procedures.
4. The effect of a drug used in psychopharmacology depends upon (a) the amount of the drug taken, (b) the individual patient's history, and (c) the expectations the patient may have about the effect of the drug.

A widely used family of chemically related drugs are the phenothiazines. The phenothiazines have been used in the treatment of all psychotic conditions except where severe depression is present (Redlich and Freedman, 1966).

A representative drug of the phenothiazine family is listed at the top of Table 7. Chlorpromazine was first used in connection with the treatment of psychotic individuals in 1952.* Within a few years that drug and the other phenothiazines were used effectively to reduce the number of patients in psychiatric hospitals (Redlich and Freedman, 1966). Oakley Ray (1972) maintains that without psychopharmacology the number of patients in mental hospitals would have reached 750,000 by 1970. Because of the phenothiazines together with some other drugs, the actual number of hospitalized psychotic individuals in 1970 was 338,600. One of the other drugs is imipramine, known more commonly by its trade name Tofranil. It is used in the psychopharmacological treatment of depression. As for the manic disorders, lithium carbonate has come to be preferred by many physicians, although its use in psychopharmacology is relatively new.

The phenothiazines, imipramine, and lithium carbonate have been used successfully in the treatment of psychotic and borderline psychotic conditions. The effective treatment of neurotic conditions is another matter. Psychopharmacology is not so clearly useful in the treatment of neurotic states, but medications are available, nevertheless. Four of them are listed in the second section of Table 7. In addition to those four drugs are a number of other compounds, which may be labeled as depressants. They do not cause emotional depression. They depress or slow down some physiological function of the human body. One of the depressants is almost famous, though not by its real name. It is called the Mickey Finn. In an ancient movie, W. C. Fields, holding a pool cue in one hand and flicking cigar ashes on the floor, turns to a bartender and asks,

---

*Between 1952 and 1956 there were approximately 1,000 published research studies involving the use of chlorpromazine. One percent of these studies can be considered as adequate and performed under careful supervision. Ninety-nine percent proved nothing (Peterson, 1966).

"Has Michael Finn been in today?" The bartender gets the signal and puts a white powder in a glass of beer that he serves to Field's opponent in the pool game. The opponent sips the beer and falls to the floor unconscious. There are moments when movies do not accurately portray life, and this is one of them. A Mickey Finn, more accurately known as chloral hydrate, does not bring fast relief from consciousness. It takes at least half a hour to do its work. Its work usually involves the reduction of anxiety and the development of sleep. Chloral hydrate and other chemical compounds such as sodium bromide, potassium bromide, and paraldehyde, which produces a potent halatosis, are known as nonbarbiturates. The barbiturates have a history that goes back a mere century—less than two lifetimes into the past. They are used to reduce anxiety,

bring about sleep, and control epilepsy. They are shown in the last part of Table 7.

In addition to the drugs mentioned so far, there is a small congregation of stimulants, such as cocaine and the amphetamines. Cocaine can be extracted from the leaves of the coca plant, a large bush. The leaves of that bush may, it appears, provide some of the ingredients for common items of our environment such as cola soft drinks.*

Cocaine—also known as coke, star dust, and snow—can bring about a short term excitation, but if taken over an extended period of time, the drug may produce convulsions and a sense of depression. In the past, amphetamines have been used in the treatment of depression, fatigue, and in weight-reduction programs. Now, however, their use—their legal use—has been restricted to the treatment of overactive behavior, especially in children, short-term weight reduction programs, and narcolepsy. (Narcolepsy is a condition in which an individual slides into sleep quickly, easily, and repeatedly no matter where he or she may be.)

All the drugs mentioned so far can be obtained illegally. They usually cost more to buy when they are purchased without a prescription, and the risks in taking them are often extraordinarily high, ranging from constipation to death. Even when they are taken under a physician's orders, risks exist. Wade (1973) reports, for example, that a million and a half people are admitted to hospitals every year because of unwanted and often dangerous-to-life reactions to drugs.

Steven

Steven was 24 years old, 6 feet tall, and weighed slightly more than 120 pounds when

Table 7. Common psychopharmacological agents*

Generic name	Trade name
Phenothiazine Family	
chlorpromazine	Thorazine
triflupromazine	Vesprin
prochlorperazine	Compazine
trifluoperazine	Stelazine
perphenazine	Trilafon
thiopropazate	Dartal
thioridazine	Mellaril
Drugs commonly used in the treatment of neurosis	
chlordiazepoxide	Librium
diazepam	Valium
mephenesin	Tolserol
meprobamate	Equanil, Miltown
Barbiturates	
barbital	Veronal
phenobarbital	Luminal
amobarbital	Amytal
pentobarbital	Nembutal
secobarbital	Seconal

*Adapted from Ray, O. S.: Drugs, society, and human behavior, St. Louis, 1972, The C. V. Mosby Co.; and McNeil, E. D.: The psychoses, Englewood Cliffs, N.J., 1970, Prentice-Hall, Inc.

*Oakley Ray has written a book titled *Drugs, Society, and Human Behavior*, which includes an historical background to the cola business and the coca bush.

he came into the clinic. He looked exhausted, and he told the intake interviewer he'd had his last fix five hours ago and was worried about getting sick. He had no money, he couldn't afford his habit any more, and besides he wanted to stop. The intake worker quickly called a psychiatrist to interview Steven. The psychiatrist noted the restlessness, the yawning, the runny nose, and the wet and tearing eyes and asked Steven if he had a heroin habit.

Steven admitted he had an addiction that cost him fifty dollars a day, and he wanted to get out of the habit. The psychiatrist gave him 10 milligrams of methadone to prevent withdrawal symptoms, and then they sat down together for a lengthy interview. Steven had been on the stuff for about two years, and when he could not get heroin, he would take bennies (amphetamines), red jackets (Seconal), or marijuana. Once in a while he drank half a pint of vodka, but only to slow down if he had taken too many bennies.

Steven was a dropout from graduate school. He had gone to Ohio State for four years, where he had earned a degree in education. He worked as a teacher in Pennsylvania for a school year, saving his money for graduate school.

He had entered graduate school to get an M.A. in educational administration, but he dropped out of school during the second semester because as he said, "I was really bored. I was really sick of school. I started school in kindergarten and went all the way through for the other twelve years and then four more years of college and then more school as a teacher, which is about as bad as being a student. Graduate school was too much on top of that, and so it was time to get out, and I got out."

He went to work as a truck driver for a gravel company, and through the spring and summer he worked a lot of overtime on a highway construction project. When fall came, he hauled gravel and sand for a company building a large office building. At a beer party in early winter someone gave him some goof balls (barbiturates), which he used up in a week. The same person gave him some more goof balls and asked him if he'd like to try some really good stuff. Steven tried the heroin and then tried some more, and suddenly it seemed

he had to start paying to get it. That was two years ago.

"For a while it was really great. Really neat. I felt like a king most of the time. Even when I was driving that truck, I felt like a monarch, but I had some bad times too."

Once he had miscalculated his own heroin dose and almost died, and another time he was stopped by the police because he had been speeding in his gravel truck. He tried to be careful after that because he did not want any contact with the police or anyone else. Nevertheless, he had three minor accidents while driving his truck, three accidents in a two-week period, and he was fired from his job.

He had saved some money, and he used that up in a week of buying more heroin. When the money was gone, he sold his books, his television set, and then the furniture in his small apartment. He sold his clothes and his shoes, and then he sold his car to get money for heroin. Then his heroin supply was used up, and there was nothing left to sell. It was at this point that he decided to walk to the mental health center.

The psychiatrist put Steven on a detoxification schedule using methadone. The amount of methadone was gradually reduced over a three-week period to a small dosage.* By that time Steven was an active participant in a Gestalt therapy group and had a new job in a grocery store. He continued with psychotherapy for six months and began taking graduate school courses again. A year later the psychiatrist received a printed invitation to Steven's graduation.

J. Maurice Rogers (1971) maintains the legal use of drugs is basically an economic and not a scientific endeavor. He states that drug manufacturers spend three quarters of a billion dollars a year on advertising directed only to physicians. Paul Hoch (1959), however, believes the use of drugs often helps to make an individual more accessible to treatment in various

---

*Heroin addiction is immersed in myths as is the use of methadone, although Americans do not seem to question these myths as the English do (Judson, 1973).

kinds of psychotherapy. But in a survey conducted by *Psychology Today* (Popoff, 1970), physicians and drug research specialists responded in ways that can be described as mixed. Drugs were viewed as useful but not a blessing, helpful but risky, and a thoroughly complicated sector of repair.

THE PSYCHOTHERAPY COMPASS

It is time to take some compass readings of the varieties of psychotherapy. In the previous discussions, we have briefly touched upon four therapies. The four can be viewed as main points on the compass as shown below.

This view of psychotherapy has some disadvantages. At first glance the different approaches may appear to be equal in some way or other. They are no more equal than elephants, deer, an electric cattle prod, and a pill are equal elements of the human environment. It may appear from the circle that each method is orthogonal, that is, highly distinct and unrelated to any other method. Such is not the case. It may seem from the appearance of the points on the circle that each approach occupies an equivalent amount of space, whether that

space involves the number of offices occupied by practitioners of the four separate approaches or the space taken up by professional journals on library shelves or the mental space each takes up in the mind of the average citizen. They all differ in these respects and in many others. So much, at this point, for the disadvantages.

The prime advantage of the compass of psychotherapies is that it is useful in roughly dividing each approach so we may explore their combinations. Combinations of the four are substantially more common than pure specialization in any one of the four directions. The combinations are central to what Lanyon (1971) calls the mental health industry.

Probably the most commonly known combination of treatments is the one used by the typical psychiatrist. He has one foot planted in the psychoanalytic sector; the other foot rests in psychopharmacology. Most psychiatrists are not psychoanalysts, but they use psychoanalytic theory in sit-up-in-a-chair, face-to-face psychotherapy with one patient at a time. When the psychiatrist believes it is advisable, he prescribes medications for the patient. On the compass the psychiatrist is more often

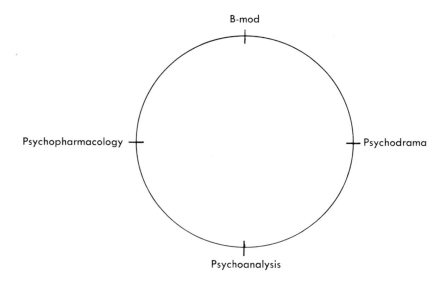

than not in a southwesterly position. There are, however, psychiatrists who have become involved with B-mod and with group therapy (including psychodrama) so much so that psychiatry is not now what it once was. The changes in the field of psychiatry have led some to wonder if it still is one of the subspecialties of medicine (Romano, 1973).

The field of psychology has so many subspecialties it covers most of the compass except the specific western point of psychopharmacology. Even there some specialized psychologists conduct research in drugs and in drug-related behavior. On the job, however, psychologists cannot prescribe medications. Other than that important distinction, many psychologists and psychiatrists work at what is called psychoanalytically-oriented psychotherapy. They do so in connection with individuals and with groups.

Group therapy is represented by psychodrama on the compass not because of the numbers of psychodrama groups that meet in different places across the land but because psychodrama has within it components of other group enterprises. No other form of group therapy has as many components. Take, to begin with, the *Begegnung*.

The *Begegnung* is also called the encounter. Individuals encounter themselves, and they encounter each other (me with me and me with you). It is a central aspect of the warm-up of step 1, and it usually leads to step 2, the psychodrama enactment. Other large numbers of groups meet and become enmeshed in the *Begegnung*, and that is all. They are sometimes called encounter groups. Sometimes they are known as sensitivity training groups or, less often, T-groups.

Encounter groups may meet together once or twice or fifty times for an hour or two. They may meet less frequently for a long-term session referred to as a *marathon*. A marathon encounter group meet-

ing lasts at least eighteen hours and often for far longer (Stoller, 1972). In short meetings and long, encounter groups become involved with some action techniques and some discussions that may become intense and emotional but that do not lead to a psychodrama. In the sequence of events, some psychodramatic techniques may be used. A frequent technique is the "empty chair" tactic mentioned as a possible aspect of surplus reality at the end of psychodrama's step 2.

Encounter group sessions may vary, depending upon the talents of the person in charge or the demands of the members of the group. Overall, however, encounter groups can be considered as something less than psychotherapy, for the thrust and orientation is in the direction of increased self-awareness at the expense of integrating and making use of that awareness. As Kurt Back (1972) has put it: encounter groups may comfort, but they do not cure anything.

There are now so many versions of group therapy they can be considered at all points on the compass except for the pure, unadulterated practice of classical psychoanalysis, the southern point. Drugs are administered to large groups of patients in mental hospitals, and in many hospitals they are the only therapy the patients receive. As for the more active types of group therapy, they can be located from the southwest in an arc that sweeps around the compass almost to psychoanalysis.

So many versions of group therapy exist that the original and innovative work done by Slavson (1943) can be merged with the earlier efforts of Moreno and the more recent ventures of Eric Berne (1966) and Fritz Perls (1951) and his colleagues; also, there are Thomas Gordon (1956) and Carl Rogers (1942, 1951, 1969). Less than ten years ago, Renata Adler (1967) encompassed the varieties of group therapy in an essay. She listed five kinds of therapy groups. Now, however, there may be an additional fifty or sixty types of group therapy, all of which may be productive and healing of psychological pain. Each type can be a blend of styles not mentioned on the compass. For example, Muriel James and Dorothy Jongeward (1971) have combined Gestalt therapy, originated by Fritz Perls, with transactional analysis (TA), which was originated by Eric Berne. As James and Jongeward put it:

> Transactional analysis gives a person a rational method for analyzing and understanding behavior; Gestalt therapy gives a person a useful method for discovering the fragmented parts of his personality, integrating them, and developing a core of self-confidence. Both methods are concerned with discovering and fostering awareness, self-responsibility, and genuineness. Both methods are concerned with what is happening now. [preface, p. ix]

They write of a way of uncovering some unknowns about the self. What they discuss in their book is an escape from a perpetual childhood and the development of alternative ways of living. What they propose is the expansion of alternatives, the enhancement of the control and regulation of one's own life. Perls (1969), the founding father of Gestalt therapy has maintained that, to him, self-regulation versus external regulation is "the most important, interesting phenomenon in all (behavioral) pathology" (p. 16).

There is only one thing that should control, and that is the *situation,* the present situation or circumstance the individual is in at this specific moment in time. Several years after Perls wrote those sentiments, Carlos Castaneda (1972) wrote that don Juan taught him freedom and an adventurous life could come only when the person was free of the past, his own past. Yet, according to Eric Berne (1961, 1964, 1966) we carry with us a perpetual child, an adult, and a parent within the mind. Each is at least a partial product of the past. The idea

Dan O'Neill/Editorial Photocolor Archives

that we have a child within, an interested, inquiring, creative, and perhaps joyful child within the mind was discussed by Brown (1959).

The idea of a child, not necessarily joyful, an adult, and a parent all living within the mind is Berne's idea, an idea that has its roots in psychoanalytic theory. Berne was on a search when he developed his ideas, and in his search, he tried to develop some ideas that might lead to a greater understanding of what people say and do to one another. It was a search for an understanding of the transactions people have with each other. Berne's ideas clearly developed out of the foundations established by Freud, but what Berne developed before he died was a more understandable, more entertaining, and perhaps a more popular view of human behavior than Freud's. In a combination of Berne's views with Gestalt therapy the questions become obvious: What is the person's child doing in this situation? What is the person's adult doing? What is the person's parent doing? —in this *present* situation, this now that is so fleeting but so meaningful. The therapist who uses a combination of TA and Gestalt must somehow assist the patient to understand the transactions taking place in the now. Gestalt therapy can be located on the compass approximately halfway between B-mod, which stresses the present moment, and psychodrama, which stresses active participation, socially, in the therapeutic endeavor. Gestalt is roughly southeast on the psychotherapy compass. TA is south by southeast, closer to psychoanalysis but involving some of the active participation of psychodrama.

Then there is the whole matter of Carl Rogers. As Charlotte Buhler (1971) has pointed out, his influence on psychotherapy has been tremendous. He can be located on the compass with only a tentative sureness. Perhaps his influence covers most of the right half of the circle. Rogers went to work as a clinical psychologist in

1927. During the nearly half a century since then, he has written a great deal, given probably half a million lectures, taught therapists how to "therap," and as Arthur Clarke does, enjoyed searching dives into the ocean. He has perhaps influenced the American psychotherapy scene at least as much as Sigmund Freud. He is a past president of the American Psychological Association, but more importantly he is a gardener. He likes to grow living things.

Roger's essential contributions to psychotherapy are many, but three stand out (Buhler, 1971):

1. He stressed the relationship the patient and the therapist have between them.*
2. He emphasized not so much the matter of "mental illness" as he did the emotional problems that result from our present era of change and instability.
3. He considered as central to psychotherapy the idea that people have a need for and can benefit from setting personal goals, appropriate goals based upon a knowledge of self and one's own potentialities. Psychotherapy was not simply a self-repair effort. It was also a way toward self-actualization.

The work Rogers has done is based upon the psychoanalytic tradition, but it seems a more intensely human, less intellectualized kind of therapy than classical psychoanalysis. Yet, like classical psychoanalysis, there seems to be little or slim success with seriously psychotic individuals (Rogers el al., 1967). Also, what he

---

*The next section of this chapter has more information about psychotherapeutic relationships. It has become a fundamental issue in almost all forms of psychotherapy, except perhaps in the more rigorous versions of B-mod and the more mechanistic, nonpersonal examples of psychopharmacology in which the main contact between therapist and patient is a pill.

proposes as psychotherapy (1951) seems to be appropriate for individuals who are verbally skilled, perhaps more educable than the average, and able to form a relationship of some kind (almost any kind [Rogers, 1957]) with the therapist.

The Rogerian version of psychotherapy is primarily nondirective. It can be used in one-to-one settings and in groups. It allows and requires that there be a closeness in the relationship between the therapist and the patient, a closeness that is sometimes called into question (Hall, 1967). Rogers responds with the idea that such closeness, which sometimes involves some self-disclosures on the part of the therapist, may cause anxiety in the therapist. From time to time it may provoke some anxieties in the patient, especially if the patient needs the therapist to be an almost inhuman tower of strength.

Rogers' first work with groups took place in 1945, at about the same time National Training Laboratories (NTL) was established in Bethel, Maine. Soon after, Esalen in California opened its seaside gates, and group therapies of great informality came into being, more on the West Coast than on the Eastern Seaboard.

Perhaps the least formal kind of group therapy is the nude group (Bindrim, 1969). Generally individuals begin fully clothed and have the opportunity to remove their clothes and swim together if it seems to the group members an appropriate or useful thing to do. Individuals in such groups understandably have some initial misgivings, and they report an onset of self-consciousness about their physical presence, a self-consciousness that fades rapidly when people discover no one looks like a *Playboy* gatefold or a well-muscled man from a woman's magazine.

A legitimate and increasingly frequent type of group therapy often has no therapist. The therapy meetings can be as revealing and as useful as any of the more formalized group orientations. They are called rap groups and have been used extensively in the ghetto (Pattison and Elpers, 1972) and among the upper middle class (Pogrebin, 1973). Rap groups talk about whatever the group members want to talk about. The orientation is part Rogers and part Moreno, for there is an emphasis on real-life problems openly shared in which personal understanding and psychological growth can result. No one is seen as omnipotent or in charge of the proceedings. The topics range from problems associated with unemployment through sexual dysfunction on to how to get a mother-in-law to move out of the house.

Somewhere on the opposite side of the compass is the application of B-mod to groups. The groups may consist of hospitalized mental patients, students in elementary schools, or cadets in a military school. The central B-mod effort consists of (1) structuring the environment so the rules and regulations as well as the rewards and punishments are well known, (2) rewarding those who follow the rules, and (3) punishing those who do not. This does not seem different from how matters usually go in group-institutional settings, but with a B-mod environment there are no exceptions to any rule, and consistency reigns.

No matter what the setting or the specifics of the endeavor, therapy is helping. The varieties are many, and perhaps that is how matters need to be, for many therapies can take into account the many styles of living that exist in our times. As Perlman (1968) has stated:

People are helped by many kinds of helpers and many forms of influence. From psychiatrists to witch doctors, from orthodox psychoanalysis to behaviorist conditioning, from miracle drugs to placebos passing as miracle drugs—many divergent and even theoretically polar forms of help have proved beneficial to people in trouble. Yet, there persists in most of us some stubborn belief that there is *one* best way. The "best way" is usually the way in which we have been indoctrinated, or have ourselves been helped, or have found compatible with our own bents and/or have found workable in its application. [p. 194]

That certain therapies may be "compatible with our own bents" may have a more specific base than is ordinarily considered. Certainly there are differences among us, varieties of lifetime styles attributable to early experiences with the pains and pleasures of our own development. These experiences, these interactions, unknowingly may cause one individual to be the sort of person attracted to psychodrama or psychoanalysis, while another individual becomes interested in B-mod or psychopharmacology. However, there may be factors beyond experiences that produce attractions.

On both specific and general matters the four points of the therapy compass represent four approaches to helping, four approaches to being helped. The few combinations of psychotherapy mentioned on these pages also differ in some specific and general ways. The differing approaches can be viewed as either (1) teleological or (2) epistemological.

Teleology is not the same as Jacques Monod's (1971) teleonomy mentioned in Chapter 1. Teleonomy, you may recall, is Monod's term for the biological purpose of organisms. Teleology, in contrast, is a very broad and sometimes intricate field of study involved with final causes. A teleologist views life as determined by or guided by some overall design or plan. Teleology and mysticism are not strangers; teleology and the study of religion of almost any kind go hand in hand. The idea of self-actualization is a teleological-like idea.

Epistemology is the study of knowledge. Epistemology has to do with the philosophy of science, with the searchings of logic and mathematics, with the total scientific endeavor, the rational and the purely cognitive as it is known in our civilization.

Teleology is a surrender to or an acceptance of nature. Epistemology is an attempt to achieve mastery and control over nature. Teleology is related to the idea of subjectivity, the sense of individual humans having separate realities. Epistemology is a striving toward objectivity. In its most condensed form, epistemology asks *what* is happening and seeks to find out. Teleology is an attempt to find out *why*. Each responds to what and why in different ways. Now, with these admittedly sketchy definitions in mind, we can sail off into a sea of speculations, not so much to find a distant shore but simply to see

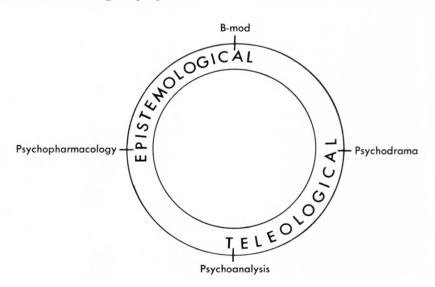

what the waves are like. Consider first the additions that have been made to the psychotherapy compass.

While psychoanalysis is a highly verbal enterprise and psychodrama a verbal-action therapy, and while TA, Gestalt therapy, and the rogerian quest are all loaded on the verbal side, the key or peak experiences for the therapist and for the patient cannot be expressed easily in words. The sudden insight, the flash of awareness, the newly discovered realization of an aspect of one's own existence is difficult to express in verbal terms. While the experience of suddenly added awareness might be called mystical or quasi-religious, it seems more prudent to characterize it as teleological. That is to say, it is highly personal and subjective, impossible to measure and make precise, but still useful or potentially useful, primarily to the patient and secondarily to the therapist.

In contrast, the epistemological aspects of B-mod and psychopharmacology seem easier to describe. In this upper left sector of the compass the therapist is a technologist, and the patient is a recipient of technology in a therapeutic effort characterized by strivings toward objectivity and a mastery or an attempted mastery over specific and finite slices of the individual's biological or social behavior. Acknowledgement of the subjective and the intuitive is at a minimum; what can be observed is what counts the most.

At this point we can sail further from wherever home port may be in our exploration of the surface waves of the psychological sea. We can add some more factors to consider. First there is the matter of structuralism (Stent, 1972). Structuralism involves the individual's control over his own perception. Powers (1973) believes that to behave is to control perception. By controlling perception the individual controls what he knows of reality, and reality becomes a highly subjective matter. Stent (1972) maintains that much information

that can be perceived is not perceived by the individual. While this unperceptiveness may be the result of denial, repression, bias, or selective inattention based upon prior experiences, the core aspect is that none of us can sense or be aware of those internal and external bits of information that we choose to ignore or that disagree with what we already believe in, especially on an emotional level.

These broad and general comments may be based upon the interaction of the human organism with the environment. This interaction begins most obviously at the arbitrarily chosen zero point of birth and becomes more complex as the individual grows physically and develops psychologically after birth. At birth and for a time after that event the infant is an incomplete organism. A part of that incompleteness concerns the brain, which, as mentioned before, is different from the mind. In a recent research study, Crowell, Jones, Kapuniai, and Nakagawa (1973) found some beginning and tentative evidence that in infants the right half of the brain is not connected so thoroughly with the left half as it is in adults. The connections between left and right sides are (1) anatomical and (2) psychological. The anatomical are there, perhaps, at birth, but the psychological connections apparently develop slowly after birth. But what is there to connect?

For a very long time physiologists believed the left half of the human brain was dominant, while the right half was of minor importance, little used, or perhaps held in reserve for reasons unknown. Recently, however, the idea that the right hemisphere was of secondary importance has been shown to be inaccurate. The right side of the brain has functions as vital as the functions of the left side but that seem far more difficult to measure or to determine with precision.

Richard Ornstein (1973) has assembled information concerning right and left

Table 8. Brain function by hemisphere

Left half	Right half
Strivings for objectivity	Subjectivity
Language development	Nonverbal recognition of what is known and named in verbal terms
Verbal reasoning	Holistic thinking
Detailed thinking	Intuition
Logic	

halves of the brain showing that each half is dominant in different ways. Table 8 presents some functions of each hemisphere.

Language development and verbal reasoning can be seen any time an individual talks. The nonverbal recognition of what is known and named in verbal terms is only slightly more indefinable. For example, an individual may go to the chalk board and talk about a triangle using the left half of his brain. As he turns to the chalk board and draws a triangle, however, he is using the right half of his brain. On a more personal level, an individual may talk of the sensual aspects of food or sex or music (left half), but to experience the sensuality in a nonverbal way (right half) is another matter. A patient in psychotherapy may talk of his own behavior (left), but to experience that behavior, or let us say, to experience the sudden insight, the flash of awareness (right?) is again another matter.

By now we have sailed far out onto the psychological sea, but there are more items to cover. At birth the psychological connections between right and left hemispheres are incomplete. They may perhaps remain incomplete for some individuals. There may be individuals who, because of early experiential interactions, grow to be adults who place a high value on rational thinking, logic, and careful reasoning. These people could be called left halfers. Right halfers may have undeveloped hemispheric connections too, but their early interactions may have fostered the development of intuitive and holistic thinking, a heavy reliance on subjectivity and perhaps a wariness of that which is only intellectual and verbal. Still other individuals, perhaps more in this instance, have hemispheric connections that are fully functioning. They are the individuals who are faced with integrating and combining an interwoven mesh of the "mystical" with the "scientific." In biofeedback, individuals are trained to do so, although it is difficult for them to describe just what it is they do when they control their own heart rate, blood pressure, or other physiological aspects. In psychoanalysis, in psychodrama, and in combinations of these therapies the patient's efforts may suggest a left-half emphasis, but the key therapeutic experiences appear to be based in the right half.

We have a society that for generations has placed an emphasis on the capabilities of the left cerebral hemisphere. Skill in verbal reasoning, in the gathering and integrating of knowledge, has been rewarded, if not economically then at least admired or preferred. It seems similar to the preference for concentrating on task achievement at the expense of process, a matter mentioned in Chapter 7. Yet, half our brain is devoted to a kind of thinking or awareness that is quite different. And who among us can dismiss that half?

There is, it appears, some need to understand more than we understand now about the functioning of the right half of the brain. Mysticism and the occult may have more meaning for mankind than is presently realized or ordinarily accepted. If we can know what it is the mystics know, perhaps we will be able to use our right hemispheres more productively than we do now in many of our activities, and that includes the activities covered by the large roof of psychotherapy.

Now that we have come this far, it is time to sail back to home port wherever it may be. Consider, though, as we return, the varieties of psychotherapy. Some are based upon what is known as rational and research-based information. Other therapies are rooted in the intuitive, and in these, subjectivity of experience is valued. These therapies were developed by a wide variety of individuals and are useful to wide varieties of patients and therapists. There is no "right" kind of therapy that is best for everyone. To borrow a statement from transactional analysis, there are different strokes for different folks. A similar statement can be used as you head for wherever your home port may be—there are different places for different faces.

THE PSYCHOTHERAPIST

Harrison

Harrison Bach drove home from work late one afternoon, and when he pulled into the driveway of his small suburban home, he saw a large pile of clothing on the front lawn. He stared for a moment, recognizing a favorite jacket, his shirts, several pairs of shoes, slacks, suits, a tumble of underwear, his books, and an empty suitcase. He got out of his car, walked to the pile and saw his golf clubs, his water skis, and his hunting boots mixed in with the clothing. He slowly turned and looked at the front door of his house. Jane was there in the doorway, sitting in a kitchen chair holding his hunting rifle in her lap. He wondered for a moment if the gun was loaded, but when he saw the look on Jane's face, he did not ask about it. He bent down, picked up the favorite jacket, and carried it to his car. He put the jacket in the backseat and went back to the pile. It took him half an hour to load his car, and during that time Jane silently watched him as she held the rifle. He said nothing to her, but as he drove away in his bright red Pontiac, he waved briefly.

That night he stayed in a motel. The next morning he called a lawyer. The lawyer said he would investigate the matter. Later in the morning Harrison received a telephone call from a lawyer Jane had retained. Jane wanted a divorce. Harrison was more embarrassed than surprised.

He found an apartment, unloaded his car, and filled the closets in his new place. He tried to call Jane, but no one answered the phone. He drove by the house and wondered if she were in there somewhere, holding his rifle. A week later he saw her in her lawyer's office. He went there with his attorney, and the four of them talked divorce.

The proper legal documents were registered with the clerk of courts two days later. A day after that Harrison received a telephone call from a mental health worker employed by the domestic relations court. They talked with one another for a few moments, and Harrison agreed to show up for an appointment the next week.

When he found the right office, he knocked on the door, walked in, and saw Jane. She was sitting in a chair talking with the mental health worker, who stopped the conversation, stood up, and said hello to Harrison. Jane, surprised, stood up too.

"Now that we're all here together," said the mental health worker, "we can sit down and talk things over."

Jane turned to the worker and said, "You didn't tell me he was going to be here."

"Well, no. No, I didn't. I didn't think you'd come if I told you."

"I'm not staying, either," said Jane.

"Let's be reasonable," said the worker.

"I am being reasonable," retorted Jane. "You haven't been."

At that moment a man walked into the room. He saw Harrison standing near the open door and noticed Jane and the mental health worker were talking in a slightly heated way.

The mental health worker quickly said, "This is Dr. Brigham. He's our consultant."

"Goodbye," said Jane. She walked out.

"What's going on?" asked Dr. Brigham.

"She's refusing to cooperate," said the worker.

"With what?" asked Dr. Brigham.

"With a setup," said Harrison. He explained to Brigham that the mental health worker had called him to come in for a conversation about the divorce. He said he hadn't been told Jane would be here, and it was evident that Jane hadn't been told he would be there.

"I'm sorry this has happened," remarked Dr. Brigham.

"So am I," said Harrison.

"But," said the worker, "they wouldn't have come in together. I had to get them together somehow."

Brigham ignored her. He put his hand out to Harrison, and they shook hands. "Sorry you had to put up with this," said Brigham. "Would you like any counseling about your marriage? Or about the divorce?"

"No," said Harrison. "No, but thank you. I think the marriage died about two years ago."

Brigham said seriously, "There's no sense in wasting any more of your time."

"Goodbye," said Harrison. He walked out of the room and down the hall.

Brigham closed the door and turned to the mental health worker whom he told to sit down. He sat down too. Then he carefully and completely chewed out the worker for using trickery in dealing with patients and clients.

We are now in an interim situation in which the typical psychotherapist is a human. How long the interim situation may last is in some doubt, for it cannot be clearly known when psychotherapy will be done by some combination of (1) psychoactive drugs that have yet to be discovered or rediscovered and (2) equipment, such as teaching machines of only slightly greater complexity than exist now.

Perhaps drugs and electronic equipment will replace the human psychotherapist in twenty or thirty years. No one can be certain. What seems certain, however, is the idea that psychotherapy as it exists now is basically a pretechnological effort (Lanyon, 1971). It is pretechnological because the training of those who do psychotherapy is usually based upon an apprenticeship idea. The beginning therapist watches an experienced therapist to see how to be a therapist. Psychotherapy is pretechnological because the very great need for psychotherapy poses problems that are being solved by large numbers of

people who are psychotherapists. To depend upon manpower rather than equipment is not technological.

Fifteen years ago George Albee (1959) reviewed mental health manpower needs. The nation, he said, was in trouble. There were armies of patients who needed psychotherapy; the armies were growing in size as the years passed. Yet, the need for a massive number of psychotherapists was not being met. Psychotherapists were, for the most part, an elite group composed of psychiatrists, psychologists, psychiatric social workers, a very few psychiatric nurses with M. A. or M. S. degrees, and several dozen certified psychodramatists. In addition, there were some clergymen engaged in pastoral counseling and faculty members of larger schools who worked part-time as psychotherapists in student counseling bureaus or in some dean's office.

Albee's review rang an alarm bell. It was included in a lengthy report delivered to the U. S. government by what was known as the Joint Commission on Mental Illness and Health. "The Report," as it came to be known, advocated great changes in the mental-health-care delivery system. Most of the elite who were psychotherapists resisted the idea of any change, claiming that psychotherapy was such an intricate endeavor it required extensive education and highly specialized experience in internship programs, in medical residency training, or in closely supervised "field placement" after at least a year of graduate school.

Perhaps the first real crack in the castle wall came when a group of housewives were trained to be psychotherapists in a two-year program (Magoon et al., 1969). That was in the early 1960s. The resistance continued, however, for the housewives had a difficult time finding jobs in mental health clinics because they did not have the proper academic credentials. They were viewed by professionals as "laymen" with insufficient training. They could, however, work as volunteers with little or no pay. But at about the same time there was a national, federally sponsored series of programs involving (1) ghetto or slum self-help and (2) the formulation of some ideas for training paraprofessionals to work in mental hospitals and mental health clinics. In the ghettos, groups of people with minor guidance from governmental authorities set up their own walk-in centers, free clinics, and neighborhood rap group centers. The formulation of some ideas for training paraprofessionals led to actual training programs, usually two years of intensive training that led to genuine jobs doing actual therapy with patients on a daily basis. The history of this development has been traced by E. Mansell Pattison and John Elpers (1972), who state that the graduates of the two-year programs have opportunities for career development and promotion based upon on-the-job performance rather than upon proper academic credentials. Pattison and Elpers (both are physicians) believe the two-years-in-training psychotherapists represent the firm beginning of a new defined profession. The term paraprofessional may quickly become obsolete.

It seems appropriate to consider the titles we now use as generally obsolete. There is little real difference in the work of most psychotherapists in their face-to-face relationships with patients. Psychiatric nurses with an M. A. or an M. S. degree and psychiatric social workers sound the same and usually behave the same in conversations with patients as psychodramatists, psychiatrists, psychologists, some high school counselors, gifted classroom teachers, the family physician, and those priests, rabbis, and ministers who have had some training in psychotherapy. The distinctions exist between all these (and others) and those physicians who merely prescribe medications in the pure application of psychopharmacology and psychologists who work solely in highly specific applications of unadulterated B-mod. Perhaps these two represent the wave of a future some twenty or thirty years from now when chemicals and technically more advanced teaching machines are available. As matters stand now, however, the psychotherapist is still a human.

Alicia

Alicia was a 35-year-old black woman who lived in a small brick house near the airport. She had been divorced for three years. Her former husband was a taxi driver who rarely gave her any money for child support, and alimony had been left out of the divorce settlement altogether. She had three sons who lived with her. Bobbie was the oldest. He was 16, over 6 feet tall, and a superb basketball player. While his grades in high school could have been better, no one really seemed to mind because he already had an athletic scholarship to college guaranteed. It seemed his pathway to a satisfying life was laid out. His younger brother, Howard, was 15. Howard was not as tall, but he was far more muscular than Bobbie. Howard wanted to grow up to be a boxer, and in pursuit of that goal, he worked out almost daily in the basement of the small house. Once in a while—every three or four months—he would get into a fight with a white boy, and he always won. Jim was the youngest boy in the family. He was 10 years old, small for his age, frail, awkward and slow, but usually friendly. No one bothered him at school or in the neighborhood because everyone knew if they taunted or teased Jim, they would quickly be faced with his formidable protector, Howard.

Alicia worked as a clerk in a federal agency. On weekends she spent one day doing simple bookkeeping at home for a small laundry and dry cleaning establishment in a shopping center three blocks from where she lived. Her total monthly income was usually about four hundred dollars. Everything seemed to be going along all right for Alicia. There were some ups and some downs, but she managed to maintain her own morale at a reasonably satisfying level until she learned the federal agency was to be closed down because of governmental budget cutbacks.

She first heard the news in March. In April she began to try to find another job. By the middle of May no new job had turned up, and she began to feel restless and frightened. On the first day of June she knew she had one last month of employment in the federal agency, and then she would be out of a job except for the one-day-a-week bookkeeping. She had difficulty sleeping, and she spent most of the night in the kitchen eating crackers and peanut butter and reading the Bible. On the tenth day of June she called her supervisor. She said she was sick and couldn't come to work. In the middle of the morning she got a large butcher knife from a drawer in the kitchen, went out into the back yard, sat down on the grass, and began to hack away at the trunk of an elm tree. By noon she had chopped half way through the tree, and she was wet with sweat and exhausted. She went back into the house and called her minister on the telephone. She asked him to come over because she needed help.

The minister came to Alicia's home, saw her, and immediately told her to wash up and put on some clean clothes. Alicia did as she was directed. When she was done, she went into the living room where the minister had been waiting for her. She sat down in a chair and began to cry. The minister continued to wait, and within a few moments, Alicia began to tell her story. Near the end she said she had chopped at the tree because the tree reminded her of her former husband, dark and silent.

The minister asked Alicia if her children knew she was losing her job in the federal agency. They didn't, she said, because she'd never told them. She hadn't told them because they had enough problems of their own.

The minister, at that point, called a physician whose office was not far away. He briefly outlined Alicia's present mental status to the physician and wondered if Alicia could get some medication to help her. The physician asked the minister to bring Alicia to his office, and within fifteen minutes he had seen her and prescribed a two-day supply of pills, suggesting Alicia go to a mental health center for help. She said she'd rather get help from the minister. She said she didn't trust those mental places because they were run by the white folks who didn't care if she had a job or not.

No, she'd rather get help from her minister. And she did.

The human therapist of whatever background might find the comments of Jerome Frank (1973) useful. Frank has a Ph.D. in psychology and an M.D. degree from Harvard. He has the proper academic credentials together with substantial experience in individual and group psychotherapy and in research in the behavioral sciences. He maintains that the personal qualities of the therapist are of more importance than whatever specialized training the therapist might have had. Furthermore, Frank believes a person with no training at all can be as successful a therapist as those who have had the most extensive training. It depends again on the human, not on the human's training. As Carl Rogers (1957) believes, special knowledge in psychology, psychiatry, or religion does not make the therapist.

Jerome Frank and Carl Rogers are in basic agreement about the conditions that make therapy what it is, an effort directed at constructive personality change. They both maintain:

1. Therapy consists of a relationship between the therapist and the patient, a relationship that can exist in a one-to-one situation or in a group setting.
2. The therapist believes in what he or she is doing, has a sense of purpose, has zeal, and centrally, the capacity to communicate to the patient an understanding of the patient's discomfort.
3. The therapist experiences an unconditional, unbroken acceptance of the patient, a positive regard for the patient as another human.
4. The therapist has a plan of action, a basic rationale or a more or less systematic approach to what can happen in the course of therapy.

Frank calls for the necessities of a plan more so than Rogers does, but both firmly state that the personal qualities of the therapist are more crucial to therapy than the details of any plan. Frank stresses the zeal of the therapist, his belief in what he is doing, while Rogers stresses the characteristic of empathy. Empathy is the ability to sense the patient's private world, to know the psychological pain, to understand. In this regard, John O. Stevens (1971) has written:

> The way to really help someone is not to help him do anything but become more aware of his own experience—his feelings, his actions, his fantasies—and insist that he explore his own experience more deeply and take responsibility for it, no matter what that experience is. [pp. 129-130]

To help anyone experience themselves in a way that leads to productive change, the therapist has, as a tool, his or her own capacities for empathy. Yet, the therapist cannot know of the patient's feelings, actions, or fantasies unless he, the therapist, is able to make contact with himself. To accomplish that the therapist must have a reasonably solid sense of personal identity. To have that identity, it may be appropriate for the therapist to have been a patient at some time or other, either in group therapy, in individual therapy, or preferably in both.

REVIEW QUESTIONS

1. From memory, can you draw the psychotherapy compass?
2. What are some of the main differences between psychoanalysis and psychodrama?
3. In what ways are the brain and the mind different?
4. Can you define CS, US, E, S, O, UR, and CR?
5. What is the stimulus complex?
6. How are exploration, integration, analysis, and synthesis related?
7. What are ego functions?
8. In what way were Freud and Fromm different? What did Fromm write about that Freud did not?
9. What are the phantasticants?
10. Which members of the phenothiazine family can you list? What are their trade names? Can you spell the generic names correctly?
11. What is epistemology?
12. What usually happens during the psychodrama warm-up? What is the *Begegnung*?

GLOSSARY

abreaction emotional reliving of a past experience. The emotions may be repressed, but in psychotherapy they may become expressed. Abreactions occur in daily living when a person recalls a past event and experiences the feelings associated with that event.

action behavior directly observable by other individuals; also known as conative behavior; one of the potentials for development present at birth.

acute brain disorder temporary disorganization of behavior due to changes in the biochemistry of the brain.

adjustment capacity to cope with change.

adolescence a vaguely defined period in life that begins with puberty and ends with adulthood; in this society a period of experimentation for the individual, a time when the prime psychological feature is the development of a sense of identity.

affect feelings.

affective psychoses severe emotional disorders in which feelings (affect) are in some disarray.

aggression purposeful behavior designed to destroy, compromise, or otherwise circumvent a frustration; often a reaction to frustration.

agitated depression usually neurotic depression in which, in some circumstances, the person may have difficulty sleeping (see also deprivation dwarfism).

agonistic behavior activities that result in fighting or in running away either physically or psychologically.

ambivalence any general tendency to respond in a conflicting manner to psychologically opposite factors, for example, love-hate, affection-anger, attraction-repulsion, commitment-withdrawal.

analysand the patient in psychoanalysis.

analysis the first part of psychoanalysis; also, an

abbreviated way of saying psychoanalysis (see also synthesis).

anamnesis a recalling to mind by the individual of his own personal history.

anger a transitory emotion brought about by frustration, injury, or threat (see also rage and hostility).

anxiety a feeling of psychological discomfort akin to fear, although the feared object is unknown. The feeling is usually accompanied by a variety of physical symptoms such as moist palms, increased heart rate, increased breathing rate.

attitude a persistent and durable mental state of readiness to react in a consistent manner to objects, people, conditions, and circumstances; has to do with conative, cognitive, and affectual perceptions and reactions.

autonomous functions the human activities not disturbed by surges of the id, such as speech, planning, physical movements, and life-purpose.

autonomous morphogenesis the concept or idea that living things are capable of self-construction.

autonomy strivings toward personal independence and the beginnings of approval of oneself; a crucial psychological development that begins to take place during early childhood (see also shame and doubt).

auxiliary ego in psychodrama, individuals who pretend to be people necessary to the protagonist.

Begegnung the encounter of "me with me" and "me with you" in the psychodrama; leads to the choice of a protagonist and the enactment of a psychodrama.

behavior modification a kind of individual and group psychotherapy that employs rigidly established techniques of reward and punishment to, respectively, reinforce and extinguish segments of behavior; based upon learning theory research with animals.

chlorpromazine generic name for a drug of the phenothiazine family; used in the psychopharmacological treatment of psychosis. Trade name is Thorazine.

chronic brain disorder permanent disorganization of behavior based upon progressive degeneration of brain tissue either from disease or aging.

civilization our environment of objects, ideas, artistic and architectural developments, language, and the wide assortment of beliefs, attitudes, and opinions held by the individual and the group (see also environment, identity system, and identity symbols).

classical conditioning a technique used in research in learning in which the learner (usually a subhuman organism) is typically passive; originally developed by Pavlov.

climax of catharsis the emotional peak of the psychodrama (see also abreaction).

cocaine drug extracted from the cola bush that provides short-term excitation; also known as coke, snow, star dust; extended use can produce convulsions and depression.

cola an extract of the cola bush. The cola bush also provides a drug called cocaine.

compazine trade name for a drug generically known as prochlorperazine.

compensation a defensive compromise in which what may be disadvantages or failures motivate or produce behavior that leads to psychological satisfaction.

conflict the concurrent existence of two or more circumstances that may be either attractive or repulsive; a feeling of being torn between two alternatives.

conflict frustration a condition that prevents or delays satisfaction by the existence of alternatives that seem at least partially equal in attractiveness or repulsiveness.

conscience an inhibitory and motivating aspect of personality that begins to be a factor in living during the years of childhood; sometimes referred to as the governor of initiative.

constitutionalist an individual who believes behavior is based only on heredity.

creating completing old and familiar tasks in new and different ways; producing a new and unique product; sometimes inventing; one of the potentials for development present at birth.

creativity the ability to do old things in new and genuinely different ways; the capacity to clearly define a given problem and find a useful and workable solution; the ability to produce a new and useful thing or idea.

Dartal trade name of a drug known generically as thiopropazate.

daydreams usually, but not necessarily, pleasant imaginings of complex objects, persons, or circumstances; typically under the control of the individual (see also fantasies).

defending behavior designed to protect oneself psychologically from a multitude of real or imagined psychological assaults; one of the potentials for development present at birth.

defensive compromise any attempt to contend with frustration in ways that lead to a reasonably consistent fulfillment of psychological needs (see also compensation and sublimation).

defensive strategies (behaviors) activities designed to protect oneself from real and imagined assaults upon the self, especially with regard to assaults that may or may seem to compromise or reduce one's own sense of self-esteem and reputation.

delusions beliefs that are not necessarily accurate.

denial of reality a defensive flight to avoid unpleasant realities; alternatively called escapism.

deprivation dwarfism short stature, a physiological result of agitated depression in which the pituitary gland fails to produce sufficient growth hormone because the individual does not sleep long enough for the pituitary to do its work.

development the steps or phases through which a person moves as he or she collects and retains a large number of personal attributes and characteristics.

discounting an aggressive defense meant to exclude from one's own attention an undesirable condition or person (see also trivialization).

disgust, despair a feeling of having wasted life, a psychological factor sometimes present in old age; the opposite of the development of a sense of integrity.

displacement an aggressive defense in which feelings of affection or anger, or both, or the proddings of a weighty conscience are shifted to an alternate, more psychologically safe individual, object, or circumstance.

double in psychodrama the person who stays by the protagonist saying aloud what the protagonist may be thinking.

E in psychological research the abbreviation for the experimenter.

ego the sector of the psychic apparatus having to do with that which is considered as rational and integrative; the arbitrator in conflicts involving the id and the superego.

emotional insulation a defensive flight in which the person withdraws into a passive state as a protection against being hurt; sometimes referred to as emotional detachment.

enactment, psychodrama the actual psychodrama itself; the second of three steps in the psychodramatic sequence.

encounter general term used to describe either the first part of a psychodrama sequence or the activities of groups involved in verbal exchange and some action techniques that may produce transitory feelings of intimacy and trust.

endogenous depression see psychotic depression; also known as primary and autonomous depression.

environment no fixed definition; generally, anything external to the individual that has an influence or a potential influence upon the person (see also civilization).

environmentalist an individual who believes behavior is based only on environmental factors.

epistemology the study of knowledge and its origins; the study of nature; the study of the limits of science (see also science).

Eros according to Sigmund Freud, the wish toward life (see also Thanatos).

exogenous depression reaction to a sense of loss; also known as neurotic depression and reactive depression.

experimental design the plan of research, including procedures, types of subjects, the experimental environment, the activities, if any, of the experimenter, and the statistical techniques used in the analysis of data.

exploration the first phase of psychodrama, which roughly corresponds to the analysis of psychoanalysis (see also integration).

external control the belief that one's own activities are decided by others (see also internal control and projection).

extinguish to condition in such a way that a response is no longer made (see also reinforce).

fantasies usually but not necessarily pleasant imaginings of complex objects, persons, or circumstances; typically not under the control of the individual (see also daydreams).

fear a feeling of often great discomfort in the presence of real, imagined, or anticipated psychological or physical danger in which the feared thing, person, or circumstance is known; tends to produce agonistic behavior (see also anxiety).

feedback what S, or the patient, in behavior modification receives in terms of information about the correctness of the response that has been made.

feeling emotional behavior; behavior directly observable; sometimes referred to as affective behavior; one of the potentials for development present at birth.

fixation a stoppage or cessation of some aspect of psychological development (see also regression).

folie à deux French for the folly of two; an extreme variation of identification (see also identification).

freudianism traditional psychoanalysis according to the precepts of Sigmund Freud.

frustration a condition that prevents or delays the satisfaction of physical, social, or psychological needs, desires, or wants.

generativity the main psychological development of middle age; an activity that involves transmitting to younger humans the essence of culture and language (see also symbolic immortality and self-absorption).

Gestalt a form of psychotherapy that emphasizes the present moment and purports to ignore the individual's past history; developed by Fritz Perls.

group therapy any psychotherapy that takes place in a group setting; often confused with sensitivity training (see also encounter).

guilt a psychological inhibitor of the sense of initiative; develops as an opposite to initiative.

guilt depression the result of a subjective sense of having broken some sort of system of rules; characterized by superficially humorous comments directed at the self and others. The humor typically has a cruel edge to it.

hallucinations a false perception that has a sense of reality; what is perceived is usually not actually present.

hallucinogen a drug that helps to generate hallucinations (see also phantasticant).

headship position a position of authority and responsibility such as boss or scoutmaster, for accomplishment of some goal; usually associated with organizations (see also leadership).

history the study and review of the records man has kept about himself.

Hollander psychodrama curve a verbally based nomograph representing the three parts of the psychodramatic sequence.

homeostasis physiological maintenance of a normal state of the blood; often used as an example to explain attempts at maintenance of a psychological state of balance.

hostility durable and persistent anger that could form the base for a wide variety of prejudices (see also rage and anger).

id the sector of the psychic apparatus having to do with deeply buried urges and impulses.

identification an aggressive defense in which the individual seeks to ally himself with someone seemingly more powerful in an effort to either borrow that power or avoid the negative consequences of that power (see also folie à deux).

identity a coherent view of oneself as an individual, a view of sense of self that begins to be developed during adolescence.

identity diffusion an incoherent view of oneself (see also identity).

identity symbols reasonably permanent fixtures of the history of a "people" that provide a foundation for the stability or persistence of the identity of a group, for example, land, language, music, dances, and heroes.

identity system a "people's" belief in certain symbols and what the symbols stand for (see also identity symbols).

industry a prime psychological development of the school age stage of behavior (see also inferiority).

inferiority a sense of being less than or somehow not as good in some ways as other; a psychological factor that is the opposite of the development of industriousness during the school age years.

initiative a central psychological development that begins during childhood (see also guilt).

instrumental learning conditioning in which the learner, or S, is an active participant; also known as operant conditioning.

integration the last phase of psychodrama, which corresponds to the synthesis of psychoanalysis (see also exploration).

integrity a main psychological development during old age, somewhat synonymous with a feeling of completeness (see also disgust, despair).

intellectualization a defensive flight in which the individual avoids whatever the issue is by being indirect and nonparticipative.

interaction the interplay of variables, one upon the other, that results in or produces behavior. At the most fundamental level, behavior is the result of the interaction of heredity, environment, and the self.

internal control the belief that one's own life is under one's own control, not under the control of others; psychologically "owning" one's own feelings and experiences (see also external control and projection).

internalize to incorporate language, ideas, attitudes into one's own mind so they eventually become one's own (see also introjection and socialization).

interpersonal what goes on between two or more people.

intimacy the primary psychological development of the early adult years; typically based upon a previously developed sense of identity (see also isolation).

intrapersonal whatever goes on, often not observable, within the mind of an individual.

introjection the "taking in" of ready-made ideas, attitudes, opinions, beliefs and making them one's own (see also internalization).

intrusive mode aggressive activities during childhood. The activities result in an expansion of the child's environment.

involutional melancholia depression, often severe, based upon feelings related to menopause.

isolation a separateness from others, the opposite of intimacy.

it another word for id.

jactation an unusual level of restlessness.

joy typically an emotion felt in the present moment characterized by highly pleasant feelings combined with observable expressions of a feeling of satisfaction or pleasure.

juvenile immature, youthful, typically an adolescent person or activity; sometimes used to refer to childlike matters (see also youth).

katasexual sexual activities in which the object or the partner is either a live subhuman organism or a dead human.

kleptomania poorly controlled impulses to steal in spite of external or observable evidence that there is no genuine or realistic need to steal.

language the spoken and written word, facial expressions, tone of voice, movements of the body; a tool or tools of communication.

latency period sometimes used as an alternate term to label the school age stage of behavior, which takes place just prior to the adolescent years.

leadership the capacity to lead; an organizational position defined and validated by members of that organization; a position of power and influence occupied by an individual accepted by the members of a group or organization (see also headship position).

learning any relatively stable change in behavior that results from experience; somewhat akin to modifiability; also, one of the potentials for development present at birth.

lithium a drug element used in the psychopharmacological treatment of manic-depressive disorders.

mania unpredictable and usually highly vigorous physical and mental activity that is generally unproductive and disorganized.

manic-depressive behavior mood swings in which the person may alternate between feeling very "up" and feeling very "down." The swings may be hourly, daily, monthly.

marathon in encounter groups or in sensitivity training any group that stays together for at least eighteen hours.

maturation physical change and growth; not equivalent to psychological development.

medications any chemical compound used in the treatment of psychological and physiological disorders.

meds generally used abbreviation for medication.

Mellaril trade name of a drug known generically as thioridazine.

mental illness an old term that implies severe difficulties in living are based upon physical factors, such as a disease in the brain; often used inaccurately.

Minderwertigkeit an overpowering sense of powerlessness, of insufficiency, of incompleteness.

mistrust the opposite of trust; a seemingly necessary attribute in a world that is not always benevolent.

modifiability the ability, capacity, or characteristic of susceptibility to change.

multiplicity of variables the causes, effects, influences that when operating concurrently (often in unknown ways) lead to or produce behavior. A human's total environment consists of a multiplicity of variables.

narcolepsy pathological condition in which the individual falls asleep with great ease.

neurotic behavior a less-than-severe level of difficulty in living.

neurotic paradox the use of behaviors that prevent the individual from getting what he wants or needs (see also self-defeating behavior).

neurotic variance a conflict between how a person sees himself and how he thinks he should be, a conflict between "should" and "actual."

nondirective therapy a style of psychotherapy first developed by Carl Rogers in which the patient is responsible for the direction therapy takes. The therapist is nondirective.

O in psychological research the abbreviation for the observer.

operant conditioning conditioning in which the learner, or S, is an active participant; also known as instrumental learning.

organic psychoses difficulties in living based upon reduced physiological functioning of the brain because of aging, accidents, or toxic conditions resulting from drugs or chemicals.

organization an assemblage of different parts, each of which performs some part of a coordinated function so that what results is a system (see also system).

organizational expansion the growth of cities.

orienting concepts anchoring points for the study of human behavior; well-established and thoroughly researched aspects of behavior.

orthogonal a term borrowed by psychology from the mathematics of matrices to describe unrelated variables, separate and uncorrelated factors in the environment and within the individual.

overload feeling that results from having to contend with an overly complex environment; synonymous with overstimulation. Overload eventually leads to withdrawal and a turning inward by the individual.

paranoid psychosis severe emotional disorder in which suspicion is high (see also projection).

perceiving a behavior based upon the physiologically determined ability to sense the environment; one of the potentials for development present at birth.

perphenazine generic name for a drug of the phenothiazine family; used in the treatment of psychosis. Trade name is Trilafon.

personality a composite of what has been inherited and what has been experienced; a tendency toward sameness or consistency of reaction, especially with regard to oneself and in relationships with other people.

phantasticant drug or chemical that influences the mind to an extraordinary degree, often to the degree of eliciting hallucinatory behavior (see also hallucinogen).

phenothiazine a general term used to describe a whole family of drugs used in the treatment of psychotic disorders.

phobia a great and intense fear of some known thing or circumstance; viewed as irrational by people who do not have the particular phobia.

power the capacity to determine what happens; the ability or initiative to do things in order to satisfy one's own desires, wants, or needs (see also internal control).

powerlessness the belief or feeling, often inaccurate, that control of one's own life rests in the hands of someone else, a system, or in the fates (see also external control and power).

primal dialogue the biological-social-psychological interaction between mother and infant; evidence indicates it is necessary for the survival of the infant.

process feelings associated with the job that must be done or should be done; also feelings about oneself and others in association with that job (see also task).

prochlorperazine generic name for a drug of the phenothiazine family; used in the psychopharmacological treatment of psychotic states. Trade name is Compazine.

projection an aggressive defense in which the individual disowns his own feelings, characteristics, and attributes them to someone or something else; a central feature of paranoid reactions that should be distinguished from fear.

protagonist the patient in psychodrama (see also sociometric star).

psychic apparatus according to Sigmund Freud, the mind and its subsectors such as the id, the ego, and the superego.

psychoactive a general term applied to drugs and other chemicals that influence the mind.

psychoanalysis a body of knowledge and of speculations about human behavior; also, one kind of highly structured and typically long-term psycho-therapy.

psychodrama intricate and complex form of psycho-therapy developed by Jacob Moreno in which pa-tients act out aspects of their difficulties in near-spontaneous dramas; a form of group therapy, but sometimes employed with individuals (see also protagonist).

psychopharmacology a type of psychotherapy in which drugs are used.

psychophobia fear of what is within one's own mind; often, the fear of what has been repressed.

psychotherapy a healing of the mind; any method, technique, or mode designed to alleviate psycho-logical pain, promote the development of alterna-tive behaviors, and enhance self-esteem and, often, self-actualization.

psychotic depression condition apparently resulting from anger directed toward the self; also known as endogenous, primary, and autonomous depres-sion.

psychotic disorder usually a severe difficulty in liv-ing.

psychotic grandeur a severely distorted and vastly in-flated view of one's own importance (see also paranoid psychosis).

psychotic persecution a severely distorted and vastly inflated sense of being in dangerous circum-stances; perhaps the ultimate of mistrust (see also projection and paranoid psychosis).

puber an individual who exists on the front edge of adolescence; an individual at the beginning of pu-berty.

puberty the time of life when an individual becomes physically capable of procreation.

rage anger that has gotten out of control (see also anger and hostility).

rationalization a defensive flight from appearing to others to be wrong or stupid or nonsensical; or just the opposite.

reaction formation a defensive flight often designed to assist the defense called *repression*. The individ-ual behaves in ways that are the opposite of how he feels.

reactive depression neurotic depression.

regression a defensive flight in which the individual seeks to avoid a present-time stress by behaving in ways that were at one time more appropriate; one avoids the present by behaving at earlier (past) levels of behavior.

reinforce to condition in such a way that a response is elicited and the connection is made more or less firmly with the stimulus (see also extinguish).

repairing actions in which the individual attempts to recover from real or imagined assaults that have produced psychological pain; informally brought into play in intimate relationships; formally, a cen-tral factor in psychotherapy; one of the potentials for development present at birth (see also defend-ing).

repression a defending behavior in which ideas, feel-ings, are excluded from conscious awareness. Blocking is sometimes viewed as a synonym, and blocking behavior as the observable aspects of re-pression.

reproductive invariance the attribute of living things to produce other living things that are essentially the same as the original.

reputation ways in which an individual is perceived by others.

respondent conditioning a term synonomous with classical conditioning.

retarded depression usually neurotic depression characterized by slowness, lowered ability to con-centrate, a slowing down but not a distortion of thinking ability, and often by an increase in the number of hours slept.

retrograde amnesia loss of memory due to accidental brain damage. In general, the greater the damage, the greater the memory loss.

rooting an infant's restless set of movements as he searches for the nipple.

S in psychological research the abbreviation for the subject. Plural is Ss.

schizophrenia see schizophrenic psychoses.

schizophrenic psychoses a diagnostic term frequent-ly used to describe severe emotional disorders usually characterized by disorganization of behav-ior and a withdrawal from reality as it is commonly known; a controversial term.

science the study of nature, including man, by man; the work of organizing information into a coherent and interconnected system; a product of scientists; an organized and usually mathematically based search for knowledge (see also epistemology).

self an abstract idea meant to capsule all that a per-son is to himself.

self-absorption a turning inward, a somewhat de-pressed state of being that is the opposite of gen-erativity.

self-actualization the fullest utilization of the poten-tials for development, perhaps most especially the potential for creating.

self-defeating behavior commonly and frequently seen activities in which an individual acts in ways that prevent the satisfaction of desires or needs.

self-esteem what an individual thinks of himself.

senile psychosis gradual deterioration of behavior based upon the aging process.

sensitivity training training in self-awareness using verbal techniques and action techniques; apparent-ly based upon activities developed in the *Begeg-nung* of psychodrama (see also encounter and group therapy).

shame and doubt the opposite psychologically to autonomy; a behavioral trend that begins to be a factor in early childhood.

social atom the people an individual requires to fulfill his social role in the several social behavior settings; a psychodramatic term.

socialization learning behaviors that are customary and acceptable as defined by the group to which the individual belongs.

socializing process the sequence of learning that begins at birth and is aimed at civilizing the individual.

sociometric process psychodramatic technique in which the group participants choose the individual who becomes the protagonist (see also protagonist).

sociometric star the person chosen by the sociometric process to become the protagonist in a psychodrama.

sociopath individual with poor judgment, no civilized conscience, loaded with swiftly expressed impulses, a vagabond who seems trustworthy and loyal but who essentially is not.

soldier's disease morphine addiction; one of the reasons why morphine is not used as widely as it once was in the alleviation of physical pain.

Stegreiftheater theater of spontaneity founded by Jacob Moreno as a part of his development of psychodrama.

Stelazine trade name of a drug known generically as trifluoperazine.

stimulus complex the environmental factors in an experiment or in behavior modification to which the subject or the patient may respond consciously or unconsciously.

striving purposeful, goal-directed behavior; one of the potentials for development present at birth.

structuralism the ability or predisposition of the individual to control his own perceptions.

sublimation a defensive compromise in which socially unacceptable or inefficient behaviors are channeled or directed into activities that are typically more acceptable.

substitution an aggressive defense much like displacement in which the target of feelings is usually in a downward direction (see also displacement).

success depression depression following some achievement.

superego the conscience.

surplus reality enhancement of the understanding and control of integration of behavior during the last part of the psychodrama; refers to the expansion and extension of the protagonist's typical or normative behavior.

survival getting enough food and water and, on a broader scale, insuring controlled procreation; based upon cerebral control of urges and impulses as well as upon the development of technology.

symbolic immortality living beyond one's own death by way of symbols left behind, the symbols representing one's own existence. The symbols may be children, works of art, graffiti, songs, memories that exist in another's mind.

sympathism an aggressive defense in which the individual spends energy to gain the sympathy of other people or to gain some form of recognition.

synthesis the last part of psychoanalysis in which behavior is redirected along more productive lines (see also analysis).

system an organization of people or of objects or of ideas in which the parts are interrelated in an orderly and durable way to make a whole (see also organization).

tardive dyskinesia disorder of the central nervous system affecting speech and producing involuntary movements of the tongue, lips, hands, fingers, and body posture; brought about by continued use of phenothiazines in psychopharmacology.

task the job that must or should be done (see also process).

technology the ways man has developed to insure satisfaction of biological and psychological needs; typically a matter of the development and use of a wide assortment of tools.

teleonomy a biological purpose that is a part of the genetic endowment of living things.

Thanatos according to Sigmund Freud, the wish toward death (see also Eros).

thinking one of the potentials for development present at birth; a many faceted aspect of behavior typically considered as being based in the brain; also known as cognitive behavior. It is not an observable behavior, ordinarily.

thiopropazate one of the phenothiazines, a drug used in the psychopharmacological treatment of psychotic states. Trade name is Dartal.

thioridazine generic name of a drug used in the treatment of psychotic conditions, a member of the phenothiazine family. Trade name is Mellaril.

Thorazine trade name of a drug known generically as chlorpromazine.

traditionalism an attachment to the past, a belief that what has happened should be repeated; the idea that new things or changed ways are not as adequate as old things and old ways.

transactional analysis a popularized version of the body of knowledge called psychoanalysis; also known as TA; developed by Eric Berne as a form of psychotherapy.

trifluoperazine generic name of one of the phenothiazines, used in the treatment of psychosis. Trade name is Stelazine.

triflupromazine generic name for one of the phenothiazines used in the psychopharmacological treatment of psychosis. Trade name is Vesprin.

Trilafon trade name of a drug known generically as perphenazine.

trivialization an aggressive defense designed to make great things unimportant or harmless, thereby maintaining or enhancing one's own feelings of self-esteem or reputation (see also discounting).

trust the belief that at least some things and individuals in the world are not harmful; a fundamental psychological characteristic initially developed during infancy.

unconditioned response a response that can be elicited before there is any conditioning.

unconditioned stimulus a stimulus that evokes a certain and definable response before there is any conditioning.

undoing excusing one's own behavior, to make amends, or to attempt repair; a technique of defensive flight designed to maintain self-esteem and, especially, reputation.

vertiginous dizzy.

Vesprin trade name of a drug known generically as triflupromazine.

youth a less inclusive term than juvenile; generally refers to persons from about age 16 to the early 20s (see also juvenile).

REFERENCES

Adler, A.: Science and evil, The Atlantic, vol. 229, pp. 87-90, Feb. 1972.

Adler, R.: The Thursday group (1967). In Toward a radical middle: fourteen pieces of reporting and criticism, New York, 1969, Random House, Inc.

Albee, G. W.: Mental health manpower trends, New York, 1959, Basic Books, Inc., Publishers.

Aldridge, J. W.: In the country of the young, part II, The Atlantic, vol. 228, pp. 93-107, Nov., 1969.

Algren, N.: The six best novels of World War II and why five died, Intellectual Digest, vol. 3, no. 8, pp. 68-69, April, 1973.

Alinsky, S. D.: Rules for Radicals, New York, 1971, Random House, Inc.

Alland, A., Jr.: Evolution and human behavior, Garden City, N. Y., 1967, Natural History Press.

Anastasi, A.: The cultivation of diversity, American Psychologist, vol. 27, pp. 1091-1099, Dec., 1972.

Argyris, C.: Interpersonal competence and organizational Effectiveness, Homewood, Ill., 1962, Dorsey Press.

Arieti, S.: Interpretation of schizophrenia, New York, 1955, Robert Brunner, Inc.

Asimov, I.: The human brain: its capacities and functions, Boston, 1964, Houghton Mifflin Co.

Avorn, J.: Beyond dying, Harper's, vol. 246, pp. 56-64, March, 1973.

Bach, G. R., and Deutsch, R. M.: Pairing, New York, 1970, Avon Books.

Bach, G. R., and Wyden, P.: The intimate enemy, New York, 1968, Avon Books.

Back, K. W.: Beyond words: the story of sensitivity training, New York, 1972, Russell Sage Foundation.

Back, K. W.: The group can comfort but it can't cure, Psychology Today, vol. 6, no. 7, pp. 28-35, Dec., 1972.

Bakan, D.: Psychology can now kick the science habit, Psychology Today, vol. 5, no. 10, pp. 14-16 and 61-67, March, 1972.

Beauvoir, S. de: The ethics of ambiguity, New York, 1948, Citadel Press, Inc.

Beck, A. T.: Thinking and depression: idiosyncratic content and cognitive distortions, Archives of General Psychiatry, vol. 9, pp. 321-327, June, 1963.

Berelson, B., and Steiner, G.: Human behavior: an inventory of scientific findings, New York, 1964, Harcourt, Brace & World, Inc.

Berne, E.: Transactional analysis in psychotherapy, New York, 1961, Grove Press, Inc.

Berne, E.: Games people play, New York, 1964, Grove Press, Inc.

Berne, E.: Principles of group treatment, New York, 1966, Grove Press, Inc.

Berreman, G. D.: Behind many masks: ethnography and impression management in a Himalayan village, Society for Applied Anthropology, monograph no. 4, pp. 1-24, 1962.

Bindrim, P.: Nudity as a quick grab for intimacy in group therapy, Psychology Today, vol. 3, no. 1, pp. 25-28, June, 1969.

Blackburn, T. P.: Sensous-intellectual complementarity in science, Science, vol. 172, pp. 1003-1007, June 4, 1971.

Blond, G.: The Marne, New York, 1962, Pyramid Publications.

Booth, E. P.: Religion ponders science, New York, 1964, Appleton-Century-Crofts.

Borsch, F. J.: The 801st man: or a man for the 21st century. In Hutchinson, J. G., editor: Readings in management strategy and tactics, New York, 1971, Holt, Rinehart and Winston, Inc.

Boston Women's Health Book Collective, Inc.: Our bodies, ourselves, New York, 1973, Simon & Schuster, Inc.

Boulding, K. E.: The meaning of the twentieth century, New York, 1964, Harper & Row, Publishers.

Brams, J.: From Freud to Fromm, Psychology Today, vol. 1, no. 9, pp. 22-24 and 58-59, Feb., 1968.

Branden, N.: The psychology of self-esteem, New York, 1969, Bantam Books, Inc.

Bridges, K. M.: Emotional development in early infancy, Child Development, vol. 3, pp. 324-341, Dec., 1932.

Brown, D.: Bury my heart at Wounded Knee, New York, 1970, Holt, Rinehart and Winston, Inc.

Brown, N. O.: Life against death, New York, 1959, Vintage Books.

Buhler, C.: Basic theoretical concepts of humanistic psychology, American Psychologist, vol. 26, no. 4, pp. 378-386, April, 1971.

Cannon, W. B.: Wisdom of the body, New York, 1932, W. W. Norton & Co.

Carnegie Corporation of New York Quarterly, vol. 9, no. 3, July, 1961.

Castaneda, C.: Journey to Ixtlan, New York, 1972, Simon & Schuster, Inc.

Charney, N.: The society—organizing for social change, Saturday Review, vol. 56, no. 7, p. 29, Sept. 12, 1972.

Chomsky, N.: Language and the mind, readings in Psychology Today, Del Mar, Calif., 1969, CRM Books, pp. 280-286.

Choron, J.: Suicide, New York, 1972, Charles Scribner's Sons.

Clark, K.: Civilisation, New York, 1969, Harper & Row, Publishers.

Clarke, A. C.: 2001: a space odyessy, New York, 1968, The New American Library, Inc.

Cleckley, H.: The mask of sanity, St. Louis, 1964, The C. V. Mosby Co.

Cohen, J. M. and Cohen, M. J.: The Penguin dictionary of quotations, Middlesex, England, 1960, Penguin Publishing Co. Ltd.

Cole, W.: Lighter-than-aircraft, Harper's, vol. 245, pp. 66-68, Dec., 1972.

Coleman, J. C.: Abnormal psychology and modern life, New York, 1964, Scott, Foresman and Co.

Coleman, J. C.: Psychology and effective behavior, Glenview, Ill., 1969, Scott, Forsman and Co.

Coles, L. S.: Computers and society, Science, vol. 178, p. 561, Nov. 10, 1972.

Coles, R.: On the meaning of work, The Atlantic, vol. 228, pp. 103-104, Oct., 1971.

Commoner, B.: Science and survival, New York, 1966, The Viking Press, Inc.

Commoner, B.: Motherhood in Stockholm, Harper's, vol. 244, pp. 49-54, June, 1972.

Coopersmith, S.: Studies in self-esteem, Scientific American, vol. 218, no. 2, pp. 96-106, Feb., 1968.

Cottrell, L.: The anvil of civilisation, New York, 1957, New American Library of World Literature.

Cousins, N.: Editorial, Saturday Review, vol. 54, p. 30, Sept. 25, 1971.

Cramer, J. B.: Common neuroses of childhood. In Arieti, S., editor: American Handbook of Psychiatry, vol. 1, New York, 1959, Basic Books, Inc., Publishers, pp. 341-382.

Crotty, W. S.: Presidential assassinations, Transaction: Social Science and Modern Society, vol. 9, pp. 19-29, May, 1972.

Crowell, D. H., Jones, R. H., Kapuniai, L. E., and Nakagawa, J. K.: Unilateral cortical activity in newborn humans: an early index of cerebral dominance? Science, vol. 180, pp. 205-208, April 13, 1973.

Crozier, M.: A new rationale for American business, Daedalus, vol. 98, no. 1, pp. 147-158, Winter, 1969.

Darwin, C.: The origin of the species and the descent of man, New York, 1936, Modern Library, Inc.

Davies, A. P.: The urge to persecute, Boston, 1953, Beacon Press.

Diamond, B. L.: Sirhan B. Sirhan, Psychology Today, vol. 3, no. 4, pp. 48-55, Sept., 1969.

Diggory, J. C., and Rothman, D. Z.: Values destroyed by death, Journal of Abnormal and Social Psychology, vol. 63, pp. 205-210, April, 1961.

Dobzhansky, T.: Changing man, Science, vol. 155, pp. 409-415, Jan. 25, 1967.

Dobzhansky, T.: Genetics and the diversity of behavior, American Psychologist, vol. 27, no. 6, pp. 523-530, June, 1972.

Dollard, J., and Miller, N. E.: Personality and psychotherapy, New York, 1950, McGraw-Hill Book Co.

Doty, P.: The community of science and the search for peace, Science, vol. 173, pp. 998-1002, Sept. 10, 1971.

Doxiadis, C. A.: Man and the space around him, Saturday Review, vol. 50, pp. 21-23, Dec. 14, 1968.

Ehrenburg, I.: A last memoir. In Cousins, N., editor: What I have learned, New York, 1968, Simon and Schuster, Inc.

Ehrlich, P. R., and Ehrlich, A. H.: Population, resources, environment, San Francisco, 1970, W. H. Freeman and Co.

Eiseley, L.: The invisible pyramid, New York 1970, Charles Scribner's Sons.

Eisenberg, L.: Student unrest: sources and consequences, Science, vol. 167, pp. 171-176, March 20, 1970.

Eisenberg, L.: The *human* nature of human nature, Science, vol. 176, pp. 123-128, April 14, 1972.

Elkin, F.: The child and society: the process of socialization, New York, 1960, Random House, Inc.

Elkind, D., and Hamsher, J. H.: The anatomy of melancholy, Saturday Review/Science, vol. 55, pp. 54-59, Sept. 30, 1972.

Elliott, G. P.: Science and the profession of literature, The Atlantic, vol. 228, pp. 61-69, Oct., 1971.

English, O. S.: Six years experience in an effort to define and treat schizophrenia. In Summaries of the scientific papers of the 119th annual meeting, American Psychiatric Association, Washington, D. C., 1963, The Association, paper no. 44.

Erikson, E. H.: Childhood and society, New York, 1963, W. W. Norton & Co.

Erikson, E. H.: Identity: youth and crisis, New York, 1968, W. W. Norton & Co.

Eysenck, H. J.: The effects of psychotherapy: an evaluation, Journal of Consulting Psychology (16) pp. 319-324, 1952.

Eysenck, H. J., editor: Behavior therapy and the neuroses, Oxford, England, 1960, Pergamon Press Ltd.

Feifel, H.: Death. In Farberow, N. L., editor: Taboo topics, New York, 1963, Atherton Press, Inc.

Ford, A. B.: Casualties of our time, Science, vol. 167, pp. 256-263, Jan. 16, 1970.

Frank, J. D.: The demoralized mind, Psychology Today, vol. 6, no. 11, pp. 22-31 and 100-101, April, 1973.

Frankfort, W.: Before philosophy, London, 1954, Penguin Publishing Co. Ltd.

Freud, A.: The ego and the mechanisms of defense, New York, 1946, International Universities Press.

Freud, S.: The ego and the id (translation by J. Riviere), London, 1927, The Hogarth Press Ltd.

Freud, S.: My views on the part played by sexuality in the aetiology of the neuroses. In Zax, M., and Stricker, G., editors: The study of abnormal behavior: selected readings, ed. 2, New York, 1969, The Macmillan Co.

Fromm, E.: Escape from freedom, New York, 1941, Avon Books.

Fuller, J. G.: The day of St. Anthony's fire, New York, 1968, The Macmillan Co.

Fuller, R. B.: Geoview: thinking out loud: physical temporality and eternal principles, Saturday Review/World, vol. 1, pp. 53-54, Sept. 11, 1973.

Gadpaille, W. J.: How the "how to" books shape up, Medical Opinion, vol. 1, no. 1, pp. 48-53, May, 1972.

Galle, O. R., Gove, W. R., and McPherson, J. M.: Population density and pathology: what are the relations for man? Science, vol. 176, pp. 23-30, April 7, 1972.

Gardner, L. I.: Deprivation dwarfism, Scientific American, vol. 227, no. 1, pp. 76-82, July, 1972.

Garnett, R., Vallee, L., et al., editors: The universal anthology, New York, 1899, Merrill and Baker.

Gerbner, G.: Communications and social environment, Scientific American, vol. 227, no. 3, pp. 153-160, Sept., 1972.

Gergen, K. J.: The healthy, happy human wears many masks, Psychology Today, vol. 5, no. 12, pp. 31-35 and 64-66, May, 1972.

Glaberman, M.: Unions vs. workers in the seventies: the rise of militancy in the auto industry, Transaction: Social Science and Modern Society, vol. 10, no. 1, pp. 85-89, Nov.-Dec., 1972.

Glasser, W.: The identity society, New York, 1972, Harper & Row, Publishers.

Glazier, W. H.: The task of medicine, Scientific American, vol. 228, no. 4, pp. 13-17, April, 1973.

Goffman, E.: The presentation of self in everyday life, New York, 1959, Doubleday & Co., Inc.

Goffman, E.: Asylums, New York, 1961, Anchor Books.

Goldstein, K.: the effect of brain damage on the personality. In Zax, M., and Stricker, G., editors: The study of abnormal behavior: selected readings, ed. 2, New York, 1969, The Macmillan Co.

Goodall, K.: The interlocking crises of father and adolescent son, Psychology Today, vol. 5, no. 12, p. 14, May, 1972.

Gordon, T.: Group centered leadership, Boston, 1956, Houghton Mifflin Co.

Graham, D. A.: The end of religion, New York, 1971, Harcourt Brace Jovanovich, Inc.

Greenberg, D.: Scoring: a sexual memoir, New York, 1972, Doubleday & Co., Inc.

Greenwald, J.: The art of emotional nourishment, unpublished material, Santa Monica, Calif., 1968.

Greenwald, J.: The art of emotional nourishment: self-induced nourishment and toxicity, unpublished material, Santa Monica, Calif., 1969.

Greer, G.: The female eunuch, New York, 1971, McGraw-Hill Book Co.

Grinker, R. R., editor: Toward a unified theory of human behavior, New York, 1956, Basic Books, Inc., Publishers.

Grinspoon, L: Marihuana, Scientific American, vol. 221, no. 6, pp. 17-25, Dec., 1969.

Grossberg, J. M.: Behavior therapy: a review, Psychological Bulletin, vol. 62, no. 2, pp. 73-88, Aug., 1964.

Group for the Advancement of Psychiatry (GAP), Committee on Adolescence: Normal adolescence: its dynamics and impact, New York, 1968, Charles Scribner's Sons.

Guibert, R.: Seven voices, New York, 1972, Alfred A. Knopf, Inc.

Halberstam, M.: The pills in your life, New York, 1972, Grosset & Dunlap, Inc.

Hall, C. A.: A primer of freudian psychology, New York, 1954, World Publishing Co.

Hall, M. H.: A conversation with the father of Rogerian therapy, Psychology Today, vol. 1, no. 7, pp. 19-21 and 62-69, Dec., 1967.

Harth, M., editor: The New York Times encyclopedic almanac, New York, 1971, The New York Times Co.

Hartt, F.: Michelangelo, New York, 1964, Harry N. Abrams, Inc.

Hawley, A. H.: Ecology and population, Science, vol. 179, pp. 1196-1201, March 23, 1973.

Heath, R.: The reasonable adventurer, Pittsburgh, 1964, University of Pittsburgh Press.

Henahan, J. F.: New dating technique, Intellectual Digest, vol. 3, no. 4, p. 66, Dec., 1972.

Heyns, R. W.: The psychology of personal adjustment, New York, 1958, The Dryden Press.

Hoch, P. H.: Drug therapy. In Arieti, S., editor: American handbook of psychiatry, New York, 1959, Basic Books, Inc., Publishers, vol. 2, pp. 1541-1551.

Hoffer, E.: The ordeal of change, New York, 1963, Harper & Row, Publishers.

Hoffer, E.: A strategy for the war with nature. In Cousins, N., editor: What I have learned, New York, 1968, Simon & Schuster, Inc.

Hoffman, M. E.: Childrearing practice and moral development—generalizations from empirical research. In Wrightsman, L. S., editor: Contemporary issues in social psychology, Belmont, Calif., 1968, Brooks/Cole Publishing Co.

Holden, C.: Altered states of consciousness: mind researchers meet to discuss exploration and mapping of "inner space," Science, vol. 179, pp. 982-983, March 9, 1973.

Hollander, C.: A process for psychodrama training: the Hollander psychodrama curve, Littleton, Colo., 1969, Evergreen Institute Press.

Holloman, J. H.: The U. S. patent system, Scientific American, vol. 216, no. 6, pp. 19-27, June, 1967.

Horrocks, J. S., and Jackson, D. W.: Self and role: a theory of self-process and role behavior, New York, 1972, Houghton Mifflin Co.

Illich, I.: Celebration of awareness, New York, 1970, Doubleday & Co., Inc.

Irving, D.: The destruction of Dresden, New York, 1963, Ballantine Books, Inc.

Ismail, A. H., and Trachtman, L. E.: Jogging the imagination, Psychology Today, vol. 6, no. 10, pp. 78-82, March, 1973.

James, M., and Jongeward, D.: Born to win, Reading, Mass., 1971, Addison-Wesley Publishing Co., Inc.

Jelliffe, S. E.: The technique of psychoanalysis, New York, 1920, Nervous and Mental Disease Publishing Co.

Jones, S. C.: Self and interpersonal evaluations: esteem theories versus consistency theories, Psychological Bulletin, vol. 79, no. 3, pp. 185-199, March, 1973.

Josselyn, I. M.: The adolescent and his world, New York, 1952, Family Service Association of America.

Judson, H. F.: A reporter at large, the British and heroin. Part II. The New Yorker, vol. 59, no. 32, pp. 70-74, 79-108, 111-112, Oct. 1, 1973.

Kahn, F.: Design of the universe, New York, 1954, Crown Publishers, Inc.

Kaluger, G., and Unkovic, C. M.: Psychology and sociology, St. Louis, 1969, The C. V. Mosby Co.

Kanfer, S.: The trivialization of evil, Harper's, vol. 246, pp. 98-101, April, 1973.

Kass, L. R.: Death as an event: a commentary on Robert Morison, Science, vol. 173, pp. 698-702, Aug. 20, 1971.

Kaufmann, W.: Do you crave a life without choice? Psychology Today, vol. 6, no. 11, pp. 78-83, April, 1973.

Keniston, K.: Toward a more human society. In Girvetz, H. K., editor: Contemporary moral issues, ed. 2, Belmont, Calif., 1968, Wadsworth Publishing Co. Inc.

King, E. L.: How the army destroyed itself, Saturday Review, vol. 55, pp. 29-33, May 6, 1972.

Klein, H.: Speech. In Wolstenholme, G., editor: Man and his future, Boston, 1963, Little, Brown and Co.

Koenig, P.: Boy in trouble: milestones in a labyrinth, Psychology Today, vol. 7, no. 4, pp. 50-51, Sept., 1973.

Krause, M. S.: Use of social situations for research purposes, American Psychologist, vol. 25, pp. 753-758, April, 1970.

Krogh, A.: The language of bees. In Coopersmith, S., editor: Frontiers of psychological research, New York, 1948, W. H. Freeman and Co. Publishers.

Kubler-Ross, E.: On death and dying, New York, 1969, The Macmillan Co.

Kuhn, A.: The study of society: a unified approach, Homewood, Ill., 1963, Richard D. Irwin, Inc.

Laing, R. D.: Knots, New York, 1970, Pantheon Books, Inc.

Laing, R. D., and Esterson, A.: Sanity, madness and the family, ed. 2, New York, 1964, Basic Books, Inc., Publishers.

Land, E. H.: Addiction as a necessity and opportunity, Science, vol. 171, pp. 151-153, Jan. 15, 1971.

Lang, D.: Ex-oracles: on the new unpopularity of scientists, Harper's, vol. 245, pp. 34-43, Dec., 1972.

Lanyon, R. I.: Mental health technology, American Psychologist, vol. 26, pp. 1071-1076, Dec., 1971.

Larson, C. A.: Edward L. Thorndike—Olympian figure, Contemporary Psychology, vol. 17, pp. 257-259, May, 1972.

Leaf, A.: Search for the oldest people, National Geographic, vol. 143, pp. 93-118, Jan., 1973.

Leavitt, H. J.: Managerial psychology, rev. ed., Chicago, 1964, University of Chicago Press.

Lejeune, J.: On the nautre of men, Mental Health Digest, vol. 2, pp. 9-14, July, 1970.

Lerner, M. J.: All the world loathes a loser, Psychology Today, vol. 5, no. 1, pp. 51-54 and 66, June, 1971.

Lessing, D.: The children of violence: Martha Quest, New York, 1970, The New American Library, Inc.

Lessing, L.: The senseless war on science, Fortune, vol. 83, no. 3, pp. 90-91, March, 1971.

Lester, D.: Self-mutilating behavior, Psychological Bulletin, vol. 78, pp. 119-128, Aug., 1972.

Lewin, K., Lippitt, R., and White, R. K., Patterns of aggressive behavior in experimentally created "social climates," Journal of Social Psychology, vol. 79, pp. 271-299, Sept., 1939.

Lifton, R. J.: Home from the war: the psychology of survival, The Atlantic, vol. 230, pp. 56-72, Nov., 1972.

Lifton, R. J.: The struggle for cultural rebirth, Harper's, vol. 246, pp. 84-90, April, 1973.

Limbacher, W.: I'm not alone, Dayton, Ohio, 1970, Pflaum/Standard.

Lumsden, M., editor: Human Behavior: The Newsmagazine of the Social Sciences, vol. 1, no. 1, pp. 40-44, Jan.-Feb., 1972.

MacKinnon, D. W.: Personality and the realization of creative potential, American Psychologist, vol. 20, pp. 273-281, May, 1965.

Magoon, T. M., Golann, S. E., and Freeman, R. W.: Mental health counselors at work, New York, 1969, Pergamon Press, Inc.

Maier, H. W.: Three theories of child development, New York, 1965, Harper & Row, Publishers.

Maier, N. R. F.: Innovation in education, American Psychologist, vol. 26, pp. 722-725, Aug., 1971.

Marks, H. H.: Characteristics and trends in cerebral vascular disease. In Hoch, P. H., and Zubin, J., editors: Psychopathology of aging, New York, 1961, Grune & Stratton, Inc.

Marx, L.: The machine in the garden, New York, 1964, Oxford University Press.

Maslow, A. H.: A theory of human motivation, Psychological Review, vol. 50, pp. 370-396, 1943.

Maslow, A. H.: Motivation and personality, New York, 1954, Harper & Row, Publishers.

Maslow, A. H.: Eupsychian management, Homewood, Ill., 1965, Richard D. Irwin, Inc.

Maslow, A. H.: Toward a psychology of being, New York, 1968, Van Nostrand Reinhold Co.

Masserman, J. H.: Experimental neuroses. In Coopersmith, S., editor: Frontiers of psychological research, San Francisco, 1948-1966, W. H. Freeman and Co. Publishers, pp. 244-249.

May, R.: Love and will, New York, 1969, W. W. Norton & Co., Inc.

Mayr, E.: The nature of the darwinian revolution, Science, vol. 176, pp. 981-989, June 2, 1972.

McConnell, J. V.: Criminals can be brainwashed—now, Psychology Today, vol. 3, no. 11, pp. 14-18 and 74, April, 1970.

McGregor, D.: The human side of enterprise, New York, 1960, McGraw-Hill Book Co.

McLuhan, M.: Culture is our business, New York, 1970, McGraw-Hill Book Co.

McNeil, E. D.: The psychoses, Englewood Cliffs, N. J., 1970, Prentice-Hall, Inc.

Mead, M.: Coming of age in Samoa, New York, 1928, William Morrow & Co., Inc.

Menninger, K.: The crime of punishment, New York, 1966, The Viking Press, Inc.

Michener, J. A.: The quality of life, New York, 1970, J. B. Lippincott Co.

Mikulas, W. L.: Behavior modification: an overview, New York, 1972, Harper & Row, Publishers.

Milgram, S.: The experience of living in cities, Science, vol. 167, pp. 1461-1468, March 13, 1970.

Miller, A. R.: The assault of privacy: computers, data banks, and dossiers, Ann Arbor, Mich., 1971, The University of Michigan Press.

Miller, N. E.: Learning of visceral and glandular responses, Science, vol. 163, pp. 434-445, Jan. 31, 1969.

Monod, J.: Chance and necessity, New York, 1971, Alfred A. Knopf, Inc.

Moreno, J. L.: Who shall survive? Beacon, N. Y., 1953, Beacon House, Inc., Publishers.

Moore, B. E., and Fine, B. D.: A glossary of psychoanalytic terms and concepts, ed. 2, New York, 1971, The American Psychoanalytic Association.

Moreno, J. L.: Psychodrama. In Arieti, S., editor: American handbook of psychiatry, New York, 1959, Basic Books, Inc., Publishers, vol. 2, pp. 1375-1396.

Moreno, J. L., and Moreno, Z. T.: Psychodrama: vol. 3, action therapy and principles of practice, Beacon, N.Y., 1969, Beacon House, Inc., Publishers.

Morgan, C. T., and King, R. A.: Introduction to psychology, ed. 3, New York, 1966, McGraw-Hill Book Co.

Morison, R. S.: Where is biology taking us? Science, vol. 155, pp. 429-433, Jan. 27, 1967.

Morison, R. S.: Death: process or event? Science, vol. 173, pp. 694-698, Aug. 20, 1971.

Mullahy, P.: Oedipus: myth and complex, New York, 1948, Hermitage House, Inc.

Muller, C.: The overmedicated society: forces in the marketplace for medical care, Science, vol. 176, pp. 488-492, May 5, 1972.

Mumford, L.: The myth of the machine, New York, 1967, Harcourt Brace Jovanovich.

Murray, H. A., editor: Explorations in personality, London, 1938, Oxford University Press.

Myers, M. S.: Every employee a manager, New York, 1970, McGraw-Hill Book Co.

Nicholls, J. G.: Creativity in the person who will never produce anything original and useful: the concept of creativity as a normally distributed trait, American Psychologist, vol. 27, pp. 717-727, Aug., 1972.

Noyes, A., and Kolb, L. C.: Modern clinical psychiatry, ed. 6, Philadelphia, 1963, W. B. Saunders Co.

Offer, D., and Sabshin, M.: Normality, New York, 1966, Basic Books Inc., Publishers.

Opler, M. K: Schizophrenia and culture. In Coopersmith, S. editor: Frontiers of psychological research, San Francisco, 1948-1966, W. H. Freeman
& Co., pp. 117-121.

Ornstein, R.: The psychology of consciousness,
New York, 1973, The Viking Press, Inc.

Palmer, S.: Deviance and conformity, New Haven,
Conn., 1970, College & University Press.

Parducci, A.: The relativism of absolute judgments, Scientific American, vol. 9, pp. 84-90,
Dec., 1968.

Parsons, T.: Societies: evolutionary and comparative
perspectives, Englewood Cliffs, N. J., 1966, Prentice-Hall, Inc.

Pattison, E. M., and Elpers, J. R.: A developmental
view of mental health manpower trends, Hospital
and Community Psychiatry, vol. 23, pp. 325-329,
Nov., 1972.

Peplau, H. E.: Interpersonal relations in nursing,
New York, 1952, G. P. Putnams Sons.

Perlman, H. H.: Persona: social role and personality, Chicago, 1968, University of Chicago Press.

Perls, F. S.: Gestalt therapy verbatim, Lafayette,
Calif., 1969, Real People Press.

Perls, F. S., Hefferline, R., and Goodman, P.: Gestalt therapy, New York, 1951, Delta Books.

Perry, H. S., and Gawel, M. L., editors: The collected works of Harry Stack Sullivan, M. D., vol. 1,
New York, 1953, W. W. Norton & Co., Inc.

Peterson, E.: Psychopharmacology, Dubuque, Iowa,
1966, William C. Brown, Publishers.

Platt, J.: Social traps, American Psychologist, vol.
28, pp. 641-651, Aug., 1973.

Pogrebin, L. C.: Rap groups: the feminist connection, Ms., vol. 1, no. 9, March, 1973.

Poland, R.: Managerial power, Western Business
Review, vol. 5, no. 1, pp. 15-21, Feb, 1961.

Poland, R., and Sanford, N.: Adjustment psychology: a human value approach, St. Louis, 1971, The
C. V. Mosby Co.

Popoff, D.: Feedback on drugs, Psychology Today,
vol. 3, no. 11, pp. 27-31 and 77-83, April, 1970.

Powell, J.: Why am I afraid to tell you who I am?
Chicago, 1969, Peacock Books Argus Communications Co.

Powers, W. T.: Feedback: beyond behaviorism,
Science, vol. 179, pp. 351-356, Jan. 26, 1973.

Quey, R. L.: Functions and dynamics of work
groups, American Psychologist, vol. 26, pp. 1077-
1082, Dec., 1971.

Raskin, M.: Being and doing, New York, 1971, Random House, Inc.

Ray, O. S.: Drugs, society, and human behavior, St.
Louis, 1972, The C. V. Mosby Co.

Redlich, F. C., and Freedman, D. X.: The theory and
practice of psychiatry, New York, 1966, Basic
Books, inc., Publishers.

Reich, C. A.: The greening of America, New York,
1970, Bantam Books, Inc.

Rheingold, H. L., and Eckerman, C. O.: The infant
separates himself from his mother, Science, vol.
168, April 3, 1970.

Rickover, H. G.: A humanistic technology. In de
Nevers, N.: Technology and society, Reading,
Mass., 1972, Addison-Wesley Publishing Co.,
Inc., pp. 21-34.

Roethlisberger, F. J., and Dickson, W. J.: Management and the worker, Cambridge, Mass., 1939,
Harvard University Press.

Rogers, C.: Counseling and psychotherapy, Boston,
1942, Houghton Mifflin Co.

Rogers, C.: Client-centered therapy: its current practice, implications and theory, Boston, 1951,
Houghton Mifflin Co.

Rogers, C.: The necessary and sufficient conditions
of therapeutic personality change, Journal of Consulting Psychology, vol. 21, pp. 95-103, Nov.,
1957.

Rogers, C.: Community: the group comes of age,
Psychology Today, vol. 3, no. 7, pp. 27-31 and 58-
61, Dec., 1969.

Rogers, C., Gendlin, E. T., Kiesler, D. J., and Truax,
C. B., editors: The therapeutic relationship and its
impact, Madison, Wis., 1967, University of Wisconsin Press.

Rogers, J. M.: Drug abuse—just what the doctor ordered, Psychology Today vol. 5, no. 4, pp. 16-20
and 24, Sept., 1971.

Rogin, G.: The fencing master and other stories,
New York, 1965, Random House, Inc.

Romano, J.: Has psychiatry resigned from medicine?
Medical Opinion, vol. 2, no. 1, pp. 27-32, Jan.,
1973.

Rose, S.: The news about productivity is better than
you think, Fortune, vol. no 2, Feb., 1972.

Rosenfeld, A.: The longevity seekers, Saturday Re-
view/Science, vol. 1, pp. 46-51, Feb. 24, 1973.

Rosenhan, D. L.: On being sane in insane places,
Science, vol. 179, pp. 250-258, Jan. 19, 1973.

Rosner, S., and Abt, L. E., editors: The creative experience, New York, 1970, Grossman Publishers.

Rotter, J. B.: Generalized expectancies for internal
versus external control of reinforcement, Psychological Monographs: General and Applied, vol. 80,
pp. 1-28, 1966.

Rubin, T. I.: The angry book, New York, 1969, The
Macmillan Co.

Rycroft, C.: A critical dictionary of psychoanalysis,
New York, 1968, Basic Books, Inc., Publishers.

Sagan, C., Sagan, L. S., and Drake, F.: A message
from earth, Science, vol. 175, pp. 881-884, Feb. 25,
1972.

Sales, S. M.: Authoritarianism, Psychology Today,
vol. 6, no. 6, pp. 94-98 and 140-142, Nov., 1972.

Sampson, H., Messinger S., and Towne, R. D.: Schizophrenic women: studies in marital crisis, New York, 1964, Atherton Press, Inc.

Sanford, N.: Self and society, New York, 1966, Atherton Press, Inc.

Schiff, A., and Schiff, J. D.: Passivity, Journal of Transactional Analysis, vol. 1, no. 1, pp. 71-78, Jan., 1971.

Schneidman, E. S.: Suicide, sleep, and death, Journal of Consulting Psychology, vol. 28, pp. 95-106, Feb., 1964.

Schneidman, E. S.: You and death, Psychology Today, vol. 5, no. 1, pp. 43-45 and 74-80, June, 1971.

Schulberg, B.: The Chinese boxes of Muhammed Ali, Saturday Review, Vol. 60, pp. 21-26, Feb. 26, 1972.

Schulman, A.: Memoirs of an ex-prom queen, New York, 1972, Alfred A. Knopf, Inc.

Seeman, M.: On the meaning of alienation, American Sociological Review, vol. 24, pp. 783-791, March-April, 1959.

Servan-Schreiber, J. J.: The American challenge, New York, 1968, Atheneum Publishers.

Shapiro, D.: Neurotic styles (The Austen Riggs Center Monograph Series, No. 5), New York, 1965, Basic Books, Inc., Publishers.

Simpson, G. G.: Biology and man, New York, 1969, Harcourt, Brace and World.

Sims, J., and Bauman, D.: The tornado threat: coping styles of the North and South, Science, vol. 176, pp. 1386-1391, June 30, 1972.

Sissman, L. E.: A little night music: the curvature of the earth, The Atlantic, vol. 229, pp. 18-20, Jan., 1972.

Skinner, B. F.: Science and human behavior, New York, 1953, The Macmillan Co.

Skinner, B. F.: Beyond freedom and dignity, Psychology Today, vol. 5, no. 3, pp. 29-42, Aug., 1971.

Slavson, S. R.: An introduction to group therapy, New York, 1943, International Universities Press.

Smith, A. (pseudonym for George J. W. Goodman): The last days of cowboy capitalism, The Atlantic, vol. 230, pp. 43-60, Sept., 1972.

Solheim, W.: An earlier agricultural revolution, Scientific American, vol. 226, pp. 34-41, April, 1972.

Sommer, R.: Personal space: the behavioral basis of design, New York, 1969, Prentice-Hall, Inc.

Spicer, E. H.: Persistent cultural systems, Science, vol. 174, pp. 795-800, Nov. 19, 1971.

Spilhaus, A.: Ecolibrium, Science, vol. 175, pp. 711-715, Feb. 18, 1972.

Spinneta, J. J., and Rigler, D.: The child-abusing parent: a psychological review, Psychological Bulletin, vol. 77, pp. 296-3f14, April, fl972.

Spitz, R. A.: The first year of life, New York, 1965, International Universities Press.

Stagner, R.: The psychology of industrial conflict, New York, 1956, John Wiley & Sons, Inc.

Steele, B. F., and Pollock, C. B.: A psychiatric study of parents who abuse infants and small children. In Helfer, R. E., and Kempe, C. H., editors: The battered child, Chicago, 1968, University of Chicago Press.

Stent, G.: An ode to objectivity, The Atlantic, vol. 229, pp. 125-130, Nov., 1971.

Stent, G.: Prematurity and weakness in scientific discovery, Scientific American, vol. 227, no. 6, pp. 84-93, Dec., 1972.

Stevens, J. O.: Awareness: exploring, experimenting, experiencing, Lafayette, Calif., 1971, Real People Press.

Stoller, F. H.: Marathon groups: toward a conceptual model. In Solomon, L. N. and Berzon, B.: New perspectives on encounter groups, San Francisco, 1972, Jossey-Bass, Inc., Publishers, pp. 171-194.

Stone, J. L., and Church, J.: Childhod and adolescence, New York, 1964, Random House, Inc.

Szasz, T.: The myth of mental illness, American Psychologist, vol. 15, pp. 113-118, Aug., 1960.

Taber, C. W.: Taber's cyclopedic medical dictionary, ed. 8, Philadelphia, 1960, F. A. Davis Co.

Tanner, J. M.: Growing up, Scientific American, vol. 229, no. 3, pp. 35-43, Sept., 1973.

Tedeschi, J. T., Schlenker, B. R., and Bonoma, T. V.: Cognitive dissonance: private ratiocination of public spectacle? American Psychologist, vol. 26, pp. 685-695, Aug., 1971.

Thackery, A.: Reflections on the decline of science in America and some of its causes, Science, vol. 173, pp. 27-31, July 2, 1971.

Thomas, A., Chess, S., and Birch, H. G.: The origin of personality, Scientific American, vol. 223, no. 2, pp. 102-109, Aug., 1970.

Thomas, L.: Guessing and knowing: reflections on the science and technology of medicine, Saturday Review/Science, vol. 55, pp. 52-57, Dec. 23, 1972.

Thompson, J.: The achievements of Western Civilization, New York, 1965, Harper & Row, Publishers.

Tiffany, D. W., and Tiffany, P. G.: Social unrest: powerlessness and/or self-direction, American Psychologist, vol. 28, pp. 151-154, Feb., 1973.

Tobin, R. L.: Murder on television and the fourteen-year-old, Saturday Review, vol. 55, pp. 39-40, Jan. 8, 1972.

Todd, R.: Notes on corporate man, The Atlantic, vol. 228, pp. 83-93, Oct., 1971.

Toffler, A.: Future shock, New York, 1970, Random House, Inc.

Tse-Tung, Mao: On the protracted war, Peking, 1952, People's Publishing House.

Veroff, J., and Veroff, J. B.: Reconsideration of a

measure of power motivation, Psychological Bulletin, vol. 78, pp. 279-291, Oct., 1972.

Wade, N.: Theodore Roszak: visionary critic of science, Science, vol. 178, pp. 960-962, Dec. 1, 1972.

Wade, N.: Drug regulation: FDA replies to charges by economists and industry, Science, vol. 179, pp. 775-777, Feb 23, 1973.

Watts, A. W.: The wisdom of insecurity, New York, 1951, Vintage Books.

Watts, A. W.: Nature, man and woman, New York, 1958, Vintage Books.

Weaver, M.: William Carlos Williams: the American background, New York, 1971, Cambridge University Press.

Weizenbaum, J.: On the impact of the computer on society, Science, vol. 176, pp. 609-614, May 12, 1972.

Werth, A.: Russia at war: 1941-1945, New York, 1964, Avon Books.

Westman, W. E., and Gifford, R. M.: Environmental impact: controlling the overall level, Science, vol. 181, pp. 819-825, Aug. 31, 1973.

White, J. G.: The use of learning theory in the psychological treatment of children, Journal of Clinical Psychology, vol. 15, pp. 227-229, Jan., 1959.

White, L.: Medieval uses of air, Scientific American, vol. 223, pp. 92-100, Aug., 1970.

Wieder, H., and Kaplan, E.: Drug use in adolescents. In Essler, R. S., et al., editors: The psychoanalytic study of the child, vol. 24, New York, 1969, International Universities Press.

Williams, H. S., editor: The historians history of the world, New York, 1904, Outlook.

Williams, T. R.: Introduction to socialization: human culture transmitted, St. Louis, 1972, The C. V. Mosby Co.

Winslow, J. H.: Darwin's Victorian malady: evidence for its medically induced origin, Memoirs of the American Philosophical Society, vol. 88, Philadelphia, 1971, The Society.

Wolpe, J.: Experimental neuroses as learned behavior. In Zax, M., and Stricker, G., editors: The study of abnormal behavior, selected readings, ed. 2, New York, 1969, The Macmillan Co.

Zdravomyslov, A. G., Rozhin, V. P., and Iadov, V. A., editors: Man and his work: a sociological study (translated by S. P. Dunn) New York, 1970, International Arts and Science Press.

INDEX